ARTIFICIAL MORALITY

ARTIFICIAL MORALITY

Virtuous robots for virtual games

Peter Danielson

Routledge
Taylor & Francis Group

LONDON AND NEW YORK

First published 1992
by Routledge
2 Park Square, Milton Park, Abingdon, Oxon, OX14 4RN

Simultaneously published in the USA and Canada
by Routledge
605 Third Avenue, New York, NY 10017

Routledge is an imprint of the Taylor & Francis Group, an informa business

Typeset in 10 on 12 point Bembo by
Megaron, Cardiff, Wales

British Library Cataloguing in Publication Data
Danielson, Peter
Artificial morality: virtuous robots for virtual games.
I. Title
006.3

Library of Congress Cataloging in Publication Data
Danielson, Peter
Artificial morality: virtuous robots for virtual games/
Peter Danielson
p. cm.
1. Robotics. 2. Artificial intelligence. 3. Virtue. I. Title.
TJ211.D36 1992
170′ .285′ 63—dc20 91-30432

ISBN 13: 978-0-415-07691-3 (pbk)

CONTENTS

LIST OF FIGURES

ACKNOWLEDGMENTS

I have thought about the problems of rationality and morality for a long time during which I have accumulated many debts. The largest is owed to David Gauthier, who encouraged me to pursue the question of fundamental moral justification. I have learned much from David's work. This book began as an attempt to implement his principle of constrained maximization. These goals changed during the project's long gestation as criticisms and replies, bugs and fixes accreted and displaced older material. If the criticisms of *Morals by Agreement* stand out, this reflects how strongly I feel the influence of this masterful piece of work.

I owe special thanks to two colleagues at York University. Peter Roosen-Runge introduced me to computers some fifteen years ago and has supplied me since with infusions of new ideas, languages, machines and courses to teach. Some of the material developed here is a joint product of our weekly lunches and ongoing computer-assisted correspondence. Not only do I appropriate this material but systematically turn it in directions that Peter finds fantastic, if not perverse. Stuart Shanker got me started with his invitation to write a book for this series.

Les Green, Chris Morris, Peter Roosen-Runge and Wayne Sumner read the first draft and suggested many improvements. David Copp, Steve Savitt and Peter Vallentyne also commented helpfully on the first draft. My research assistant, Blair McDonald, proofread a second draft. Two anonymous readers read the second draft and suggested many improvements. Some of these readers disagree with much of what I say. In any case, they bear no responsibility for what follows.

Robert Axelrod, David Gauthier, Chris Morris, Jean Hampton, Richmond Campbell, Howard Sobel and Holly Smith supplied unpublished material from which I learned a great deal. The free software community deserves recognition for providing almost all the tools with which I created this book. Thanks in particular to Prabhaker Mateti for Guläm (for my Atari), Richard Stallman for Emacs, my text editor, Leslie Lamport and Donald Knuth for LaTeX and TeX, and the Prolog, unix, and NeXT communities for providing fabulous tools.

Early versions of this research were presented at the American Philosophical Association, the Canadian Philosophical Association, the Conference on Contemporary Contractarian Thought (London, Ontario), Bowling Green State University, Simon Fraser University, the University of British Columbia, the Ontario Philosophical Society, the Fourth Annual Conference on Computers and Philosophy at Stanford University, the University of Washington, and the Canadian Institute for Advanced Research in Vancouver. I owe special thanks to those who commented on these presentations, especially Arthur Ripstein, Alan Gibbard, Bill Harper, and Leslie Burkholder, and to the audiences for their questions and suggestions. There is some overlap between the material in this book and Danielson (1990a).

Many students have contributed to my research. Andrew Rau-Champlin, Lew Lowther, and Alex Kean deserve special thanks. I also thank my students who for many years have tolerated the weird and sometimes nasty games I tested on them.

My research has taken me to computer science and back to philosophy. I was fortunate to teach at York University, which tolerated these wanderings and supported my need for computing resources. The University of British Columbia has also been generous with computer support and the time to finish this book.

I fondly dedicate this book to my wife Margie, without whose generous support it never would have been written.

Vancouver 1991

HOW TO AVOID READING
SOME OF THIS BOOK

Ideally, you should use a computer to help you avoid reading some of this book and read the rest more effectively. The models used in the book are written in an executable form of the predicate calculus, called Prolog (for *Pro*gramming in *Log*ic). Many of my claims are testable within these models. More important, you can use these models to modify my premises. For example, by adding new agents to my toy tournaments you can test the robustness of my claims. Finally, with a computer you can submit your new agents to real tournaments I plan to hold on the Internet.

I will provide computer support for this book at the e-mail address: artmoral@unixg.ubc.ca. Mail to this address will get you further information about how to download programs for agents and tournaments, as well as instructions for and results of current tournaments. You will need a Prolog interpreter to run these programs. Prolog is available both for mainframe computers at universities and personal computers. I will post an up-to-date list of sources of public domain and shareware versions of Prolog for the most popular small machines.

There is a division of labour here. Books should contain what is better put on paper and servers should provide what is better distributed electronically. Prolog programs are not fun to type nor easy to read (but easier than most other computer programming languages) and tend to have bugs in them, so they should be downloadable, executable and regularly updated, via the Internet. This leaves the book to state the fairly constant core of the theory, examples (including examples of programs) and bibliography (although a current machine-readable bibliography is also available from my server).

I do not wish to discourage you from reading this book without the help of a computer. I have tried to make it as readable as possible. But one of the theses of *Artificial Morality* is that the subject is too complex to explore with book and armchair.

Part I

METHOD

1

RATIONALITY
AND
MORALITY

1.1 THE PROBLEM

It is rational to be moral? Morality has evident advantages. A group of moral agents, able to co-operate by trusting one other, will do better than a group of amoralists. Co-operative civilized life is better for each than unconstrained conflict (the so-called state of nature). But this argument goes too fast. We can agree that morality generates social goods but rationality speaks to individuals. From the individual perspective the advantage of morality is problematic. Morality involves – at least – constraint; it requires that an agent sometimes act contrary to her own interests in favour of mutual advantage. Therefore moral behaviour generates a *public good*, available to all. However, rationality recommends *free riding* on public goods. The rational advice seems to be: let others practice moral constraint; remain amorally free to collect the benefits of others' constraint. Of course, when all follow this advice, we end up in the state of nature, where no one is foolish enough to constrain herself.

Therefore from the point of view of rationality, morality is deeply problematic. This comes out in several ways. Our most developed social science, economics, is overwhelmingly cynical about moral motivation and pursues a programme of finding institutional replacements for morality. The received theory of rational choice, by defining rationality as unconstrained choice, makes morality irrational by definition. On the other side, most moral theorists have abandoned the attempt to provide a justification of morality in terms acceptable to a wider audience. The common methodological assumption that morality is an *autonomous* realm underscores the distance between morality and the sciences of rational choice.

3

I find this situation unsatisfactory. It seems to me that the rational challenge to morality is real but answerable. On the one hand, some received moral theories are defective from the rational perspective; it would be foolish for a rational agent to adopt them. On the other hand, moral constraint cannot be irrational by definition, as this conceptual legislation closes substantive issues (for example, between internal moral and external institutional solutions to social problems) on weak *a priori* grounds. This is a sign that the received theory of rational choice is also too narrow and dogmatic. By introducing new moral conjectures and broadening the rationality test we should be able to make some progress on the rational justification of morality.

1.1.1 A solution

In this book I show that there are moral agents which are rational in the following sense: they successfully solve social problems that amoral agents cannot solve. The obvious way to test my claim is to build worlds with social problems and see if moral agents are differentially successful in them.[1] One of the most important elements in social success is the ability to deal with other agents' reaction to one's own and other's behaviour. This *strategic* interaction is intrinsically complex, so I will need to keep matters workably simple. I will borrow techniques from game theory to reduce some social problems to their abstract essence and construct artificial agents that interact in these small, toy worlds, using tools borrowed from artificial intelligence. None the less I will try to avoid the strong axiomatic assumptions (employed by game theory) or strong moral idealization (employed by moral theory).

My results are a challenge, not a *refutation* of the standard rational choice (that is, decision and game) theory because I reach my deviant conclusions from deviant premises. In contrast, a refutation would work within the axiomatic tradition of rational choice. My successful agents are deviant; they are *thick* (they are software robots) and *weird* (they can read each other's minds). Their situation is also non-standard. In the place of simple games between symmetrically rational agents, I propose to test varied populations that form complex artificial ecosystems around mixed-motive games such as the Prisoner's Dilemma and Chicken. Furthermore, my conclusions are qualified in several ways. Most notably, rationally successful agents are not as moral as we might like, nor are they completely successful in ridding their world of amoral predators. Yet, I hope to show, we have much to learn from them and their (partial) success.

1.1.2 The challenge of H*Land

Let us design a small world to test our thinking about morality. This world, (we might call it Hobbesland or Humeland – H*Land captures both with a hint of computerese) should be both promising and problematic. H*land is roughly characterized by three features. First, it has *economic potential*: it promises to return benefits to those who co-operate to exploit its natural resources. However, it is initially barren of moral, political and legal institutions. Therefore the returns to co-operation are only potential; agents may not co-operate and co-operators may be exploited. Second, this world is a *virtual* place; only software entities are permitted. Indeed, it has been decided that each of us (humans) can send one representative, which I will call a *player*, whose net proceeds from the expedition will be ours to claim.[2] Third, this place is *computationally active*; the environment supports rudimentary *intelligence*. In particular, a logically precise description of your player suffices to generate the described behaviour.

Obviously this is a world that is barren only in certain respects; in others it is praeternaturally rich. I am not trying to model a minimal set of assumptions. Rather, the idea is to set a particular problem in a maximally fruitful problem-solving environment.[3] H*Land is a world that poses a challenge common to Hobbes and Hume in a way that allows us to use powerful tools we owe to the tradition in computer science. (Incidentally, these are the sort of logical tools of which Hobbes and Leibniz dreamed.)

I hope that you are tempted to send a player on your behalf. I suggest that you read this book first, as it should help you design your player. It will also help you decide whether your player should be a morally constrained co-operator or an amoral predator, or perhaps something in between. Consider what follows to be a manual for success in this test, for prospering in H*Land, and an argument that this challenge is an appropriate way to address the issue of the rational justification of morality.

You may find my challenge fantastic. This is a mistake. What I propose – my moral olympics – is not science fiction.[4] Similar contests have been constructed; I am merely generalizing what is found in the literature of experimental sociology and economics, and the growing field of Artificial Life.[5] More important, the technology to support ideas like this is readily available. For example, the high-level computer languages and computer-assisted communication which allow widespread participation in my scheme are available free to most academics.

You may find my challenge frivolous. Why create and populate a problematic artificial world when we have a surfeit of unsolved social problems in our real world? I am sympathetic to this criticism. I will argue that my artificial game world *models* important real moral problems. Therefore players successful in my world may teach us something about how to deal with our real world. I take up some real problems momentarily. Why then did I start with my science fiction challenge? Because I suspect that the peculiar approach that I offer will appeal to an audience at the intersection of philosophy, computer science, evolutionary theory and science fiction.

1.2 THREE REAL PROBLEMS

1.2.1 My commuting dilemma

Consider a trio of practical problems. The first one confronts me daily. I live in a beautiful suburban community where most people who work commute across a narrow bridge each day. This creates a typical social problem. If most of us rode the bus, or car-pooled, the reduced traffic would flow smoothly. Yet each is better off driving her own car. (One additional car does not make a traffic jam and personal point-to-point travel is far more convenient than sharing schedules.) When we all drive alone in cars, we create massive traffic jams twice daily. The traffic-clogged bridge that separates my home from the city of Vancouver is legendary.

1.2.2 The Greenhouse Dilemma

The second problem has greater significance. Each of us (where the agents may be people, families, firms, cities, provinces, states or empires) faces a choice of two general policies: burn more or less fossil fuels.[6] Again, we all prefer that all burn less to more, since the latter threatens runaway atomspheric warming with uncertain but likely disastrous effects on our climate. But we are addicted to fossil fuels; restricting their use is individually costly. If others give them up, I (or we) do better to use them; if others use them, I do better to do so as well.[7]

In each of these cases it is puzzling how rational agents could fare so badly. We should look more carefully at the structure these situations share. The problem is clearest in the abstract form of a two player game, the Greenhouse Dilemma, depicted in Figure 1.1.

		You burn	
		less	*more*
I burn	*less*	good for both	my worst, your best
	more	my best, your worst	bad for both

Figure 1.1 The two-player Greenhouse Dilemma

The matrix depicts the situation of two players, you and I. Each of us has two alternatives: to burn less or more CO_2 releasing fuel.[8] Why call this situation a *dilemma*? Because there are two plausible lines of argument supporting a decision. First, I consider what I can do independently of your decision. As we have seen, this is particularly easy in situations of this structure, as the same action is best for me regardless of what you do. If you burn less, I do better (best is better than good) by burning more as I gain the advantage of cheap dirty fuel. Alternatively, should you burn more, I also should burn more (bad is better than worst; mutual profligacy is better than one-sided conservation). Since you must either burn more or less, we have what appears to be a conclusive logical argument for the rationality of my choosing to burn more.[9] This is the first horn of the dilemma. The other horn considers the symmetry of our situation, which makes it rational for you to do what I do. It would be better for us both to burn less, not more, if we could act together. But so long as we act independently, the first argument is conclusive, and rational individual players end up with only their third best outcome. It is important to feel the force of this practical dilemma, the conflict between what is better for both and what is individually rational.

1.2.3 Virtual communities

A third real problem comes closer to my virtual game world of H*Land. Consider the Hacker's Dilemma. If you are skilled in computer-assisted communication, you possess a strong analogue of Gyges' ring.[10] You can enter many computer systems and do what you will with a miniscule risk of punishment. So you face two alternatives. Defect by taking what you like (information, money, prankish fun) or co-operate by non-invasive use or creating useful public tools. Hackers have gone both ways, from the fabulous Free

Software Foundation to the surprising success of the Internet Worm. This is no small problem. The joys of hacking attract some our brightest minds and almost everything in our world is converging on the dominant digital control technology.[11] Therefore the scope of the Hacker's Dilemma is increasing rapidly and without obvious limit.

Evidently it is difficult for our natural ethics to get a grip here:

> Much of the time when we work on computers, even when that work deals directly with other people's lives, there is no sense at all of another person.
>
> This distancing makes it easy to relax ethical behavior . . . .
>
> Unlike other kinds of human communities which are constituted around the physical presence of their members, the virtual community cannot teach or enforce a code of ethics by example. We always have depended heavily on the physical presence of others to remind us we need to behave ethically. In a community of the mind, there is no physical presence.
>
> (Robbinett 1991, p. 16)

Although Robbinett may overstate the problem, there are real difficulties civilizing our new virtual frontier using traditional ethical theories and techniques. Therefore this third practical problem suggests a bridge from practical natural human morality to my proposed virtual world. As our world becomes more artificial, techniques of artificial morality may become more useful.

Considering how similar they appear, it is important not to misunderstand the relation of my virtual world to this last practical problem. They differ in the values at stake and the range of techniques available to solve their respective social problems. First, in my created world the only point is to explore the relation of morality to rationality. My world is a play world; it is a game. The only costs are to the self-esteem of the players. In the real computing world, there is real work and real losses at stake. Second, it is appropriate to explore all manner of techniques to humanize virtual communities. But employing these techniques would be to misunderstand the point of H*Land. If my player co-operates with yours because I know you and like you and would not want to show you up, we will have learned nothing new from artificial morality. (We already know this much about decent behaviour.) Artificial morality is supposed to be the blindest experiment, the longest of arm's length tests. Therefore the links between players and people should be thoroughly anonymous, else what we know about human morality may leak into our new world to the detriment of our chance to learn something new from it.

1.3 WHY THESE PROBLEMS ARE DEEP

So far I have suggested that many real problems share a rough common structure. In this section I identify this structure and argue that it indicates why these problems are deep as well as numerous and serious.

1.3.1 The Prisoner's Dilemma

The practical problems have a common structure; they are called Prisoner's Dilemmas.[12] Abstracting further, in each situation, the player can choose between a more or less co-operative action; call the former C and the latter D (for defect). Then we can arrange the possible outcomes in a 2 × 2 matrix and represent the worst to best ranking with an integer scale from 0 to 3. (See Figure 1.2.) If both do

	C	D
C	2,2	0,3
D	3,0	1,1

Figure 1.2 The Prisoner's Dilemma

the less co-operative action, D, both do worse than if both do the more co-operative action, C. Yet each does better doing the less co-operative action. Thus these situations reveal a conflict between what we might call the moral and the rational points of view. From the moral point of view, where we consider what all should do, it is clear that we should choose C, and get the optimal result of joint co-operation. From the rational point of view, where we consider what each should do, it is clear that each should choose D. Rationality condemns us to non-optimal outcomes.

Hence the Prisoner's Dilemma is widely considered to be a deep problem for the theory of rationality. In an excellent introduction to the problem, Richmond Campbell accounts for the 'deep attraction' of this problem:

Quite simply, these paradoxes cast in doubt our understanding of rationality and, in the case of the Prisoner's Dilemma suggest that it is impossible for rational creatures to cooperate. Thus, they bear directly on fundamental issues in ethics and political philosophy and threaten the foundations of the social sciences. It is the scope of these consequences that explains why these paradoxes have drawn so much attention and why they command a central place in philosophical discussion.

(Campbell 1985a, p. 3)

1.3.2 The compliance problem

Another way to plumb the depths of the Prisoner's Dilemma is explore the structure of attempts to solve what I call the compliance problem. Consider the result of pairing two players, one a simple Moralist, who always co-operates, and the other an Amoralist, who does not.[13] Figure 1.3 indicates the outcomes for the row strategy when playing PD with the column strategy. Moralists do well

Player	Moralist	Amoralist
Moralist	2	0
Amoralist	3	1

Figure 1.3 Compliance failure

with Moralists but Amoralists do even better in this case. Also, Amoralists do better with Amoralists than Moralists do. Indeed, the situation should seem familiar; this pairing of players replicates the original Prisoner's Dilemma at one level removed. The proposed moral solution to the compliance problem generates a situation with the same problematic structure of the original Prisoner's Dilemma.[14] This indicates the depth of the compliance problem posed by the original dilemma. If moral solutions to the compliance problem must lead to a compliance dilemma, they are rationally doomed.

It appears to be irrational to be moral but also stupid to be rational. We might call these problems, respectively, moral and rational failure. The compliance problem challenges both received theories of morality and rationality, and the disciplines based around them. Moral theories tend to be too *idealistic*, focusing on what is best from the moral point of view. Contemporary moral theory fails to give a convincing answer to the old question, why be moral? On the other hand, the social sciences based on the theory of rational choice tend to be too *cynical*, often ignoring the possibility and instrumental usefulness of moral motivation.

1.4 GAUTHIER'S SOLUTION

I believe that there is a solution to the compliance problem. The solution derives from a family of theories we can group under the label of *instrumental contractarianism*, associated historically with Thomas Hobbes and recently with David Gauthier. These theories promise to bridge the gap between the moral and the rational points of view, between ethics and social science, respectively. The central idea of this approach is that some agents might agree among themselves to co-operate because this commitment allows them to fare better than amoral rational agents. We can see instrumental contractarianism as using the moral point of view to generate agents and agreements, which are tested from the rational point of view. For example, Hobbes claims that a political agent, capable of subjecting herself to sovereign authority, passes this test. Gauthier makes a similar claim for a moral agent, the constrained maximizer.[15]

The compliance problem is the central problem addressed by David Gauthier in his book *Morals by Agreement*. Gauthier proposes to break out of the compliance dilemma by introducing a more sophisticated moral principle: constrained maximization. To be rational, moral constraint must be *conditional* upon others' co-operation. Gauthier uses this conditional disposition to rebut the dominance argument in favour of non-co-operation:

> Since persons disposed to co-operation only act co-operatively with those whom they suppose to be similarly disposed, a straightforward maximizer does not have the opportunities to benefit which present themselves to the constrained maximizer. Thus [the dominance] argument . . . fails.
>
> (Gauthier, 1986a, p. 172)

Gauthier's constrained maximizer does not co-operate when faced with an exploitative amoralist, which Gauthier calls a straightforward maximizer (SM).[16] In the Prisoner's Dilemma, a constrained maximizer (CM) refuses to open herself to exploitation by acting co-operatively with an amoral straightforward maximizer. Her conditional disposition is a new option that gives rise to a new set of payoffs in the choice of dispositions for dealing with partial compliance. These new payoffs are shown in Figure 1.4.[17] Gauthier's proposed CM moral strategy fares better than the unfortunate moralist in Figure 1.3 when paired with the SM amoralist.

Agent	CM	SM
CM	2	1
SM	1	1

Figure 1.4 Compliance success

Gauthier's constrained maximizers do as well or better than straightforward maximizers. They escape the compliance dilemma and show moral constraint to be individually rational. This claim is obviously significant. Derek Parfit writes about an earlier version of Gauthier's compliance argument:

> If this argument succeeds, it has great importance. It would show that, in many kinds of case, it is rational to act morally, even when we believe that this will be worse for us. Moral reasons would be shown to be stronger than the reasons provided by self-interest. Many writers have tried, unsuccessfully, to justify this conclusion. If this conclusion is justified by the argument that I am discussing, this argument solves what Sidgwick called 'the profoundest problem of Ethics'.
>
> (Parfit 1984, p. 19)

Does Gauthier's argument succeed? Does constrained maximization solve the compliance problem? I believe that Gauthier's theory is a major advance in our understanding of the rational justification of morality. His formulation of Sidgwick's problem in terms of rational choice in games like the Prisoner's Dilemma, and his appeal to conditional strategies to solve the compliance problem are sound. It seems to me that they should be taken as the basis for further work relating morality to rationality.[18]

Has Gauthier solved the basic compliance problem? Gauthier's principle of constrained maximization is highly controversial. Like many others, I do not think that Gauthier's theory succeeds in rationalizing morality. I will focus on its central difficulty: the existence claim that there is a type of agent that can beat rational agents at their own game, namely strategic interaction. I suggest that constrained maximization is unsatisfactory because it is too conservative. Gauthier, attempting to stay as much as possible within the received theory of rational choice, suggests that the moral agent is but a small modification of the rational agent. I submit that this is mistaken. Introducing a new type – i.e. conditionally constrained – of agent, as instrumental moral contractarianism must, greatly complicates social interaction. It becomes difficult to say what these agents will do in various situations. For example, there are real questions as to whether such agents are coherent, let alone more successful than traditional rational or moral agents.

Spelling out this criticism and my constructive response will occupy the rest of this book. We can get started by sketching six problems that Gauthier's theory, morals by agreement, does not adequately address.

1.4.1 Coherence and construction

First, there are questions about the procedural rationality of conditional dispositions. Gauthier's constrained maximizer is a conditional co-operator. If we are both constrained maximizers, I will co-operate only if you will and you will only if I will. We seem to be stuck in a vicious circle. This may turn out to be a benign co-ordination problem but some critics suggest that it points to a deeper problem. I argue that they are right; builders of constrained maximizers need to explore radical procedural options. To test Gauthier's and competing conjectures we need to *construct* agents. We must move from the level of axiomatic game theory to a more procedural approach.

1.4.2 Pluralism

Second, Gauthier moves us from what we might call motivational monism (that focuses on the ideal situation where all agents reason in the same way) to motivational dualism. Setting out the conditions of constrained or moralized rational choice, Gauthier notes that 'A just person must however be aware that not all (otherwise) rational

13

persons accept this reading ... "rational response" remains ... open to several interpretations' (Gauthier 1986a, p. 158). The move to motivational dualism is a major advance away from the utopian monoculture that plagues rational and moral theory. It allows Gauthier's theory to begin to address the problem of partial compliance.[19] Gauthier demands that rational moral principles prove robust enough to resist amoral predators. However we should ask, why stop at motivational *dualism*? What about the other sorts of agent – in particular other sorts of morally constrained agent? Gauthier does not consider this complication although it creates new problems for his theory. I shall argue that when we reintroduce the naive unconditional co-operator, a new sort of constrained agent, the reciprocal co-operator, becomes attractive. Reciprocal co-operators exploit naive unconditional co-operators and so do better than Gauthier's constrained maximizers. Therefore pluralism leads in unexpected directions.

1.4.3 Ecosystems vs games

A plurality of distinct agents gives rise to the third problem: how should we judge substantive rationality in a complex environment where various kinds of agents interact? Gauthier falls back on the received theory of rational choice, working with the concepts of game theory in an attempt to rationalize morality at the level of decision theory. (Crudely, at some level, one's straightforwardly maximizing choice is to become an agent who eschews straightforward maximization in action.) I am unable to offer an alternative *deep* rationalization of morality. But I can see several reasons to avoid premature use of the apparatus of what I will call *strong game theory*. The main reason is that game theory makes assumptions incompatible with the whole project of instrumental contractarianism and begs what I see as crucial moral questions. Strong game theory makes the following recursive assumption. All agents are (i) identical – that is, symmetrically rational – and (ii) fully and freely informed about assumptions (i) and (ii). However these assumptions are falsified by the possibility of an instrumental social contract. First, constrained maximizers make themselves different from amoral non-contractors. Second, moralized contractors need to communicate their dispositions to each other but SM have no such need. It will beg the moral/amoral question to assume that this information is freely available.[20]

I will argue below that we can capture the useful contribution of game theory without these problems if we think in terms of ecosystems instead of games. Chapters 5 and 8 will explore the differences between these two concepts of the situation in ethics. The conclusion of that argument is that once we relax the assumptions of strong game theory, we generate ecosystems where a variety of different agents co-exist for whom the cost of information is a crucial consideration, thus confirming the negation of the two assumptions.[21]

1.4.4 Morality

Fourth, the strategy of reciprocal co-operation, which I introduce to cope with the problem of pluralism, opens the gap between morality and rationality again. Reciprocal co-operators exploit innocent unconditional co-operators. Since this exploitation is apparently immoral, the compliance dilemma threatens again, with rationality pointing to reciprocal co-operation and morality pointing to – what? Difficult problems arise here, both in the treatment of naive agents and the use of sanctions against agents like reciprocal co-operators who exploit them. I take up the general problem of morally evaluating our agents in Chapter 6 and turn to the special problems of threats and sanctions in Part III. Of course, these are not problems for Gauthier, since it is I and not he who introduces the nasty strategy of reciprocal co-operation (which he does not wholeheartedly embrace). But it remains a problem for the extension of the theory he defends.

1.4.5 Autonomy

Fifth, the reciprocal co-operators that solve the Prisoner's Dilemma are rigidly fixed agents. They fall short of the ideal of morality: autonomous moral choice that somehow combines freedom and constraint. Is it possible to combine these features? One way might be to introduce *learning*. Agents that learn while interacting will also make our ecosystems more robust, by freeing our tournaments from direct and constant human input.

1.4.6 Beyond the Prisoner's Dilemma

Sixth and finally, Gauthier is especially concerned to unite rationality and morality in situations like the Prisoner's Dilemma, where the natural strategic equilibrium conflicts with the co-operative optimum. While this is a difficult situation, it is not the least tractable, as the success of Gauthier's constrained maximizer, or at least my modification of her, the reciprocal co-operator, indicates. In particular, the Prisoner's Dilemma is especially friendly to the solution of the compliance problem by means of public commitments to co-operate. The cost of sanctioning defectors is low in the Prisoner's Dilemma. If we increase this cost, leading to the game of Chicken, we find a new moral problem crops up: should one defend morality against transparently committed amoral threatening agents? Here we see the techniques of artificial virtue turned to support vicious aggression.

1.5 ARTIFICIAL MORALITY

Others have criticized Gauthier's attempt to derive a morality from rational choice. Unlike most of them, I do not see my criticisms as a reason to reject Gauthier's entire project of rationalizing morality. Gauthier is ambitious, and, perhaps, too traditional in his methods. But nothing that follows undercuts his vision of a theory of morality free from irrationality and firmly within the tradition of rational choice, *broadly conceived*.

1.5.1 'Rationality' hijacked

I stress 'broadly conceived' because of difficulties with the term 'rationality.' I would love simply to claim that it is rational to be moral. There is, after all, ample historical justication for taking 'rationality' to be the highest standard of practical reason. The most successful agent(s) deserve to be labelled rational. And my moral agents are socially successful agents, hence in this sense, they are rational. But while this is tempting, it would be confusing. We cannot ignore the fact that the term 'rational' has been successfully hijacked by a particular theory of choice (Binmore 1987, p. 181). Simply to use 'rational' for something else would be misleading.[22] On the other hand, we should not acquiesce to this appropriation of the term that marks the ultimate practical value. Therefore, when I claim that my successful agents are rational, I intend this in the widest sense; they best achieve the goal of instrumental rationality. I will sometimes substitute less theoretically loaded terms, like 'useful,' for successful agents and I will avoid using 'rational' in the narrow sense as this would reinforce a usage that begs important questions.[23] I propose to use Gauthier's term for the received theory that dictates preference maximizing choice at every point: straightforward maximization (SM).

There is more than terminological clarity involved in this matter. The theory of rational choice is an important theory that provides powerful tools for thinking about interaction. It is not clear to what extent my revisionist account can be integrated into this theory. It seems better to mark the differences from the start, to issue a warning, as it were, against importing ideas and procedures from the received theory too easily.

1.5.2 The goal of this book

In this book I shall develop an elementary version of a small part of this broader theory in a new way. I propose that we actually build the agents proposed by the contending theories and test them instrumentally. This promises to resolve questions about the coherence and efficiency of moral agents. It will also, as we shall soon see, generate a host of new problems. My overall proposal is that a new method, which I call *artificial morality*, is the appropriate way to deal with these problems. Artificial morality combines game theory and artificial intelligence to develop instrumental contractarianism. Game theory simplifies the compliance problem, stripping it down to basic elements: what sort of agents, amoral or moral, do better playing a series of representative games? The constructive resources of artificial intelligence allows us actually to build (most of) the desired agents and manage complexities that result from their interaction.

My approach involves both more and less than one expects to find in moral philosophy. *More* because I find that verbal arguments do not suffice; it is unusual to claim that computers are necessary to providing a justification of morality. *Less* because the agents that I propose to study are minimal agents, programmed robots. The received opinion is that morality pertains only to much more complicated agents, capable of complex thinking and communication. I have no *a priori* defence of these deviations from accepted practice. I hope that my methods will be fruitful and invite you to try them.

The goal of this book is to introduce a new method for studying the relation between rationality and morality. I should admit here, near the beginning, that I do not yet have a clear idea of how best to develop this method nor do I know where artificial morality will lead. My goal is to explore, and to help and encourage others to explore, an area of which we know too little, not to prove some particular results.

I find myself building a method as well as building agents. Most likely most of what I do at both levels will be supplanted by others.

1.5.3 The design of this book

This prospect has influenced the way I conceive the book. Rather than build one tightly inter-connected – and therefore fragile – argument, most of which might be misconceived, I have instead sketched several different strands that seem important to the method. My guiding metaphor is a toy building set (I am a Lego and Meccano fan), not a crucial structure (like a suspension bridge or spaceship). This approach will not appeal to everyone interested in a constructive approach to morality and rationality, so I should denote what follows with a proper name: Artificial Morality (AM).

Here is how the main strands fit into the book, which is divided into three parts. Part I introduces Artificial Morality as a method. Chapter 2 sets out the goal of fundamental justification and compares my project with David Gauthier's. Chapter 3 relates AM to two neighbouring disciplines, sociobiology and artificial intelligence. Part II presents the initial results of my theory. Chapter 4 shows that conditional co-operation is a rationally attractive strategy by constructing an elementary responsive agent. Chapter 5 introduces the complicating factor of a varied population of agents, in which environment a new and nastier agent, the reciprocal co-operator, does best. This is a rational success but a moral disappointment. So Chapter 6 introduces some moral tests for our initial results which suggest another new agent. Part III extends the theory beyond the extremely simplified initial model. Chapter 7 introduces learning and other flexible agents. Chapter 8 argues that when the costs of information are considered, it is not rational for all agents to be similiar responsive co-operators. Chapters 9 and 10 take us beyond the Prisoner's Dilemma to the game of Chicken and the problem of supporting moral constraint through sanctions.

2

FUNDAMENTAL
JUSTIFICATION AND GAMES

Artificial Morality is a method for providing a fundamental justification for moral constraint. It shares this goal with David Gauthier's *Morals by Agreement*. 'We are committed to showing why an individual, reasoning from non-moral premises, would accept the constraints of a morality on his choices.'[1] In this chapter I use the goal of fundamental justification to focus my argument by choosing its starting points. Fundamental justification leads us to the compliance problem as a crucial problem and to games as the best models of this problem.

This chapter also defines Artificial Morality in terms of two contrasts. First, Artificial Morality is closely related to contractarianism so I contrast my approach with the well-known contractarian theories of Hobbes, Rawls and Gauthier. Second, Artificial Morality uses games somewhat differently from the theory of games.

2.1 FUNDAMENTAL JUSTIFICATION

The idea of a fundamental justification – a justification of a realm that does not appeal to any of the concepts of that realm – has enormous philosophical appeal.[2] The easiest way to argue for fundamental justification is to consider the alternatives. In general, anything short of a fundamental justification of morality, by assuming some moral premise(s), begs the central question of ethical theory. I realize that many philosophers think that begging this question is necessary. It may be that ethics is not possible unless one assumes the automony of the field. Or it may be that some moral premise is deeply true of human beings. Perhaps, but notice that both of these methodological moves make strong claims and should be seen to do so. I am inclined to

19

make do with weaker claims, to seek a fundamental justification by reducing morality to something simpler and clearer.

An obvious candidate is amoral instrumental rationality. Instrumentalism provides the motivation necessary to a practical theory; ends provide reasons for pursuing means. (Without this motivation, we would have an *explanation* not a justification.) Amoral ends guarantee that the justification will be fundamental (with respect to morality). Examples include Hobbes' attempt to give a fundamental account of the political realm and Kant's proposal of a theory of justice applicable to amoral devils. I join Hobbes, Kant, and now Gauthier, in making a case for moral constraint addressed to naturally unconstrained agents. These arguments share a general strategy: they attempt to show that morality corrects a defect in the social relations of amoral agents. Therefore we should consider the social problems rational agents are likely to face.

2.1.1 Why the compliance problem is central

Following Hume, Alan Gibbard gives a succinct account of the major social problems confronting rational agents:

> We might classify three chief puzzles under the names Hume used for three distinct virtues: *justice, fidelity,* and *allegiance.* By *justice* I shall mean arriving at shared standards of fairness in social dealings. Fidelity and allegiance are matters of abiding by those standards. Allegiance concerns large groups, whereas fidelity concerns small groups – often bilateral arrangements.
> (Gibbard 1990, p. 792)

Three difficult problems; too much to take on at once. But we can make some headway by noticing that solving the first problem is unmotivated without a solution to the second and third. It makes no sense to worry about rules that no one will follow. Concerning the latter two, there is controversy about which, if either, of morality or politics is the more basic problem. My interests and skills incline me to work from bilateral cases up to larger groups, but I can see that other methodologies might begin with larger scale interactions.

This focuses our attention on fidelity. The hard case for the rationality of fidelity is the compliance problem. As we saw in Chapter 1, the appropriate problem to test the rationality of fidelity is the one-play, two-player Prisoner's Dilemma (PD), where there is only one optimal outcome, joint co-operation (CC), which we can identify with following the agreed standards of justice. We can restrict our focus even more. For repeated Prisoner's Dilemmas, there appear to be straightforwardly rational strategies to obtain optimum outcomes.[3] 'This leaves the problem of a Prisoner's Dilemma where it is known there will be no further interaction.'[4] Achieving optimal outcomes in the one-play PD calls for a stronger virtue, which we might call *high fidelity*. Following Gauthier, I will focus on this case, because easier cases (with expected future interaction) do not call on the particularly moral ability to choose against one's preferences.[5]

2.1.2 The Extended Prisoner's Dilemma

Consider the simplest case where high fidelity can claim a significant result: a Prisoner's Dilemma extended in time, so that one player (II) can react to the prior move of the other (I). I will call this one-play sequential game an Extended Prisoner's Dilemma (XPD). In this situation, the ability of player II to keep a promise to co-operate could induce player I also to co-operate. But player II's ability to commit itself to keep a promise is problematic. Thus this case puts the virtue of high fidelity to an instrumental test. Gauthier tells a story to illustrate the problem:

> You and I are farmers. Next week my crops will be ready for harvesting; the following week, yours will be. And then, the harvest season over, I am selling my farm and retiring, far away from where we now live. Each of us can bring in the harvest unaided. Or we can help each other. Each of us would prefer to help and be helped, than to work alone. But giving assistance to the other is in itself a cost. And so I face a problem. My best course of action, I realize, is to offer you my assistance in return for yours. But a fortnight hence, whether or not you have helped me get in the harvest, I will do best not to help you. For helping you is a cost, and I can expect no benefit in return. Either I already have received the benefit – your assistance with my crops, or there is no benefit. But in either case, I have nothing to gain by now helping you. But you know this. Indeed, it's common knowledge. So I'm not in a position to promise sincerely that I will assist you if you first assist me, and you are not going to accept any so-called promise that I offer.[6]

It may be helpful explicitly to lay out the situation in time. The tree diagram in Figure 2.1 depicts the choices facing the two agents.[7] The farmers' problem is a Prisoner's Dilemma. Each farmer faces two alternatives: *C* (for co-operate) stands here for aiding; *D* (for defect) stands for not aiding. There are four possible outcomes to which I assign labels of the path leading to them. For example, if player I helps but II does not, this yields outcome *CD*. The numbers record the value of the outcomes to each of the agents. It is worst (0) to help without being helped, bad (1) neither help nor be helped, good (2) to both help and be helped, and best (3) to be helped without helping. For example, the value of *CD* is 0 for player I and 3 for II. (It is the best outcome for player II.)

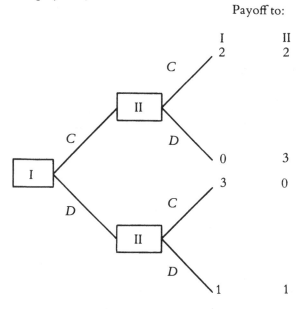

Figure 2.1 Extended Prisoner's Dilemma

2.1.3 Strategic failure

In the story of the farmers Gauthier presents the case for the failure of straightforward maximizers. Assuming that player II is a straightforward maximizer, she always chooses the alternative that leads to her best outcome. If player I has chosen *C*, II should choose *D* and get her best and his worst outcome. If player I has chosen *D* then II should also choose *D* and bring about the second worst outcome for both. Therefore as an unconstrained rational agent player II cannot make a promise – in any sense that performs the function of promising

– to help in return. Since player II cannot promise, player I does best choosing D (guaranteeing the bad outcome for both) because choosing C will be worst for him. Straightforward maximizers are doomed to sub-optimal outcomes. The DD outcome is worse for both of them, according to their own values, than the accessible outcome CC. The problem is that CC is not accessible *for them* because as creatures of the received theory neither player can ever choose what is worse for itself. It is a tragedy of their own making; it would seem that a moral agent – an agent who could constrain its choice – would do better.

2.1.4 Moral failure

In Chapter 1, in the discussion of the compliance dilemma, I wrote that moral failure paralleled strategic failure. Now I would like to support that claim. I am not suggesting that *all* moral theories fail; but significant and popular theories do and do so in ways that reinforce the appeal of the project of fundamental justification.

There are many more strands of moral theory and tradition and consequently many more flavours of moral agent, than is the case for rationality. This variety makes it difficult to pin morality down. I shall focus on a determinate problem and show that one kind of morality fails to solve the farmers' social problem. Probably the most fully developed and probably the most influential theory of morality is utilitarianism. Utilitarians are secular moralists who typically care about solving social problems. So it will be pertinent to ask: will things go better if player II is a utilitarian, that is, if she chooses the action that is best for *both* agents?[8]

The answer seems obvious since player II can now keep a promise. Therefore it is worthwhile for her to make a conditional promise to help if helped and player I – even if not morally constrained – should rationally choose C to get 2 instead of D and get 1. However this argument moves too fast to its happy conclusion. Player I should think further; strategic agents consider all alternatives and consider what the other agent can be expected to do in response to each of them.[9] Player I should consider his other alternative. What if he chooses D? Then player II faces the alternative of choosing D, leading to the joint outcome value of $1 + 1$, or C, leading to the joint outcome value of $3 + 0$. Remember: player II is a utilitarian. Since 3 is better than 2 (utilitarians ignore distribution in the final sum), player II ought to choose C. Utilitarians are committed to making the best of a bad situation and they count all agents, moral and non-moral, in their globally impartial goal. But – and this is crucial – this means that the conditional aspect of player II's promise is not believable. Indeed, it is not a promise but a threat. Given player II's utilitarian goals, she threatens to make both worse off (get them a joint utility of 2) than they would be without her promise (getting 3). As a utilitarian, she cannot carry out this threat. Therefore her promise is not credible and player I will not help her, knowing that player II will help him anyway.[10] I conclude that one prominent strand of the received theory of morality also fails to achieve optimal outcomes in the farmers' situation. Moral failure parallels strategic failure.

2.1.5 An objection

Need a utilitarian agree that this is a story of failure? After all, given a *utilitarian* valuation of outcomes, player II does as well as possible in her situation. (The social utility is 3 instead of 2.) But, I rejoin, this makes two mistakes. First, strategies need to be evaluated by how they structure one's alternatives. II is faced with making the best of a bad situation because of her utilitarian principle. (Act utilitarianism inherits this narrowness from the theory of rational choice.) Second, player II does gets the worst outcome – 0. Softening this defeat by appeal to utilitarian – that is, a species of moralized – evaluation must be avoided if we are to provide a fundamental justification of moral constraint. It begs the crucial ethical question to assume utilitarian valuation.

Conclusion

I conclude that the compliance problem is a crucial problem standing in the way of providing a fundamental justification of morality. As we have seen, this is a difficult problem from the point of view of rational and moral theory. I need to demonstrate the usefulness of the virtue of high fidelity in situations like that the farmers face. I have suggested modelling situations as games. I will look more closely at this proposal in §2.3. The next section uses the idea of the social contract to elaborate on fundamental justification and the compliance problem.

2.2 THE SOCIAL CONTRACT

The idea of a social contract illuminates my goal of fundamental justification and can also help us to focus on the compliance problem.

However, Artificial Morality is a narrower theory than contractarianism and I indicate some contractarian assumptions that I hope to avoid. In this section I will use three contractarians, Rawls, Hobbes and Gauthier, to distinguish some features of my own approach.

The idea of a fundamental justification is intimately connected with the modern contractarian tradition that runs from Hobbes, through Kant, to Rawls and Gauthier.[11] In a contractarian argument, justification proceeds by showing that in an appropriate situation, rational agents would agree to certain principles. Artificial Morality is contractarian in this wide sense. John Rawls' theory of justice is a sophisticated example of the general contractarian method: 'Principles of justice may be conceived as principles that would be chosen by rational persons. . . . In this way conceptions of justice may be explained and justified' (Rawls 1971, p. 16). More generally, the contractarian method puts rational agents in a preferred situation and argues that their choice of X provides a fundamental justification of X, where X typically ranges over institutions or principles. Rawls describes the method:

> as a procedure familiar in social theory. That is, a simplified situation is described in which rational individuals with certain ends and related to each other in certain ways are to choose among various courses of action in view of their knowledge of the circumstances. What these individuals will do is then derived by strictly deductive reasoning from these assumptions about their beliefs and interests, their situation and the options open to them. Their conduct is, in the phrase of Pareto, the resultant of tastes and obstacles.
>
> (Rawls 1971, p. 119)

I shall work within this broad contractarian framework, asking what special assumptions should be made about agents and situations to secure a fundamental justification of morality. This will draw our attention to the differences that distinguish various contractarian arguments.

2.2.1 Varieties of contractarian justification

Weak vs strong contractarians

First, we might distinguish *weak* from *strong* contractarians.[12] Rawls is an example of weak contractarianism because he works *within* morality, attempting to derive principles of justice from a situation constrained by prior general moral constraints. In contrast, strong contractarians, like Hobbes and Gauthier, argue from premises of amoral individual rational choice.[13] On this account, weak contractarians do not attempt to give a fundamental justification of morality. Rawls is clear about this; his construction starts from widely held moral assumptions. Therefore my plan is to follow Hobbes and Gauthier, not Rawls, on this point.

Moral vs political

Weak and strong contractarians differ in the strength of their premises. We can draw a second distinction in terms of the conclusions that contractarian arguments seek to support. *Moral* contractarians (such as Rawls and Gauthier) stress individual self-constraint in their conclusions; *political* contractarians like Hobbes and Buchanan (1975) aim to provide a justification for an *institutional* solution to the problem of unstable social co-operation.

This contrast is less clear than the previous one. On the one hand, moral contractarians see the need for some institutions. On the other, political solutions typically require some sort of moral underpinning. None the less, we can imagine at one extreme a purely moral – that is to say, anarchistic – solution to the problems of social order and at other, coercive institutions that called for no moral restraint on the part of subjects. Hobbes is closer to the second extreme and Gauthier is closer to the first. The project of providing a fundamental justification of morality aims at avoiding the second extreme. It stresses, in terms I adapt from Gauthier, the visible hand of morality, not the visible foot of a coercive sovereign. Therefore I follow Gauthier, who sees in constrained maximization the solution to the compliance problem by *moral*, not political means.

While there are reasons to doubt the Hobbesian solution, my point here is not that it is inferior, but simply *different*.[14] Morality is a particular sort of control on behaviour, focusing on individual self-control, to which there are alternatives. In contrast, Hobbes argued for coercive institutional control in place of internal moral controls. For now the important point is to distinguish the internal moral solution that I seek to justify from the external political alternative.[15]

Notice that I am not claiming that social problems like those modelled by the Prisoner's Dilemma cannot be solved by institutional means. Obviously they can be. Institutions can give straightforward maximizers reasons to behave co-operatively. My point here is that moral constraint is different from externally motivated co-operation.

Summing up, Artificial Morality joins Gauthier and Hobbes in seeking a fundamental justification, and Gauthier in seeking such a justification of morality as a particular form of social control.

2.2.2 Without a social contract

Having used the social contract to help define my own project, I must now mark some differences. First, I will avoid any appeal to a social agreement or contract. In this way my theory will be more radically individualistic than Hobbes' or Gauthier's. I will begin with individual agents and may never reach a social agreement of all the agents. Indeed this lack of agreement, by constantly reminding us of the alternative(s) to and within morality, will keep us focused on the crucial problems of compliance and toleration. This difference will come out especially in Chapter 7, where I discuss ways that agents might co-ordinate their strategies. Second, and more obviously, contractarians like Hobbes, Rawls and Gauthier limit their accounts to what is feasible for human agents, while Artificial Morality has a wider range of application.[16]

Foundationalism

Another, related, difference is the attempt to secure contractarian assumptions as true – even necessarily true – of humans. Hobbes and Gauthier take this tack. They seek to provide a *foundation* for their conclusions; I shall avoid this quest for reasons I set out in this subsection.[17]

My label 'fundamental' may mislead one into thinking that I give too much independent justificatory weight to considerations of rationality. A contrast with foundationalism will be useful here.

> In a foundationalist theory, some sort of consideration is held to support a particular form of political order, without itself depending on any substantive assumptions about the legitimacy of particular forms of human interaction. Hence the metaphor of a foundation, which holds up an edifice without itself being supported by anything else.
>
> (Ripstein 1987, p. 116)

That is, a foundationalist theory purports to be a *sound* argument; it claims (the justificatory analogue of) a true premise. For example,

Hobbes seeks to establish the truth of his motivational premises. He attempts to provide a deep account of the springs of human conduct, literally reaching down to a mechanical explanation of our goals, that shows why men must give strong (lexicographic) priority to individual self-preservation. If Hobbes were right, his argument would provide a foundational justification for the state. In contrast, fundamental justification claims merely to be valid, based on a counter-factual premise, adding that the premise and conclusion are independent in a specific sense. Mine is a counter-factual argument that attempts to establish a connection between two seemingly independent and opposed realms, the rational and the moral. A less misleading term would be 'reductive justification'. I seek to reduce (some instances of) the question: why be moral? to questions about rationality. This makes my argument fundamental. I do not go further and seek a foundation by attempting to answer the question: why be rational? The point of premises is to block regress of this sort. All arguments are relative to assumptions; one must start somewhere. Artificial Morality begins with the assumption that amoral rationality matters.[18]

Gauthier's natural foundation

As a contrast to my refusal to argue for rationality as a foundation of my argument, consider Gauthier's account of the foundations of his theory:

> The underlying ideas of [moral theory as rational choice theory] are simple and, I believe, natural. What distinguishes human beings from other animals, and provides the basis for rationality, is the capacity for semantic representation. . . . Since in representing our desires we become aware of conflict among them, the step from representation to decision becomes complicated. We must, somehow, bring our conflicting desires into some sort of coherence. And there is only one plausible candidate for a principle of coherence – a maximizing principle. We order our desires in relation to decision and action, so that we may choose to maximize our expectation of desire-fulfillment. And in so doing, we show ourselves to be rational agents. There is simply nothing else for practical reason to be. . . . Can we introduce morality without postulating any features either of the world or of persons over and above those

which naturally suggest themselves if we think of human beings as animals with this one peculiar and distinctive capacity – a capacity that brings with it, on the surface, only the apparatus of rationality?

(Gauthier 1988a, pp. 1–3)

While I welcome this defence of naturalism in a broad methodological sense, Gauthier's claims go far beyond the conjecture that moral theory can make do without supernatural motivation. I do not find these additional claims to be convincing, for three reasons. First, one can think of 'plausible candidates for a principle of coherence' other than a maximizing principle. Notice that what Gauthier is doing here is providing a transcendental argument for maximization based on bare agency. This is a dubious move that I would like to avoid. In addition, it is not obviously true that a rational agent must maximize. I can imagine agents who employ the alternative structure of lexicographic preferences: first take care of pain, then take care of kin, then find food . . . and so on. It is not even clear that maximizing is an *easier* way to make complex decisions than a set of ordered rules. (For example, many working expert systems use the latter form of decision-making.) I suspect that the appeal of maximization is due in part to making strong assumptions about the availability of a great deal of information, neatly packaged and priced in utilities. But then most of the work of deciding has already been done. Second, note that Gauthier's defence of his purported foundation rests on an argument from a failure of the imagination. Such arguments carry little weight.[19] Third, a morality built on human capacities fails to apply in the first instance to supra-human organizations although Gauthier does apply his theory to states (Gauthier 1984). I conclude that Gauthier's attempt to provide a foundation for his theory does not succeed.

The point of fundamental justification

Of course, foundationalists like Gauthier and Hobbes may have a goal which make their method appropriate. Both of them are sceptical about received morality; both seek a rational foundation for a replacement for that morality. Critics of morality need strong arguments and a foundation built on a true account of human rationality is attractive in this respect. Indeed, what is the point of a fundamental justication if its premises are not true and therefore

29

moralists need not accept them? I should stress that Artificial Morality is not directed against received moral theory but against the received theory of rational choice, which is sceptical of all moral constraint. Rational choice theorists do accept my instrumentalist premises, so this criticism should be effective.

2.3 MORAL PROBLEMS AND GAMES

In this section I consider which situations should be used to test agents. I argue that games are good models of the relevant aspects of situations, and that mixed-motive games are the appropriate games for the compliance problem.

2.3.1 Games and fundamental justification

My goal of fundamental moral justification leads me to model moral problems as games. Abstract games are especially suited to fundamental accounts. A game consists of two parts: players and a situation. This allows an explanation of what happens in a game to be divided between what the players want and what the situation allows. There is a general *a priori* reason why this sort of factoring is necessary for a fundamental account, be it explanation or justification. Unless complex output is explained by the interaction of (at least) two sources, the entire output must be attributable to a single source. This leaves the single source with the same complexity as the output and one hasn't reduced the problematic complexity at all.[20]

In the case of morality, a split between motivation and situation seems appropriate. The alternatives to factoring an explanation between these two elements are unsatisfactory. Either all outcomes would be determined by the situation, with no room for action, or all outcomes would be the simple result of what players want, in which case we would have no fundamental explanation, since we would need to go on to explain their wanting what they do. In other words, one way to get a fundamental account is to look for unintended consequences and games model the simplest cases of unintended consequences. The players want various outcomes (e.g. *DC*, one-sided defection in the Prisoner's Dilemma) but they can only choose from the two actions (*D* or *C*). No one player can determine the outcome so game outcomes are often unintended. This makes games attractive to social scientists seeking fundamental explanations and to moralists seeking fundamental justifications.

Which games need moral robots play well? The short answer is: *all* games. That is, I need to show that moral players do as well generally as amoral players. But I also need to show that they do better in some situations, and these are the games on which we should focus. As I have already stressed, mixed-motive games like the Prisoner's Dilemma model the compliance problem and form our crucial test.

This choice of subject is confirmed by a quick classification of games. On the one extreme are games of pure conflict. Here one player's losses are the other's gain. There is no room for mutually beneficial moral constraint and hence no place for moral constraint that could pass the test of instrumental justification. At the other extreme lie co-ordination games. It is true that moral rules might help stabilize co-ordination problems, but so can any regularity that indicates a salient outcome. The special constraining force or morality is unnecessary for co-ordination problems. So I conclude that we should attend first to mixed-motive games (so called because the attraction to the joint gains from co-operation are opposed by the pull of individually dominant defection).

2.3.2 Pure conflict

My proposal to sidestep problems of pure conflict is common in instrumental moral theory.[21] None the less, some will find it confusing. This section takes up a few objections. On the one hand, my use of games to model moral problems may seem to require attention to games of conflict. After all, the games with which most of us are familiar (e.g. tennis, chess) are games of pure conflict. But we can abstractly describe any situation which can be modelled in terms of moves and payoffs as a game, so this confusion should be short-lived.

On the other hand, moralists have given situations of conflict a great deal of attention, so my rejection of these situations as morally irrelevant needs explanation. Consider an example from Michael Frayn's *The Tin Men*, a delightful parody of artificial intelligence and what I call Artificial Morality:

> Macintosh has concentrated all his department's efforts on the Samaritan programme. The simplest and purest form of the ethical situation, as he saw it, was the one in which two people were aboard a raft which would support only one of them, and he was trying to build a machine which would offer a coherent

ethical behaviour pattern under these circumstances. It was not easy. His first attempt, Samaritan I, has pushed itself overboard with great alacrity, but it has gone overboard to save anything which happened to be next to it on the raft, from seven stone of lima beans to twelve stone of wet seaweed. After many weeks of stubborn argument, Macintosh had conceded that the lack of discrimination in this response was unsatisfactory, and he had abandoned Samaritan I and developed Samaritan II, which would sacrifice itself only for an organism at least as complicated as itself.

(Frayn 1965, p. 23)

Frayn has isolated what we shall see is the crucial cognitive problem for Artificial Morality: the ability to discriminate between those whom one should and should not treat morally.[22] However I disagree with Frayn's character, Macintosh, about what should count as 'The simplest and purest form of the ethical situation'. The Samaritan series of robots seems to be designed to deal with pure conflicts of interest. I will argue that situations like this are unlikely to have moral solutions subject to fundamental instrumental justification. The important point is that there is no mutually beneficial outcome in this situation. Therefore the rules of instrumental morality would presumably ignore such conflicts; nothing can be done to civilize this type of interaction.

This conclusion needs to be carefully circumscribed. In the first place, conflict needs to be defined and in the second, conflict needs to be limited. I take these up in order. We must be careful to distinguish conflicts of interest from conflicts of preference. Interests do not always conflict when preferences do. Our model of a situation is more complex if we have the means to distinguish *interests* from mere revealed *preferences*. For example, following Hardin (1988, §§7–9) preferences can be opposed in cases where morality still finds much to say. In particular, our *interests* may only be partially opposed yet our preferred actions may totally conflict. Consider the textbook case of me, the poor swimmer, falling into a pond and you, the good swimmer, passing by. Our preferences may be opposed: I prefer that you save me; you prefer not to ruin your clothes. But our interests need not conflict to the same degree. I stand to gain enormously at your relatively small loss. This sort of case shows us that we can only relegate cases of pure conflict outside the moral pale by assuming a conflict of interests. A conflict of preferences does not make the point. On many accounts of morality, utilitarianism being the best example, one important job of morality is precisely to tell you that you ought to rescue me in spite of our conflict of preferences.

There is another way in which my conclusion that a pure conflict of interests is beyond the power of morality may seem obviously wrong. Doesn't morality have anything to say about conflicts like war? Aren't pure conflict games such as football and baseball esteemed as ways of building moral character? Something seems to be missing from an analysis that sees no moral importance in following the rules of the game, even in games of pure conflict. Something *is* missing. Most real pure conflict games are embedded in a larger situation. This is signalled by the terms of my critic's rhetorical question: he has shifted from choices within the rules of the game to the external question of whether one should follow the rules of the game. The possibility of following the rules or not places the player in a new situation. Typically, this is also a *different* situation because the choice whether to follow the rules of a game of pure conflict does not lead to another game of pure conflict.

For example consider a fantasy based on a notorious incident that dominated the local news as I wrote the first draft of this book. Ben and Jerry are to compete in a 100 meter sprint.[23] One will win, the other lose. It appears that they are in a pure conflict situation. Now consider that they have two options with respect to the rules regarding the use of performance-enhancing drugs. Ben may follow the rules or cheat, say by taking some banned steroid. With these new options they enter a new situation, modelled by a new game. The new game is not a game of pure conflict, as becomes obvious when we ask: would they all prefer to run with or without drugs? Presumably they would all like to avoid the predicted dire consequences of a high-steroid diet, as well as the risks of exposure and sanctions. Therefore they all do better running clean than dirty. This shows that our runners are not in a pure conflict of interests; there is an optimal outcome (all run clean) and a jointly worse outcome (all run dirty). The situation is complicated by the fact that in this higher-level game they are choosing what sort of lower-level game to play, and they can choose between different games of pure conflict.

We are now in a position to answer the original objection. Many of the situations of pure conflict, such as sports contests and military battles, are embedded in larger situations structured by rules (no drugs; kill no prisoners) about which interests do not simply conflict. These are situations in which we all can do better and all do worse. We can all lose in these situations if we end up in the dirty versions of games and wars. Thus sports and war have moral import in spite, not because, of their purely conflictual elements. The moral aspect is due, I submit, to the mixed-motive structure of the larger game. We could all gain but each is tempted to break the rules. Even the lifeboat problem is embedded in a larger mixed-motive situation if the two castaways face the alternative outcomes where one peacefully jumps or both violently try to remain, with the result that both drown.

2.3.3 Abstraction and strategies

As we have seen, abstraction can be confusing. A situation can be seen as purely conflict at one level of abstraction and as admitting mutually beneficial outcomes at another. The difference is often related to the amount of freedom open to players to choose moves of varying complexity. Consider another example from the short history of artificial morality, Warren McCullough's speculations about the moral powers of simple automata. He describes a game-learning machine, imagines a tournament and then draws an interesting set of distinctions:

> a machine who desires to play and secondarily to win, if he knows what constitutes winning, need not be told the rules of the game, if only his opponent will not play unless the machine abides by the rules. He can derive them by induction, with exactly the same circuits and memory that he used to improve his play when he already knew the rules of the game.
>
> Let us therefore envision a day in the not too distant future when there are half a dozen or perhaps a hundred of these machines, some of whom have the game of chess and are eager to play . . . they will start playing; and once playing try to win. They have joined themselves into civilities at least, in order to enjoy what neither can enjoy alone. To this degree their conduct is social. Now let us distinguish three possible varieties of machines: the first and most interesting is the one we have just described; the second has the rules of the game programmed into them in advance; the third has their components so connected that they can play only according to the rules. I shall call the first ethical machines. They are free in the sense that we, their creators, have neither told them what they ought to, nor so made them that they cannot behave inappropriately. The second machine is like a man who enjoys a religion revealed to

him personally or through tradition. I shall call him a moral machine. He would have been free, had he not been programmed with the rules of conduct. The third machine is likewise not free. He is at best naturally virtuous, like the Noble Savage.

(McCullough 1965, p. 199)

I quote this fascinating passage at length because it suggests several important points. The most obvious concerns McCullough's focus on chess. This is a classic game of pure conflict of interests, but McCullough's conclusions about morality (and learning) depend on embedding chess in a mixed-motive framework as I did for the sprinting example above. I suggest that we now carry abstraction a step further, by removing altogether the underlying game of chess which complicates the situation. From the point of view of fundamental justification, the interesting choice is between these two alternatives: to follow the rules (of chess) or to cheat. These are the sort of abstract alternatives that we present to players in the Prisoner's Dilemma.

Now we can return to the question about the alternatives the players face. In chess the simple actions are moving white rook to Q5 and the like. I have suggested above that we move to higher-level alternatives. What are these? Are they simply to play fair or to cheat? I think not. McCullough assigns preferences for playing over winning that make the game mixed-motive. Since each prefers winning, it seems that we would each cheat regardless of what the other did. (Recall the reasoning for running dirty.) But McCullough concludes that one would learn not to cheat, so something is missing. What is missing from my pessimistic account is the availability of more complex conditional strategies. McCullough assumes that players can play the conditional strategy: play fair only while the other plays fair. With this strategy available, the game stabilizes into a co-ordination problem; both players do better to play fair. Therefore McCullough's conclusion is similar to Gauthier's; the moral solution is to adopt conditional constraining strategies that convert nasty mixed-motive situations into simpler co-ordination problems. This reminds us why it is important that co-ordination problems are morally tractable; otherwise this solution by conversion would lead in a circle. It also reminds us we need to give more content to the alternatives that games present only abstractly if we are to develop moral solutions. We need to know if it is possible to employ conditional strategies. I shall argue in Part II that this depends on the cognitive makeup of the players and features of their situation.

The third point connects the first and the second; it concerns another cost of focusing on chess. McCullough claims speculatively that the same program ('exactly the same circuits and memory that he used to improve his play') that would learn to play good chess would learn by simple induction not to cheat. I believe that he underestimates the difference in cognitive structure needed for the two tasks and overestimates the power of simple induction. Of course his reference to circuits offer an historical excuse; he is thinking of robots in terms of specialized hardware. I am not making the (cheap) anachronistic point that he doesn't see that software is better. My point is deeper: the structures needed for rational antagonistic play, even in a game as profoundly difficult as chess, are different from those needed to solve a moral problem by enforcing a conditional rule of responsive play. I return to this topic in Chapter 7 which takes up learning and thereby considers the differences between McCullough's moral and ethical robots.[24]

2.4 GAMES WITHOUT GAME THEORY

While using games to model situations suits the abstract style of this book, it may mislead us as well. In particular, I would like to use games without the full apparatus of game theory. My models of players and situations both differ from standard game theory; this section makes these differences explicit.

2.4.1 Players

Consider the players that populate our games. Game theory would allow us to complete this picture very quickly; its agents simply reflect their situations. Indeed, the 'agents' of game theory are vanishingly thin; they can simply be identified with the straightforwardly rational action at each choice point. I shall argue that our project of fundamental justification requires more complicated players and thus provides a reason for abandoning some of the stronger assumptions of game theory. (See §4.1.3 for further discussion.)

The theory of rational choice is in some respects remarkably simple. On the one hand, it advocates a minimal *psychology*: players reflect their situation described as a matrix of outcomes ranked by preferences. Simon (1981) puts this point graphically; the rational agent is like the ant, whose path looks complex but simply mirrors environmental complexity processed by a exceedingly simple mind. On the other hand, rational agents are all alike and are assumed to share common knowledge about themselves and their situation. This results in a minimum *sociology* as well. This simplified model has its purposes, but it is too simple to allow us to state our problem. The psychological assumption stops us from representing moral agents; the sociological assumption oversimplifies the crucial epistemic problem of discriminating friend from foe.

2.4.2 Interests and preferences

What do the numbers in our game matrices represent? It is usual in the theory of games that they represent subjective *preferences*. I will follow the lead of Russell Hardin and David Schmidtz and use *interests* instead. In this section I sketch the difference this makes for our game models and argue that interests are more appropriate for the purpose of Artificial Morality.

> I view numbers in the matrix as representing interests rather than preferences, specifically those interests brought into conflict by the situation at hand. (In other words, the numbers represent the actual stakes – e.g. monetary values or lengths of prison terms – rather than the agents' subjective reactions to those stakes.) This allows us to conclude without any residual uncertainty that the conflict of interests depicted in a matrix such as Figure [1.2] is indeed a Prisoner's Dilemma. . . . Taking the numbers to represent only those interests brought into conflict by their dilemma allows us graciously to admit that agents in such situations may have interests above and beyond their interest in maximizing incomes or minimizing prison terms. . . . On the other hand, when I say individuals prefer [defecting to co-operating], I will be assuming that their preferences track their interests in the case at hand. This saddles us with a residual uncertainty concerning whether preferences track interests in a given case. But the uncertainty here is produced by reality rather than by our model of reality. Obviously we cannot always be sure that people will do – or even want to do – what is in their best interest.
>
> (Schmidtz 1991, p. 61; figure renumbered)

It may seem strange to concur with Schmitz's empiricism for my *artificial* worlds. But I do concur. Our players should know as much as possible about the structure of their situation, but given the open-endedness of the population, they cannot know how other players will react to this structure of interests. Furthermore, scores should represent interests rather than subjective preferences because the players I introduce are typically too simple to have full subjective preferences. The tournament test that I will introduce in Part II will help to ensure that the population consists mainly of players whose preferences track their interests in the game.

There is an unresolved methodological tension here. It would be simpler to follow the received theory of rational choice, as Gauthier does, in its assumption of subjective preferences. This would allow my argument to serve as an internal criticism of these two theories. It may also seem that my argument would have weaker premises in this case. However, this last point is not so clear, as theories that assume subjective preferences plus common knowledge must also assume some other interaction where subjective preference information is revealed. (Preference revelation is non-trivial for mixed-motive games.)

CONCLUSION

It will be useful to summarize this chapter in terms of the differences between my approach and its closest neighbour, David Gauthier's morals by agreement. Both seek fundamental justifications for distinctly moral principles. Gauthier claims that his premises are true of people; I do not. Gauthier's theory is also much wider, as he offers a theory of justice as well as of compliance. (Neither of us discusses allegiance.) Within the compliance problem, both of us treat the issue as one that can be represented in terms of mixed-motive games, such as the Prisoner's Dilemma. Both of us allow players who can choose against their preferences. However, I use a weaker theory of games than Gauthier; I do not assume equal rationality or common knowledge of subjective preference information.

3

NATURE AND ARTIFICE

THE SEARCH FOR CONSTRAINT

Artificial Morality borders on fantasy. Writing moral principles for imaginary creatures playing abstract games sounds like science fiction. Indeed, Artificial Morality *is* science fiction – imaginative fantasy constrained by science. All simulation is; this is not grounds for dismissal.[1] A problem remains. Without scientific constraint, fantasy can be tedious.[2] And I appear to be doing all that I can to cut myself loose from any such mooring. In particular, I seem to ignore recent advances in the scientific understanding of behaviour. Sociobiology claims to explain many kinds of behaviour, including the moral phenomenon of altruism, within a methodologically attractive framework of individualistic rationality.

Sociobiology is attractive and I do wish to avoid fantasy. Indeed, this book began when reading Richard Dawkins' splendid *Selfish Gene* convinced me that my moral intuitionism was methodologically embarrassing. So this project began with sociobiology and owes most of its methods to research in that field. None the less one cannot build a fundamental justification of morality on the basis of the main results of sociobiology: kin and reciprocal altruism. The first provides no fundamental justification of morality; the second is not about morality (strictly speaking) at all. I shall set out these reasons in detail in the first two sections of this chapter. This leaves me free of nature; is there any source of constraint left? Yes, there are the boundaries of what can be constructed using the most general and adaptable of means, a programmable general purpose automatic symbol interpreter: a computer. Artificial Morality takes its source of constraint here, from the limits of what is procedurally possible.

3.1 SOCIOBIOLOGY

As the initial exaggerated controversies that marked its reception have died down, the contribution of sociobiology to moral philosophy has become evident. Sociobiology has inspired a new naturalism, an impatience with moral obfuscation and a willingness to apply models from game and decision theory in new ways. I am happy to be working in such exciting times and proud to identify Artificial Morality as Darwinian in this broad sense:

> Darwin advocated a natural and testable theory based on immediate interactions among individuals (his opponents considered it heartlessly mechanistic). The theory of natural selection is a creative transfer to biology of Adam Smith's basic argument for a rational economy: the balance and order of nature does not arise from a higher, external (divine) control, or from the existence of laws operating directly upon the whole, but from struggle among individuals for their own benefit.
>
> (Gould 1980, p. 67)

I find Darwinism profoundly liberating, both intellectually and politically, as it frees us from oversimplified models of central (divine or political) control of our affairs.[3] Sociobiology provides deep and satisfying fundamental *explanations* of some apparently moral behaviour. The application of Darwinism to ethics as an empirical phenomena, resulting in the discovery of natural laws like kin and reciprocal altruism, is attractive. But sociobiology is a specific application of Darwinian theory to animal behaviour and in this form, I shall argue, it can mislead us in our quest for fundamental justification.

3.1.1. A common problem

Readers familiar with sociobiology will find my formulation of the problem of social co-operation familiar. I ask: how should a rationally self-interested agent play mixed-motive games such as the Prisoner's Dilemma? As Richmond Campbell explains in his excellent introduction, this is similar to the central problem in sociobiology, the problem of altruism:

> Since there is some uncertainty in the biological literature on this point, it is worth emphasizing that co-operative behavior in a PD situation fits the biological definition of altruism. If organism *A* behaves co-operatively, organism *B* will have a

higher level of fitness and *A* will have a *lower* level of fitness (than if *A* had behaved nonco-operatively) no matter which choice *B* makes. In other words, *A*'s co-operation produces a net gain in fitness for *B* and a net loss for *A*. The explanation of mutual co-operation in such cases is a genuine challenge to the orthodox understanding of natural selection.

This challenge is indeed virtually identical to the difficulty of explaining how mutual co-operation in a PD is individually rational – rational according [to] rational egoism – given payoffs measured in units of individual utility. Natural selection favors the behavior with the higher expected individual fitness; rational egoism favors the behavior with the higher expected individual utility.

(Campbell 1985b, p. 285)

In view of such a striking similarity of problem, the question arises, why don't I simply apply the results of sociobiology to answer my question about rational morality as well? The answer is that in spite of these striking similarities, there is a crucial difference. Sociobiology is concerned to show how something like morality is possible for biological creatures. It is not concerned with justifying morality fundamentally. This leads to two differences between sociobiology and my project. First, sociobiology has a different model of motivation; for example, it explains some morality – kin altruism – as a fact given by an organism's biological nature. It shows how some unselfish behaviour is natural by virtue of other-regarding motivators built into organisms by evolutionary processes. In contrast, Artificial Morality justifies moral constraint even for agents without other-regarding preferences, by giving them reasons to enhance their natural preferences by means of cognitive and cultural artifice. Second, sociobiology need not focus on morality *per se*; indeed we shall see that the explanation of reciprocal altruism falls short of addressing a moral problem at all, because it sets agents in a situation, the Iterated Prisoner's Dilemma, that does not require moral constraint. Therefore, I shall argue, the results of sociobiology are irrelevant to Artificial Morality. Since these are controversial claims, I shall proceed carefully.

3.1.2. Kin selection

Kin selection is sociobiology's distinctive contribution to our understanding of the limits genetics may set for morality.[4] The basic idea is that one's genetic nature – how one's natural kind of creature came about – can drastically affect one's motivation. The rough idea is that because siblings share genes, they share genetic interests as well. Since my sister and I share more genes than you and I share, my genes will likely incline me to more altruistic behaviour towards my sister. The stock example has me sacrificing myself if the chance of saving one of my siblings is greater than one-half. Since I share one-half of my genes with each sibling, from the genes' point of view, this is a good deal; the trade-off is directly advantageous for my family's genes.

For all of its power, kin selection does not answer any question about instrumentally useful morality. We can reformulate its problem as: when, if ever, should selfish genes cause organisms to co-operate?[5] The main defect in the theory of kin altruism is that it fails to account for an organism's constraint as useful *for that organism*. Kin selection concludes that constraint on the part of an organism is rational from the point of view of its genes. In a case of altruism due to kin selection, I do not benefit from my self-sacrifice in order to save my sister; my action is rational only from the point of view of my genes. The question I seek to answer is different. How can it be useful *for me*, the agent, to constrain myself? Because of its motivational premise, the sociobiological concept of kin selection is irrelevant to this question of fundamental justification of morality.

Let me add that kin selection is not irrelevant to another way to approach ethics generally. We might ask a different question: why, as a human, need I not be constrained to sacrifice my interests for the sake of my daughters? I want to do this; it comes naturally to me as a parent. In this case I do not *need* morality; it is straightforwardly rational for me to act on my other-regarding desires. The question of the *instrumental* rationality of these attitudes does not arise, for the simple reason that they play no instrumental role. When one loves his children, as I do, this is what one wants, and instrumental rationality takes agents' wants as its motivational primitive. The question of rationality arises when we consider Hume's second class of moral duties, the artificial duties of justice, fidelity and allegiance, by which one's 'original inclination . . . or instinct, is here checked or restrained'.[6] How can it be rational for an agent so to restrain itself for the sake of others (or all impartially)?

Here sociobiology explains why egoism is generally false; nepotism is a better empirical premise for predicting what humans will do (Campbell 1986). Kin selection explains but provides no fundamental justification of these ethically significant desires. In conclusion, the sociobiological explanation by appeal to genetic interests spanning kin falls short of a fundamental justification by appeal to the agent's interests. While the selfish gene theory might answer the question how selfish genes can lead to less selfish organisms, it is irrelevant to the question why selfish organisms should be non-selfish.

3.1.3. Reciprocal altruism

Kin selection may explain why an agent may in fact care about its relatives; it provides no reason why an agent ought to so care. A justification must be addressed to the interests of the agent, not those of his genes. The second sociobiological model, reciprocal altruism, need not suffer this defect. The interests of the agent and his genes can be identified when kin are out of the picture. But reciprocal altruism faces two equally serious objections. First, the problem reciprocal altruism solves is not a moral problem. I take this up in the next section where I argue that iterated games are morally irrelevant. I turn to the second problem now: the evolutionary defence of reciprocal altruism invokes the mechanism of differential survival. This mechanism only applies where the values involved are *fitness interests*. However, fitness interests are inappropriate values for a fundamental justification of morality. Instrumental justification must appeal to something that the agent wants, or, at least, should want. I have taken up the latter alternative, and tied my justification with successful pursuit of objective interests. Still, an agent's interests need not include reproductive fitness. It is true that it will be generally useful for a moral agent to be copied by other agents, but this is an indirect, not an intrinsic reproductive interest. Things could go otherwise. For example, it is generally useful for an exploitative wolf in sheep's clothing to have others copy her sheepishness. I conclude that while genetic reproduction leads to organisms with intrinsic reproductive interests, artificial justification need make no similar assumption. Our agents should care about scoring but scoring need not be connected to reproduction.

The foundations of sociobiology

The previous argument requires that I separate selection and rationality. However this creates a problem for the rational choice approach. Crudely put, we cut ourselves off from their answer to the question: why start with self-interested rationality? Sociobiology provides a splendid answer: the basic mechanism of evolution entails that there will be selfish somethings – whatever is the basic unit of selection. For Dawkins (controversially) these are genes:

> At the gene level, altruism must be bad and selfishness good. This follows inexorably from our definitions of altruism and selfishness. [An entity, such as a baboon, is said to be altruistic if it behaves in such a way as to increase another entity's welfare at the expense of its own. Selfish behaviour has exactly the opposite effect.] Genes are competing directly with their alleles for survival, since their alleles in the gene pool are rivals for their slot on the chromosomes of future generations. Any gene which behaves in such a way as to increase its own survival chances in the gene pool at the expense of its alleles will, by definition, tautologously, tend to survive. The gene is the basic unit of selfishness.
>
> (Dawkins 1976, pp. 4, 38–9)

If Dawkins is right, sociobiology provides a true fundamental explanation, that is, in my terms, a foundation of selfishness. Genes are truly selfish and they have an interest sometimes in building altruistic organisms. In contrast, I have argued that a fundamental justification must start at a higher level, with the agent (the organism). At this level, as we have seen, there is no such general reason to think most organisms will be selfish. On the contrary, sociobiology provides strong reasons to expect natural nepotism and altruism. This is another reason to emphasize the *counter-factural* aspect of my motivational assumption. I do not *assert* that agents are truly egoists (psychological egoism) nor do I argue for egoism as a moral conclusion (ethical egoism). Instead I ask, if agents were selfish, why and how could they become morally constrained? Perhaps I should call this *hypothetical egoism*.

I hope that it is clear that I do not claim that artificial agents are necessarily self-interested. Starting with artificial agents is permissive, not determining.[7] Artificial agents impose no goals, self-interested or otherwise. Their job is to impose a weak procedural constraint on means. Indeed, if there is any connection between robots and selfishness it is the opposite of what a foundational account requires. On the one hand, Oldenquist (1980) argues that robots should tend to be naturally selfless, not self-interested. On the other hand, we should only expect selfishness where some mechanism selects for it.[8] This is arguably true in the case of genes and perhaps for firms and states. But it will only be true for robots if we *make* it true. We make it true by imposing the scoring regime that sets the task for our tournament of games.

Conclusion

I reject what is distinctive about sociobiology as irrelevant to the fundamental justification of morality for quite traditional reasons. Both kin selection and the appeal to fitness interests in the account of reciprocal altruism fail as justifications. Neither factual family connections nor probable reproductive success need be relevant to the interests of an agent.

3.2 THE ITERATED PRISONER'S DILEMMA

Some of the appeal of sociobiology stems from its application of game theory to a new range of problems. Why, for example, do predators *not* fight each other very often? Sociobiology rejects the traditional and morally reassuring explanation that this behaviour is 'for the good of the species'. Intra-specific limits on aggression *are* good for the species but unfortunately, as I have been at pains to stress by emphasizing the compliance problem, benefits to all need not rationally motivate each. So how do non-kin manage ever to co-operate?[9] The sociobiological answer – reciprocal altruism – amounts to showing that in some games the co-operative outcome is also straightforwardly rational. That is, agents who can recognize other agents and are likely to interact with them again, are playing *iterated* games.[10] Some of these are quite easily resolved by reciprocal strategies: if you remove my ticks, then I will remove yours.

I hope that two things are immediately clear from my rough description. First, these solutions have nothing whatsoever to do with biology in general or genetics in particular. For example, Robert Axelrod's general and accessible discussion of reciprocal altruism (Axelrod 1984), begins by applying the theory to legislators, not to lower animals. Second, since iterated games can be solved by straightforwardly rational agents, they are not morally significant problems. This second point is likely to be controversial, so I will defend it in detail in this section.

3.2.1 The moral triviality of Tit for Tat

Tit for Tat is the principle of co-operating initially and then matching one's co-player's previous action. As Axelrod has shown, TFT effectively induces widespread co-operation. Therefore it is an impartial, mutually beneficial principle. None the less, TFT is not a moral principle because in the Iterated Prisoner's Dilemma it is straightforwardly in an agent's interests. Given the expectation of future interactions, and other agents' responsiveness, each of the choices required by TFT is directly maximizing.[11] Since straightforward maximization suffices here, there is no need for a new kind of principle, namely a moral principle constraining an agent's self-interest. Therefore, I agree with Gauthier that agents following TFT 'exhibit no real constraint'.[12]

It is tempting to see TFT as a moral principle, as I did in Danielson (1986). This is mistaken; TFT is no more moral than are the other choice rules subsidiary to straightforward maximization, such as the maximin decision rule for games of pure conflict. The Iterated PD may be represented to look like the one-shot Prisoner's Dilemma, where D would be dominant. But the appearance of similarity is misleading. In an iterated game, players get to choose from a large number of sequential strategies; this is called a supergame. In the supergame, the strategy of always choosing D is simply short-sighted because the repeated situation allows the other player's future behaviour to be influenced by the player's present action. With the prospect of an indeterminately ending series of two-player games with the other player capable of responding to one's actions, the consequence of choosing C is a series of Rewards (value = 2) and the consequence of choosing D is a series of Penalties (value = 1). For a player who weighs future payoffs prudently (that is, with a sufficiently low discount rate), the C choices required by TFT are straightforwardly better than D. Tit for Tat exercises no constraint over the player. My mistake was to define morality too widely. Not every secondary rule specifying the egoistic first principle should count as a moral rule. Otherwise, we trivially incorporate all of economics, game and decision theory into morality.

3.2.2 Indirection

Because Tit for Tat is not obviously a straightforward maximizer, it provides a good contrast against which to sharpen our sense of what is required for a principle to count as constraining an player.[13] I shall argue that Tit for Tat is the straightforwardly rational strategy in the Iterated PD despite Richmond Campbell's claims to the contrary. The problem is that one can think of *more* apparently straightforward strategies for the iterated PD. I can speak of this with some feeling. I once spent the better part of a weekend working on what I took to be the strongest straightforward maximizer, who worked by doing a sophisticated appraisal of many different alternative strategies. Unfortunately, my Look-ahead player lost and TFT won (in a class of thirty computer science students). My player (based on Axelrod (1978)) looks like a maximizer; TFT doesn't. But what is crucial to straightforward maximization is not the look – or any procedural suggestion – of maximizing but the inability to choose against one's own preferences. In Parfit (1984)'s terms, straightforward maximizers are 'never self-denying'. TFT never denies herself; since TFT is the most effective player of this sort, she best exemplifies straightforward maximization.

Richmond Campbell disagrees in two respects. First consider the situation from the point of view of the player using the TFT strategy. The strategy *appears* to constrain because it requires that one initially choose *C* when *D* is dominant. Campbell (1985b, p. 288) writes,

> the rational egoist's use of TFT . . . does constitute altruism toward many *other* individuals. In interactions with pure co-operators, for example, the fact that the rational egoist has chosen TFT over pure nonco-operation yields a net gain to the pure co-operator at a net cost to the rational egoist.

I think that Campbell is mistaken here. He neglects the context that informs Axelrod's results. Axelrod applies what he calls an 'ecological analysis' to his tournaments, selecting only the most successful players. Therefore, no unconditional co-operators survive after the first few rounds. In a population with many unconditional co-operators, TFT does worse than quite a few other strategies submitted; indeed, *every* strategy does better than TFT against random players (Axelrod 1984, p. 194).[14] The only reason that TFT co-operates with unconditional co-operators or random players is because otherwise it would pay costs later. Attempts to find out whether one faces one of these easy victims evidently cost more in an environment selected for success. Campbell ignores these epistemic costs. Once again, I conclude that TFT shows no constraint.

In another discussion, Campbell (1988b, p. 207) contrasts TFT with an agent who is free to choose:

> The Tit for Tat 'agent' is a paradigm of mechanism and utterly devoid of libertarian free will . . . agents with libertarian free will . . . would, in effect, make up their decision rules as they go along, deciding whether or not to cooperate move by move, unbound by any predetermined response pattern.

Although Campbell does not strictly identify these libertarian agents with straightforward maximizers, he does call them 'smart' and draws the contrast between them on one side and TFT and constrained maximizers on the other.[15] Again I believe that Campbell is mistaken. 'Straightforward' should not be confused with 'simple.' The theory of straightforward maximization includes all of decision theory, game theory and economics (most of which is not simple for me). Some of its recommendations require highly complex algorithms. Conversely, an agent who simply chooses what *appears* to be best at each point is evidently *not* a straightforward maximizer in a situation, like the IPD, where there are costs to trial-and-error learning.[16] Straightforward maximization is a criterion of (one theory of) rational action. It requires that an agent never choose what is worse by his preferences; it does not identify any particular decision procedure.[17]

These conclusions are confirmed when we shift to the point of view of another player contemplating co-operation in the IPD. Need this player know that her co-player is constrained in order to be assured sufficiently to choose C? As I will argue in Chapter 4, in the one-shot PD, she does; she needs to know how her co-player is constituted and that this constitution constrains the other player. But in the IPD, it suffices to know that the other player is straightforwardly rational and not short-sighted for, as Axelrod argues, he will then follow TFT. This contrast brings out an important epistemic cost of the strategies like constrained maximization. Straightforward maximizers need not know *how* other straightforward maximizers work, only *that* they do indeed straightforwardly maximize. Knowing that another is a straightforward maximizer, which one might know due to the optimizing or other selective pressures in the environment, suffices to predict her behaviour. But constrained maximizers must know more; they must know how the other works. To put the contrast graphically, in the IPD one can afford to co-operate with an opaque, *black box* player, while in the one-shot PD one needs assurance that can only be gotten if the other is a transparent *glass box* player.

3.2.3 The significance of Tit for Tat

However, this is not to say that the iterated case is not morally interesting.[18] It is, in two ways.

Moral Anarchy

The main moral significance of TFT and reciprocal altruism is negative. They show us that we don't need to use morality to achieve co-operation in a certain class of situations, namely Iterated Prisoner's Dilemmas. In this respect there is a parallel between the IPD and the market, at least under the description of it as a 'moral anarchy'.[19] In both cases moral constraint is unnecessary; straightforward maximizing suffices to achieve optimal outcomes.[20] TFT in the IPD is interesting because it often achieves joint co-operation without moral constraint. The IPD does not require a moral change in the player; co-operation is rational because of the situation. Therefore Axelrod's results belong in abstract sociology, where they parallel Hobbes' in political science and Adam Smith's in economics. Each points to a type of situation (iteration, the state, the market) in which straight-forwardly rational players will achieve unexpectedly beneficial outcomes. I call such solutions, which are alternatives to internal moral constraint, *institutional solutions*. Of these, Axelrod's situations are minimally institutionalized and interesting in this respect. On the one hand, Axelrod's results greatly extend and thereby strengthen the externalized institutional theory of co-operation, which, as I see things, is a competitor to the internalized approach characteristic of morality. On the other hand, by relieving morality of some burdens, institutions that promote co-operation make morality's job easier. Morality need not support the *entire* social world by chains of obligation.

Tit for Tat as a model

Second, the responsiveness of other players creates the environment in which Tit for Tat is rational. Similarly, the rational success of the responsive moral principles that Gauthier and I defend depends on others' responsiveness. Therefore Gauthier exaggerates when he claims that there is *no* parallel between constrained maximization and TFT.[21] Both depend on artificial selection: the social success of each depends on other players discovering an appropriate discriminating strategy. Axelrod rightly points out that transparency and responsiveness are important because they allow others to discriminate TFT from less co-operative strategies and can be achieved even by simple organisms (and organizations) in the iterated case. A central problem for Artificial Morality is to show how to extend these ideas from Iterated Prisoner's Dilemmas to other, less tractable games: the single play PD, Chicken, and eventually to multi-player situations.[22]

Conclusion

I conclude that morally significant games should not be iterated, as this supports an institutional, in contrast to an internalized moral, solution to the problem of unstable social co-operation. Notice that I do not defend my focus on the extreme, one-shot, PD on grounds of realism. Doubtless, many actual social situations are better modelled by Iterated Prisoner's Dilemmas. But some are not and these are crucial for isolating the special technique of impartial self-constraint that I identify as distinguishing morality. I focus on one-shot games on methodological grounds; they are crucial cases to test the claim of morality to contribute uniquely to instrumental rationality. Indeed, if one-shot games did not exist, moral theorists would need to invent them. In order to focus on situations that require morality as a particular form of cognitive technique, we must eliminate iteration. Thus non-iteration is the situational analogue of my assumption of narrow, self-interested motivation. Neither is true; each is chosen to specify our problem of fundamental moral justification. Finally, removing iteration makes the problems of constructing discriminating moral players more difficult as we shall see in Part II.

3.2.4 Beyond sociobiology

I have surveyed two reasons to distinguish Artificial Morality from sociobiology: the motivation of the agents and the character of the situations studied by biologists are inappropriate to my task of fundamental justification. There is a third difference as well, one that should be obvious but is easily forgotten. Animals and plants mostly feed on each other by force. Co-operation is the exception, not the norm for natural interaction. Sociobiology is news because it explains what ethnology reveals: the small but unexpected amount of co-operation in nature. In contrast, human life is characterized by – indeed our civilized mode of life is only possible because of – extensive co-operation.[23] It seems obvious that a theory that justifies widespread co-operation as the norm must go beyond sociobiology. Co-operation apparently depends on the ability to communicate in ways unavailable to most animals. In this respect, Artificial Morality will need to move beyond sociobiology in order to enrich its models with enhanced means of communication and commitment.

3.3 PHILOSOPHY AND ARTIFICIAL INTELLIGENCE

As an alternative to sociobiology, I find a source of constraint in the constructive task of building successful players. Therefore I turn to artificial intelligence, considered as the science of engineering intelligent agents, and its relation to philosophy.

3.3.1. Moral engineering

The field of artificial intelligence (AI) is conventionally divided into two parts. One, cognitive engineering, tries to discover ways to build intelligent machines. The other, cognitive science, tries to build mechanistic models of human psychological abilities. The latter is tied to what nature has already accomplished in the case of people; the former is unconstrained and can study intelligence as such. Artificial Morality is a branch of cognitive engineering; it is moral engineering.[24]

The distinction is sometimes drawn to begin an argument that the goal of cognitive engineering is ill-formed. This is an argument that I should consider, since it speaks against my decision to follow the engineers and abandon the human paradigm. Haugeland (1987, p. 5) puts the argument in an interesting context:

> Artificial Intelligence in this sense (as a branch of cognitive science) is the only kind we will discuss. For instance, we will pay no attention to . . . [cognitive engineering] systems . . . that make no pretense of developing or applying psychological principles. . . . My own hunch, in fact, is that anthropomorphic prejudice, 'human chauvinism', is built into our very concept of intelligence. This concept, of course, could still apply to all manner of creatures; the point is merely that it's the only concept we have – if we have escaped our 'prejudice', we wouldn't know what we were talking about.
>
> Be that as it may, the only *theoretical* reason to take contemporary Artificial Intelligence more seriously than

51

clockwork fiction is the powerful suggestion that our own minds work on computational principles. In other words, we're really interested in AI as part of the theory that *people* are computers – and we're all interested in people.

Haugeland suggests in the first paragraph that without the instance of human intelligence we simply would have nothing upon which to pin the concept of intelligence. Therefore he concludes (on the next page) that AI is wedded to Turing's test, that determines X to be intelligence by asking whether X is indistinguishable in (cognitive) behaviour from a normal human (Turing 1953). Haugeland continues in the second paragraph quoted above by suggesting that without the goal of modelling human abilities, AI would be only slightly more constrained than science fiction, off on an endless quest for fancier contraptions. These claims are plausible in the case of intelligence; I shall not dispute them. What about the case of morality? To many it will seem that Haugeland's conceptual conservatism (no instance, no concept) has an even stronger basis in the case of morality. Indeed, having rejected the sociobiological attribution of morality to lower animals in the previous section, it would seem that I must hold that the only morality we know is human morality.

However, morality and intelligence differ in this important respect. We are not exemplars of morality. In the case of intelligence, we humans occupy a privileged and commanding position. We possess a formidable natural intelligence that we should challenge AI to match. In contrast we are not at the pinnacle of morality; indeed we don't know what it is or even if there is such a thing. Of course we have moral ideals but they are many and often incompatible. And it isn't that some are immoral in the way that some are simply stupid. The problem is that how much and which way to be moral is fundamentally contested by people, especially 'morally smart' people. This indeed is one reason I am interested in a fundamental justification. I hope that it will shed some light on what rational morality might be like. There is a sense in which rational morality, unlike intelligence, still needs to be invented.

3.3.2 Reductive explanation and justification

Artificial Morality differs from AI as portrayed by Haugeland in a second respect. AM does have a goal distinct from modelling human moral behaviour. Rationality provides this goal. Unlike intelligence, where there is arguably no independent criterion apart from normal human performance, we can subject morality to the test of substantive rationality. This provides a way to cut through the thicket of moral disagreement. We assume that morality is a means to agents' ends and test it by the standard of means-ends rationality.

This is a reductive approach to morality. Certainly human ethical life has many facets that may be lost in the reduction to what is individually rational. What is lost in richness may be made up in rigour and enlightenment. This brings us back to cognitive engineering, with its commitment to reduce the mysteriously mental to layers of machinery, each of which is transparent. One way to state the goal of cognitive engineering is to construct an intelligent agent using non-intelligent parts. When successful, this yields a fundamental explanation of some bit of intelligence, one that makes no appeal to intelligence in its premises.

> To explain the mind, we have to show how minds are built from mindless stuff, from parts that are much smaller and simpler than anything we'd consider smart. Unless we can explain the mind in terms of things that have no thoughts or feelings of their own, we'll only have gone around in a circle.
>
> (Minsky 1986, p. 18)

The goal of Artificial Morality is similar. I aim to construct a moral agent starting with non-moral motivation. To do this I use the tools and methods of one prominent tradition of AI: symbolic information processing using logic programming in artificially simplified toy domains.

3.3.3 Two contrasts

My title, Artificial Morality, may suggest two other projects from which mine should be distinguished.

Moral expert systems

First, moral philosophy is a broader inquiry than my quest for a fundamental justification of moral constraint. Many moral philosophers are prepared to accept some moral principle or principles as premises and focus on the problems that arise further on in the argument. For example, it is problematic how a deontological agent, that is, one constrained by moral rules, can make these rules both consistent and complete. I suspect that the simulation techniques found in Artificial Intelligence can advance our understanding of these problems; one could attempt to build moral expert systems. One would begin with a set of rules or goals, attempt to implement them mechanically, and then test them against increasingly difficult problems.[25] I do not deny that this is an important area for research. Indeed, unless my agents can move from highly simplified games to increasingly realistic moral problems, my approach deserves to be criticized as 'artificial' in the pejorative sense. But I follow a strategy of divide and conquer. Moral philosophy asks both *why* and *how* an agent should constrain itself. This book focuses on the first – and to me prior – question: why should a rational agent constrain itself at all? This question directs us initially to simple situations that pose the conflict between moral constraint and amoral self-interest most clearly. I leave to another occasion the further problem of how to build agents able to deal with the complexities of a richer moral life.

Moral science fiction

Second, I should distinguish another link between Artificial Intelligence and morality, one that takes a different path through science fiction. Some have argued that if AI were ever to be successful at creating something intellectually on a par with a normal human being, then that thing ought to have moral standing. It would *be* a person (Leiber 1985). I have no quarrel with these arguments from the possibility of artificial persons but my argument is different. I need not claim that (so-called 'strong' (Searle 1981)) AI could be fully successful, nor that the mechanisms that I build are agents in some strong sense, fully capable of action in a real world, much less capable of understanding or solving real human moral problems. I am not concerned with full, rich, human persons but instead with one of the core problems of moral theory: how can moral constraint be rational. I claim that actual programmed mechanisms – agents in a minimal sense – clarify and solve some of these problems. Indeed, that artificial players can solve some abstract moral problems is scientific fact, not fiction.

3.3.4 Theory and practice

Why should someone interested in moral theory actually attempt to build a (software) robot? One lesson of AI has been the enormous distance between plausible philosophical theory and workable computational practice. Two celebrated theorists testify to the beneficial effects of this high-level methodological pragmatism:

> Artificial intelligence cannot avoid philosophy. If a computer program is to behave intelligently in the real world, it must be provided with some kind of framework into which to fit particular facts it is told or discovers. This amounts to at least a fragment of some kind of philosophy. . . . The next plausible alternative might be to build our programs to seek and represent knowledge in accordance with the tenets of one of the philosophies that have been proposed by philosophers. This also has not been possible. Either no one in AI (including retreaded philosophers) understands philosophical theories well enough to program a computer in accordance with their tenets, or the philosophers have not even come close to the required precision.
>
> (McCarthy 1988, pp. 305–6)

I hope to show that moral philosophy will prove more tractable than epistemology. My theory is an attempt to implement part of David Gauthier's theory of morals by agreement which, contrary to McCarthy, I find almost precise enough to be implemented mechanically.[26] To test this understanding, as well as to meet objections, I must actually build some agents.

As Dennett suggests, the rigour of implementation will force us to confront many problems that can be ignored in philosophical thought experiments:

> Most AI projects are explorations of *ways things might be done* and as such are more like thought experiments than empirical experiments. They differ from philosophical thought experiments not primarily in their content but in their methodology: they replace some – but not all – of the 'intuitive', 'plausible', hand-waving background assumptions of philosophical thought experiments by constraints dictated by the demand that the model be made to run on the computer. . . .
>
> The constraints imposed serve to discipline the imagination – and hence the claims – of the thought experimenter. There is very little chance that a philosopher will be surprised (or more exactly, disappointed) by the results of his own thought experiment, but this happens all the time in AI.
>
> (Dennett 1988, p. 289)

I can attest to the power of these methods to discipline speculation. The agents presented in Parts II and III are nothing like what I first imagined they would be. Some problems, like solving the co-ordination problem of principles, or deciding whether to copy another agent's principles with variables or constants, simply didn't arise in my original thought experiments.

Finally, while I agree with Dennett that my constructions – my games and players – are more like thought experiments than real experiments, realizing them as computer programs pushes them in the empirical direction. By sharing the programs for generating and testing players, and hosting a tournament for the creation of others, we can construct an (incrementally richer) environment in which the results tend to have more empirical validity.

CONCLUSION

I set out to ask whether morality is rational, which led us, in Chapter 2, to explore fundamental justification. In this chapter I have argued that in spite of the appeal of Darwinism, sociobiology provides an inappropriate framework. Fundamental justification forces us to consider the hard case of the compliance problem, not the easier Iterated Prisoner's Dilemma, and it aims at a rationale for morality applicable to any possible agent. The limits of nature, whether human, mammalian, animal or even biological are irrelevant. The only relevant limits are the constraints posed by what it is to be an player interacting with other players. These are the purely procedural limits on motivation, cognition and communication. I ask what an agent must be that it may be moral and rational. Artificial intelligence seems the best place to start this constructive task, which I take up in the next chapter.

Part II

RATIONAL
CONSTRAINT

Part II presents the central result of Artificial Morality, a constructive demonstration of how it is rational to be moral. I will develop problems incrementally, as I introduce logic programming as a method for implementing players and their situation. Chapter 4 uses my method to defend something close to David Gauthier's principle of constrained maximization against several objections. The next chapter is more critical; I propose a new player, the reciprocal cooperator, that trades moral nastiness for rational gains. Chapter 6 turns to the moral problem of evaluating these results. Part II considers only the Prisoner's Dilemma under idealized conditions of full information and small, hand-selected populations of players. Part III extends the argument.

4

CONDITIONAL
CO-OPERATION

Critics have objected to constrained maximization (CM) for several reasons. Some criticize CM because it deviates from the received theory of rational choice. Others find CM impossible because of the procedural complexities of conditional co-operation.[1] In this chapter I defend the possibility of constrained maximization *from the point of view of artificial morality*,[2] by focusing on this pair of criticisms, the first methodological and the second procedural. To the first I reply that the possibility of indirect choice must be allowed if we are to *argue for* (rather than assert) the received theory of rational choice. I address the second by actually implementing a working CM player in the simplest sequential case. I strengthen this argument by implementing a CM player for the procedurally more difficult simultaneous case.

4.1 A NEUTRAL CRITERION OF SUCCESS

I am attempting show how morality can be instrumentally efficient; how some mutually beneficial constraining principles are the best means to a player's ends. Following David Gauthier, I want to argue for the rationality of indirect choice, where principles constraining a player's immediate choices are his best means in some situations. Both this argument, and those of critics of indirection, should appeal to a neutral criterion for success, which leaves open whether straightforward or indirect choice of actions is better. I develop one such criterion in this section.

The quest for a fundamental justification of morality properly begins with instrumental rationality, for two reasons. A justification must be embedded in a normative theory and the premises of a fundamental justification must be non-moral. Taken broadly, rational choice provides the non-moral normative framework that we need:

The theory of rational choice is, before it is anything else, a normative theory. It tell[s] us what we ought to do in order to achieve our aims as well as possible. It does not tell us what our aims ought to be. . . . Unlike moral theory, rational-choice theory offers conditional imperatives, pertaining to means rather than to ends.

(Elster 1986a, p. 1)

The received theory of rational choice goes on to identify rationality with a particularly direct connection of means to ends. But we should hesitate here. I propose remaining at the broadest level, to use this overarching instrumentalism as our highest standard of rationality. The job of the criterion of substantive rationality or instrumental success is to characterize the substantive aim of rational players in abstract terms.[3] 'The aim of rational choice seems straightforward: to maximize the number of units of payoff received in the outcome of the choice' (Campbell 1985a, p. 40). Scores generate a ranking over outcomes, rational action is that action that leads to the best outcome (or outcomes). This criterion is abstract and empty of any guidance to the player as to how best to select the best action. The criterion of rational success gets its normative force from recommending efficient means to the player's ends. We presume that the player does want what is in his interest, the theory presumes that he ought to want the best means thereto.

4.1.1 Theories of rational choice

The job of a *theory* of choice is to provide more determinant grounds for choice. This task is trivially easy in the case of choices between pairs of actions which each result in single outcomes with certainty. It grows more difficult as one proceeds to uncertain choices and then to games against rational players. Indeed, up to and including zero-sum games of pure competition, the received theory of choice is almost universally accepted. Deep controversy begins with mixed-motive games, such as the Prisoner's Dilemma, where the optimum outcome is not an equilibrium of rational choices.

In the face of situations like the Prisoner's Dilemma, it is not obvious *how* to achieve successful outcomes. We need to continue to distinguish two parts of the general theory of instrumental choice: the *criterion* of success which sets the rational goal and various *theories or conceptions* of rationality purporting to tell a player how to select instrumentally successful acts. On this account, the received theory, which, following Gauthier I label straightforward maximization (SM), is one possible theory of rational choice, not to be confused with the criterion of rationality. It is a well developed theory, which defends the thesis that maximizing at each choice point is the best way to maximize. This elegant, strong thesis may be true. To determine whether it *is* true I suggest testing it against a criterion of substantive rationality. The received theory must show that players who follow it reach better outcomes (in terms of their own interests).

However, many advocates of the received theory do not distinguish a neutral substantive criterion from their favoured theory of rational action. This leads me to wonder how they plan to argue for their theory without a standard against which to test it. Do they think that their theory is true by definition, self-evident or obvious to intuition? Such moves tend to evacuate the theory of rational choice of all content. On my account, in contrast, the received theory is significant. It asserts that direct choice is best; straightforward maximizing is the best way to maximize. This has content, and – I hope to show – it is false. Indirect, morally constrained choice does better, as we shall soon see.

4.1.2 A utilitarian parallel

There is a parallel with utilitarianism. The criterion of rational action, like the utilitarian criterion, is *objective*. It tells players to be whatever sort of thing would best further their interests. The difference is that the rational criterion aims at maximizing only the player's interests while the utilitarian criterion aims at maximizing the interests of a larger set of players. To apply either criterion to action, a player needs a theory of rational or utilitarian choice, respectively. Utilitarians debate whether players should try directly to maximize utility or instead, indirectly to follow (collective utility maximizing) rules. Similarly, there is now a debate among theorists of rational choice, over whether the best way to satisfy the criterion of rationality is straightforwardly to maximize or indirectly to follow (individual utility maximizing) rules. In this debate I join Gauthier and McClennen in advocating an indirect theory of rationality, where, in particular, the rules are moral principles. Roughly, we advocate rule egoism while the received theory favours act egoism. One of my main theses is that the neutral rationality criterion is best satisfied by a two-level, indirect, decision procedure.[4]

4.1.3. Players and actions

To what does the criterion of rationality apply: actions or players? Of course, we can ask of *either* players or actions whether they are rational, but which is more basic? I shall argue that individual players are the appropriate focus of our theory, for two reasons. First, testing different theories of rationality creates the possibility of mixed populations of players. In this environment, the question of the best action is poorly defined. One needs the best set of actions given many interactions, with several different (kinds of) players. Players are sets (generators) of actions; this is the appropriate level for speaking of success or failure.

My constructive approach gives us a second reason to focus on players rather than actions. Actions do not exist without players. To construct a generator of actions is to construct a player and evaluation should acknowledge this. The actions alone cannot be evaluated without the context of the player that generates them. For example, as we shall soon see, the action of choosing to co-operate is rational if one is the sort of player that can assure other players in various ways, but not otherwise.

Does making players the subject of rational evaluation beg the question between theories proposing direct and indirect rationality? I think not. After all, players are not principles or dispositions, so my proposal doesn't beg the question. It is still open whether successful players commit themselves to principles or remain straightforward act-by-act maximizers.

Finally, note a possible source of confusion. Since the criterion of substantive rationality is not a criterion of rational action, it may select, as the best sort of player for satisfying A's goals, a type of player inaccessible by means of A's actions. For example, it might be substantively rational for a Ma & Pa store to fire Pa and get a proper manager or for a cheetah to grow wheels. What a player can do by its own action is an additional constraint of procedural, not substantive rationality. This is likely to become confusing when advocates of the received theory point out that my recommendations are not actions that a straightforward maximizer could possibly undertake. This is true but not an objection to the criterion of substantive rationality. (It is an objection to the received theory.)

4.2 RESPONSIVE PLAYERS

I turn to the task of improving upon the straightforward maximizer proposed as rational by the received theory of rational choice. The compliance problem introduced in Chapter 1 is caused by a failure to discriminate. Recall the naive moral player, the unconditional co-operator (UC), who co-operates indiscriminately with all players. Unconditional co-operators fail to protect themselves from exploitation by straightforward maximizers. UCs do not know how 'to make the best of a generally bad situation' where some other players are not morally constrained.[5] Unconditional co-operators fail to satisfy the rational analogue of what Lyons, discussing utilitarianism, calls 'minimizing conditions'. To protect herself from exploitation, a would-be rational moral player must discriminate. She must distinguish friend from foe and attempt differentially to co-operate only with other co-operators. The ability to discriminate in this way, which I call *responsiveness*, is the key to solving the compliance problem. It leads to the two main problems that artificial morality addresses: *where* to draw the friend/foe line (the tolerance problem) and *how* to distinguish friend from foe (a procedural problem). I will take these problems up gradually, adding complications as we go along.

4.2.1 Constrained maximization

I begin with the best known proposal, David Gauthier's principle of constrained maximization (CM). Constrained maximizers are responsive; they embody a conditional disposition; 'the just person is disposed to comply . . . in interacting with those of his fellows whom he believes to be similarly disposed' (Gauthier 1986a, p. 156). Simplifying somewhat, I identify this component of constrained maximization as the strategy of conditional co-operation:[6]

Conditional Co-operation (CC): co-operate with and only with those who one expects to co-operate.

The principle of conditional co-operation protects a player from exploitation, allowing the player to escape the compliance dilemma. Figure 4.1 displays the possible outcomes open to two players each of whom can choose between straightforward maximization and conditional co-operation as strategies for the Prisoner's Dilemma. The availability of conditional co-operation has changed the compliance problem from a Prisoner's Dilemma into a benign co-ordination game. If I choose CC, I am protected should you choose SM, as I will then defect as well, so CC meets minimizing conditions. Moreover, my choice of CC makes CC your best choice, so choosing CC is the dominant equilibrium choice. Finally, since we both do better choosing CC than choosing anything else, the outcome is optimal. Conditional co-operation seems to be rational *and* moral. Gauthier's principle of constrained maximization appears to solve the compliance problem.

Player	CC	SM
CC	2	1
SM	1	1

Figure 4.1 Compliance success

4.2.2 Responsiveness

Conditional co-operation bridges the gap between morality and rationality because it is responsive.[7] It is easy to underestimate the importance of this simple feature:

> Of the contingent strategies, Tit-for-Tat elicits consistently the most cooperation in the [Iterated] Prisoner's Dilemma. Obviously it would be fatuous to interpret this result as a vindication of the 'eye-for-an-eye' principle. The success of Tit-for-Tat may be no more than that of a simple reinforcement schedule in a two-choice situation, devoid of ethical overtones.
> (Rapoport *et al.* 1976, p. 343)

Rapoport makes too little of Tit for Tat here. I (now) agree that Tit for Tat has little moral importance but only because it solves a morally insignificant problem, as I argued in the previous chapter. We should not attribute Tit for Tat's irrelevance to its responsiveness, a morally significant feature that it shares with conditional co-operation. Restricting the benefits of co-operation – via the 'simple re-inforcement' of conditional response – is crucial to the rational success of morality in the Prisoner's Dilemma. One must not extend impartiality to include toleration of non-co-operators.

Without responsiveness there is no hope of making impartial constraint rational. This is because moral constraint is a public good.

The benefits of impartial constraint naturally flow to all while the moral player pays the costs of constraint herself. The publicness of morality's benefits gives rise to the compliance problem. Each is tempted to free ride on other players' moral constraint. The point of responsiveness is to impose an artificial connection between the cost of my moral constraint to me and its benefit to you.

4.2.3 A moral price system

How do responsive co-operators solve the compliance problem? They generate new artificial incentives to co-operate. Responsive co-operators put a *price* on constrained behaviour. Conversely, faced with a responsive player, a would-be free-rider is forced to pay the costs of her defection. This makes it individually rational for her to co-operate. In this way responsive players meet the following objection addressed to the individualism implicit in my rationality criterion.

> Mind in this sense [the capacity to absorb exceedingly complex principles that enabled the body to move more successfully in its own environment] consists less of testable knowledge about the world . . . more in the capacity to restrain instincts – a capacity which cannot be tested by individual reason since its effects are on the group.
>
> (Hayek 1988, pp. 22f.)

It is true that in a naturally unresponsive environment I cannot test the effects of various moral and amoral principles, since some of their benefits fall to others. But the same is true in any situation lacking a price system. Without prices on various emissions, I cannot determine whether it would be better for me to invest in a more fuel-efficient water heater. A price system internalizes costs; it signals me the costs that others will bear. Similarly, responsive co-operators send other players signals – the price of co-operative and unco-operative behaviour.[8] Therefore it is ironic that Hayek, who strongly stresses the price system as the central economic device, neglects its analogue in facilitating the rationality of mutual moral constraint.

Complications

I should not make matters appear simpler than they are. The two-player Prisoner's Dilemma is particularly amenable to solution by responsive principle. By defecting, I impose a cost on you without imposing one on myself; the *CD* outcome which I avoid is worse for me than the *DD* outcome with which we end up. Therefore I have an incentive to be responsive. I can afford to link your participation in moral constraint directly to your benefit. In contrast, things are not so simple in situations involving many players, where I may hurt other would-be co-operators should I defect, so my incentive to be responsive is weakened and the connection between participation and benefit tends to be looser. Similar complications arise in two player situations where the *DD* outcome is worse than the *CD* outcome. I will take up these problems in Part III. Even within the two-player Prisoner's Dilemma the argument for responsive principles is not conclusive. Conditional co-operation is but one instance of the class of responsive co-operators. We need to go on to consider others and the means to decide between them in terms of instrumental success in the next chapter.

4.3 CONSTRUCTING PLAYERS

In a constructive theory, rationality is ultimately a matter of procedure. We must be able to implement players that we describe abstractly. I have suggested that a responsive player embodying the strategy of conditional co-operation (CC) will be more successful than a straightforward maximizer (SM). This initial argument for CC's instrumental superiority is thin because it ignores procedural issues entirely. I specified that CC would co-operate when this sufficed to guarantee the other player's co-operation. But not every process that we can specify can be carried out. For example, every player in our games wants most – in some sense – to get to her favoured outcome, *DC*. Why doesn't some player outmanoeuvre CC into unrequited co-operation? This is not logically impossible. It only appears to be impossible because we defined CC to make it impossible. So why can't we define an even more clever player, a CC-demon?[9] I can't answer this crucial question without entering the procedural level. I must show that it is possible to build a responsive player that will reliably discriminate friend from foe and impossible to build her demon.

It will turn out that the most difficult problem is to discriminate a fellow responsive player without getting caught in a loop, where each co-operates conditionally upon the other co-operating. This problem comes up in the standard simultaneous version of the Prisoner's Dilemma, which requires players to choose simultaneously. The two players face a co-ordination problem due to the need to choose strategies at the same time. I propose to separate this co-ordination problem out (and leave it for the next section) by beginning with the Extended Prisoner's Dilemma (XPD) introduced (with the Farmers' Problem) in §2.1.2. This will allow us to practice implementing simpler players first.

4.3.1 Players as logic programs

I will model players as computer programs in the language Prolog (which stands for *Programming* in *Logic*). A player is a decision *function* that returns either C or D when asked to make a move in a game. In sequential games, player II faces a different situation than player I, since she knows the other player's first move. I will assume that players can find themselves in either role. Therefore players for sequential games consist of two functions, for the first and second move, which I will label **move1** and **move2**, respectively and define as Prolog predicates.

4.3.2 Unconditional players

Let us begin with the simplest unconditional players. Here are implementations of an unconditional co-operator, UC1, and an unconditional defector, UD1:

```
% '%' begins a comment
% unconditional co-operator

    m1(uc1,Other,c).
    m2(uc1,Other,Anymove,c).

% unconditional defector

    m1(ud1,Other,d).
    m2(ud1,Other,Anymove,d).
```

The **m1** predicate returns a move of C or D given the moving player's name and another player; the **m2** predicate needs, in addition, the other player's first move, to which it is a response. (I should mention Prolog's confusing capitalization conventions. In standard Prolog variables begin with capital letters and constants with lower-case, which is contrary to English practice. To keep things straight, I shall write all Prolog in **boldface** font. Variables (like **Anyone**) will be capitalized and constants (such as **ud1**) will not. In English I will continue to use italicized capitals for variables and roman capitals for properly named constants like UD1.) UC1 always returns *C* and UD1 always returns *D*.

Why Prolog?

What is the point of taking the trouble to express our principles as procedures in Prolog? Because this extra trouble allows us fully to automate the testing of decision procedures. The definitions of players in Prolog are the premises of an argument. We can put these definitions to work by posing questions; the answers are conclusions determined by Prolog's theorem prover.

Here are some sample queries; notice that they begin with '?-' to distinguish them from additions to the premise set, which have no initial mark, and the Prolog interpreter's solutions, marked with '⇒'.

?- m1(ud1,uc1,Whatmove).
⇒ **Whatmove = d**
?- m2(ud1,ud1,d,d).
⇒ **Yes**
?- m1(uc1,uc1,Whatmove).
⇒ **Whatmove = c**
?- m2(uc1,ud1,d,d).
⇒ **No**

The answers returned assure us that the unconditional players perform as intended; UD1 chooses *D* first and second, UC1 chooses *C* first and fails to respond to a *D* with a *D*.

It is interesting to note that although I designed these players to return **c** or **d**, the definitions may be used in other ways. For example, we might ask who could ever generate the pattern of returning *D* for *C*:

?- m2(Who,ToWhom,c,d).
⇒ **Who = ud, ToWhom = X**

The answer is that UD1 can generate this pattern with anyone.[10] The ability to use (most) Prolog predicates in any direction, as it were, reminds us of the ideal of the language: to allow us to program in logic. We define *predicates*; our query specifies a question (a pattern of constants or variables) and asks if it is *true*. We are asking a descriptive question (is this true?) not issuing a procedural command (produce the output appropriate to this input!). Of course, we are still ultimately commanding the interpreter to seek out this truth by its theorem prover and we shall soon find that not all procedural considerations can be banished. None the less, Prolog goes a remarkable way towards that philosophical dream, the automatic argument testing machine. Of course, UD1 and UC1 are so simple there is little to test. Let us turn to a more demanding task.

4.3.3 Conditional players

A rational player who would be moral faces two difficult problems, one primarily motivational and the other epistemological. On the motivational side, she must resist the temptation (T) to defect.[11] She must somehow commit herself to choose the individually worse co-operative reward (R). And she must do this in a way that assures others that her co-operative intentions are effective. Call this the *assurance problem*. On the epistemological side, she must be able to detect players of the first sort, that is, those who can assure her that they are worthy of her risking co-operation. Call this the *prediction problem*. In the standard simultaneous PD both problems must be solved by each player, since their situations are symmetrical. The XPD simplifies the task of building players by separating the two problems. Player I has no need to commit himself psychologically; he commits himself in fact (externally, if not physically) by moving first. Therefore player II has no prediction problem; player I has already moved and knowledge of his move is passed to player II in the course of the game. On the other hand, player II confronts the assurance problem in pure form: how to convince player I that she, player II, will do the costly co-operative act *after* player I has moved. Note that player I cannot monitor nor enforce (by strictly speaking reciprocal means) player II's compliance. Player II's position is causally privileged (she is temporally downstream); this makes her assurance problem the more severe, worse even than in the standard PD. Player I has the correspondingly difficult prediction problem. He must predict what player II will do in the future when he has already moved and thereby has lost the ability further to monitor and control, by reciprocal means, her action. The Extended Prisoner's Dilemma clarifies while it simplifies, factoring the two problems into two predicates that comprise a player, **move1** and **move2**.

A conditional co-operator

I shall start with CC1's predicate for **move2** because it is simpler than **move1**.

m2(cc1,Other,c,c).   **% respond to c with c**
m2(cc1,Other,d,d).   **% respond to d with d**

The other player has already moved, so CC1 can simply react to a C with a C and a D to a D. This half of CC1 is the same as Tit for Tat. CC1's **move2** need not call the other player's **move1** since the output of **move1** is a matter of known fact. All that remains is assurance, which is secured by the simple promise to return like for like and permitting all players to test this out (which we shall get into shortly).

CC2 is a more elegant implementation, which uses a single variable to insure that **cc2** reacts to any move with that very same move:

m2(cc2,Other,Move,Move).   **% respond to any move**
                                        % with the same move

From principles to predicates

These conditional co-operators are complex enough to raise some important questions about implementing players in Prolog, which I take up here. Notice that we have moved down a level of specificity, from principles (or strategies) to players. CC1 and CC2 are particular players.[12] They are to be distinguished from the principle CC discussed up to now. Players embody principles specified as decision procedures. This specification has two dimensions. First, where principles can be incompletely specified, with *ceteris paribus* clauses and the like, players must be definite. They must consist of rules (to draw out the contrast due to Dworkin (1977)). I shall fill this gap in two steps. While players can consist of various *procedures* – small experts or productions that may or not pertain to various contexts – they must compose to a single, *decision function* that outputs a legitimate move in the specified game. For example, CC1 has a separate rule to cover each of the two possible cases, where player I chooses C and D. Second, players may vary; several players may implement one principle differently, as CC1 and CC2 do. Players are particular procedural conjectures about possible ways to make principles work. By making this move from principles to players, Artificial Morality attempts to gain more content by making stronger, more criticizable, procedural claims.

Players may consist of any number of predicates. Minimally, they need top-level predicates to select the moves of the game; in the case of the XPD, they need to generate a first and second move, with the predicates **m1** and **m2**.[13] Predicates consist of a head (the predicate's name) and any number of argument slots. For example, in the move predicates, the heads are **m1** and **m2**, respectively. In both **m1** and **m2** first slot identifies the player and the final slot is the move selected.

m1(Player,Other,Move1).   %structure of
                                      move1

m2(Player,Other,OthersMove,Move2). %structure of
                                      move2

In addition, note that **m2** has an extra slot (compared to **m1**) to carry the result of Player I's move. Arguments can be variables or constants. For example, in **m1(ud1,Other,d)**, the first and third arguments are constants and the second is a variable because player UD1 selects a constant move of **d** against any player. As in predicate logic, an unbound (free) variable is true of any constant. Thus our first two players are unconditional because they leave all possible sources of conditioning information as unbound variables. In contrast, CC2 uses a variable to return like for like. Constants are used to identify a player (**uc1**) and to specify its move (**c**).[14]

Individual players

This brings us to the problem of individuating artificial players. Players are individuals; we need a way to distinguish the predicates that make up one from those that make up another. I will introduce a convention that a predicate's first argument slot is filled with the player's unique name such as **ud209**. Player's names individuate but are otherwise meaningless. For example, an unconditional defector could be named **uc42** (perhaps in an effort to fool an exceedingly stupid CC player). I impose no conventions giving meaning for names to players; I will avoid misleading names for the sake of exposition. Since they serve to connect players to our game apparatus, the **m1** and **m2** predicates have *all* their argument slots dictated by convention. For example, **m2(W,X,Y,Z)** tells us what player *W* will do after player *X* makes move *Y*; she will make move *Z*. The last argument, **Z**, is the value of the function associated with the predicate. However, not all predicates are so governed by convention. Players are free to have (in principle) unlimited predicates of their own devising. (In Chapter 7 I shall consider how players might add to their cognitive equipment.)

Self-ownership

Not all predicates belong to players. For example, the predicate **member(Element,List)**, which is true of an element, like blue, and a list (a structured set) like {red, white, blue}, does not belong to any player. This brings up three important points about the *limits* of our models. First, the game is managed by impersonal predicates; they are available to all players. In contrast, a player consists of private predicates which can only be directly accessed by their owner, named in their initial argument slot. Abstractly, one could imagine the manager to be another player, a referee.[15] I do not make the referee a player because this role stands outside our theory. I take the game to represent the given situation, not a result of some player's choice.[16] Second, much is assumed by our models. For example, all players can freely use unowned predicates; they share a common language. Therefore I am not trying to prove that players can start with no common ground and establish co-operative interaction. Third, when I speak of players *owning* their predicates, I mean this literally. The owner and only the owner is free to use and to change her predicates. No non-owner has these rights. These two principles define a regime of (minimal) self-ownership. I am well aware that ownership *can* be a moral institution. But it is not moral in our model because it is enforced by external not internal constraints. No poaching or meddling players are allowed in the model; ideally the referee program enforces access privileges (I develop some primitive examples below). In any case, these restrictions are enforced. The important point is that these property rights are premises, not conclusions, of our model. I assume players that own their own minds (they have no bodies) and derive the possibility of moral constraint from this.

Prediction

Returning to the implementation of a conditional co-operator, we now take up the problem of predicting player II's move. The prediction problem is simplified in the Extended PD by the sequential layout of the game. None the less, CC1's first move is much more difficult to implement than the second. There is no assurance problem but the prediction problem requires more apparatus than we have yet encountered. In particular, the **move1** predicate has no argument slot that could trigger a conditional, reflecting the fact player I must move first, without information about what the other player has done. But there may be information available about what the other is committed to do and CC1's **move1** is based on this.

```
m1(cc1,Coop,c):-              % co-operate if
   pubmove2(Coop,cc1,c,c).    % player II will co-operate
m1(cc1,NonCoop,d).            % otherwise defect
```

Here is a new operator, ':-', the logical 'if'. CC1 co-operates with another player if that player is publicly committed to responding to co-operation with co-operation. The condition that makes this strategy conditional is formed by this 'if' based clause, and completed by the second **move1** predicate that implements the default: otherwise defect with every other (that is, non-co-operating) player. I have replaced the variable **Other** with the more descriptive variables **Coop** and **NonCoop** to indicate with whom the two conditions match. This construction makes use of Prolog's backtracking apparatus. Prolog tries to prove the first clause of **m1**. If it should fail (for example, because the other player will respond to C with D), then Prolog tries to prove the next clause of **m1**. Therefore, the *order* of the rules is important. Were CC1's two **m1** rules to be reversed, CC1 would always defect. Do you see why?[17]

Now that we see CC1's **move1** predicate, it looks suspiciously circular. However, it is not. Player I calls player II – literally: it executes the other player's **move2** predicate to test it – but when CC1 moves second it does not execute player I's decision. Expectations are grounded in the Extended Prisoner's Dilemma by the fact that player I's move precedes player II's. Responsive players need not loop in the XPD.

Reading minds

CC1's strategy depends on being able to find out what player II is committed to doing. He solves the prediction problem by directly testing player II's decision procedure. It would obviously be a mistake to assume that player II is simply subject to such a search. The ability of players to examine – and even invoke – other players' decision procedures and principles suggests a degree of transparency incompatible with interpreting our predications as separate players. Players may need a private inner life; this is incompatible with general public access to their decision procedures. As we discussed earlier, this inner life is implemented by the convention that private predicates are owned by the player whose name appears in its first argument slot. I extend the ownership to include *intellectual property*: the rights to read, copy, or execute information. The default will be complete privacy; the right of privacy will be enforced by the tournament as a non-moral external constraint. However, there is no need to require privacy to be permanent. Intellectual property is a right; it may be revealed, shared or given away.[18] A player may choose to reveal its inner workings; it may have reasons to open its mind to others. To specify the degree to which it makes its decision procedure public, each player may add permissions of the following form to the database:

permit(Player,Permitted_Player,Permitted_Action).

Permitted actions include executing and reading one's principles.[19] For example, my implementations of UC1, CC1 and CC2 should allow other players to execute their principles, while UD1 permits no access at all to anyone, so I add the following:

permit(uc1,Anyone,execute).
permit(cc1,Anyone,execute).
permit(cc2,Anyone,execute).

UD1 needs no **permit** predicate because no permission is the default. Implementing voluntary transparency complicates the Prolog for agents. The basic idea is that one agent should not be able to call another's **move** predicate without permission. For example, the **pubmove2** predicate in CC1 checks for the required permission before executing player II's **m2**. More details can be found in Appendix B, §B.1.

I realize that my decision to to allow players to read (some) other player's minds is controversial. Let me stress that it is a *decision*; I do not believe that players are naturally transparent (or opaque). We must choose how to model our players and there are good reasons to allow optional transparency. I conjecture that without publicity, the one-play simultaneous Prisoner's Dilemma admits only a sub-optimal straightforwardly maximizing 'solution' of *DD*. As I argued in Chapter 2, we should focus on situations where we are likely to get interesting results. By slightly weakening the informational constraints on the PD, we can get an optimal solution. Notice that this change is less drastic that it may seem. First, transparency is voluntary; no player is forced to reveal anything. Therefore the straightforward maximizer cannot complain that anything his theory requires to be secret (the key to the randomizer generating mixed strategies, for example) is forcibly revealed. Notice as well that the received theory really has little to complain about, since straightforward maximizers presumably have no use for information of the sort we are revealing. That is, according to the received theory, rational (i.e. SM) players in a PD have nothing to say (worth taking seriously) to each other, so adding an information dimension shouldn't make any difference.[20] Since this information does make a difference, it is significant and supports my criticism of the received theory.

Second, even if transparency is necessary for conditionally constrained players it is not a sufficient means to achieve co-operation. For example, if unconditional co-operators effectively communicate their decision procedure, this does little to improve their hopes to co-operate generally. Third, it is easy to take effective communication to be a stronger assumption than it is. I do not make any *moral* assumption about players, namely that they are committed to some principle of veracity. I simply stipulate a world in which some sorts of deception (claiming falsely that one is committed to CC, for example) are impossible.

None the less, publicity does strengthen our premises and thus weaken our argument, at least initially. In particular, I do not allow players to lie about their decision procedures and I assume that players make no mistakes about each other. These are strong assumptions. But they are preliminary, simplifying assumptions. Chapter 7 admits misleading, if not deceiving, agents and Chapter 8 considers the effects of epistemic mistakes.[21] The important point is that I will assume optional publicity in the models of Part II.

Finally we can test out our stable of players. I set up a tiny tournament by defining a roster of players and letting Prolog pair up all permutations.[22] Notice how the first move is passed via the **M1** variable.

player(uc1). player(ud1). player(cc1). %a roster of 3 players

**?- player(P1), player(P2), move1(P1,P2,M1),
    move2(P2,P1,M1,M2).**
⇒ P1 = uc1, P2 = uc1, M1 = c, M2 = c;
⇒ P1 = uc1, P2 = ud1, M1 = c, M2 = d;
⇒ P1 = uc1, P2 = cc1, M1 = c, M2 = c;

⇒ P1 = ud1, P2 = uc1, M1 = d, M2 = c;
⇒ P1 = ud1, P2 = ud1, M1 = d, M2 = d;
⇒ P1 = ud1, P2 = cc1, M1 = d, M2 = d;

$\Rightarrow$ **P1 = cc1, P2 = uc1, M1 = c, M2 = c;**
$\Rightarrow$ **P1 = cc1, P2 = ud1, M1 = d, M2 = d;**
$\Rightarrow$ **P1 = cc1, P2 = cc1, M1 = c, M2 = c;**
$\Rightarrow$ **No**

P1 generates row headings and P2 the column headings. We can see that CC1 behaves as expected. It co-operates with itself and UC1 but not with UD1 and it does not loop with itself. Therefore my implementation of conditional co-operation, CC1, behaves in the way Gauthier requires in his argument for constrained maximization. This instrumentally attractive responsive moral strategy is possible, at least in the procedurally simple case of the Extended Prisoner's Dilemma.

Conclusions

I have introduced my method of modelling players in Prolog in the domain of the Extended Prisoner's Dilemma. We have seen how the Extended Prisoner's Dilemma factors the compliance problem into elements of assurance and perception. We have also seen the need to allow players to publicize their principles. I have implemented a working conditional co-operator, CC1, and tested it against itself and the basic unconditional players, UC and UD. CC1 meets this rudimentary test and does better than the unconditional players.

Several cautions are in order. First, this test is quite tentative and rudimentary. I shall argue in the next chapters that more players need to be introduced even in the simplest XPD context fully to test the rationality of strategies like CC. Second, while I introduced the XPD as a primer in Artificial Morality, it proves to be a surprisingly rich micro-world as well. For example, while the XPD simplifies the construction of conditional players, it complicates the implementation of straightforward maximizers. I gloss over this problem for now (by conflating SM and UD) and return to it in Chapter 8.

4.4 THE COHERENCE PROBLEM

The Extended Prisoner's Dilemma is an asymmetrical decision problem for which a CC player can be coherently defined. In contrast the standard Prisoner's Dilemma requires players to choose simultaneously in a symmetrical situation. Richmond Campbell criticizes Gauthier's principle of constrained maximization (CM) as indeterminate in this situation:

> The first question is whether 'constrained maximization' has a clear meaning and one that has a clear application in the basic PD decision problem. One may have doubts on this score. Recall my brief characterization. . . . 'If a CM believes that the other party will cooperate, then the CM will too; otherwise not.' Isn't there a problem of circularity? . . . I am disposed to cooperate if you will. You are disposed to cooperate if I will. But that doesn't settle what each of us will do. . . . We seem to be led to an impasse.[23]

4.4.1 Looping

Campbell's criticism shows how the simultaneous PD intensifies the two problems we discussed earlier. Most obviously, it poses a serious prediction problem. In the Extended PD I used the device of invoking the other player's decision function as a way of predicting what it would do. If I define players for the simultaneous PD using this same prediction device, some definitions will be circular. To see why, I will modify the CC1 procedure for playing the one-shot PD. A single **move** replaces **m1** and **m2**. A conditional co-operator should select C if the other player selects C. Here is a pair of *defective* attempts to implement CC:

```
permit(loopy1,Anyone,Anything).
*move(loopy1,Other,c) :- pubmove(Other,loopy1,c).
 move(loopy1,Other,d).

 permit(loopy2,Anyone,Anything).
*move(loopy2,Other,c) :- pubmove(Other,loopy2,c).
 move(loopy2,Other,d).
```

Each of Loopy1 and Loopy2 will co-operate with whatever will transparently co-operate with her. For example, both pass the basic discrimination test and co-operate with the following unconditional co-operator but not the unconditional defector:

```
 permit(uc2,Anyone,Anything).
 move(uc2,Anyone,c).

 move(ud2,Anyone,d).
```

?- move(loopy1,uc2,What).
⇒ **What = c**
?- move(loopy1,ud2,What).
⇒ **What = d**

But pairing Loopy1 with Loopy2 will produce an error condition. The Prolog interpreter is unable to terminate its search because **move(loopy1,loopy2,c)** invokes **move(loopy2,loopy1,c)** which invokes **move(loopy1,loopy2,c)** again and so on.

The second problem is more subtle. It comes to the fore in Holly Smith's formulation of the coherence problem as an objection to Gauthier's principle of constrained maximization.

> Let's simplify matters by assuming that you have already chosen CM, and of course I know this. What should I predict you will do if I choose CM? Gauthier seems to assume that I may simply predict that you will form the intention to [co-operate]. But matters are much more complex than this. Given your choice of CM, what I *can* predict is that you will [co-operate] if and only if you predict that I will [co-operate]. But how can I assume you can make this prediction about me? Your position vis-a-vis me is perfectly parallel to my position vis-a-vis you. Even if you know that I choose CM, all you can infer from this is that I will [co-operate] *if and only if* I predict you will [co-operate]. You cannot infer that I will [co-operate], simpliciter.[24]

Smith brings out a deeper reason why conditional co-operators might lapse into incoherence that is related to Gauthier's conception of constrained maximization as a form of moral impartiality or equality. In our formulation of the CC procedure above, each Loopy player asks for more from the other – that is, co-operation – than the conditional co-operation she is willing to offer herself.[25] This is another form of the assurance problem: CC conditional co-operators demand more assurance than they offer.[26]

A serious problem

I conclude that the objections of Campbell and Smith raise a major problem of coherence. Gauthier underestimates the procedural complexities that his conditional principle introduces, even for artificial players:

> If one thinks of morality, not only as artifice, but as intended for such artifacts as corporations and governments, then one need

consider only problems of institutional design. In principle, a constrained maximizer is no more difficult to construct than a straightforward maximizer.

(Gauthier 1988b, p. 417)

This is not so. The compliance problem requires that if constrained maximizers are to be rational they must be responsive. But for responsive players to co-operate together, they must interact in ways entirely different from straightforward maximizers. As we saw, in the XPD, responsive agents need to execute each other's decision procedures; it is not clear that straightforward maximizers need to do this.[27] However, the obvious way to construct a conditional co-operator for the simultaneous PD, Loopy1, *is* incoherent.

4.4.2 Matching

Smith is sceptical about the prospects of solving the coherence problem, which she sees as a trilemma:

> It might be hoped that a reformulation could be found according to which it would necessarily be the case that if two transparent partners both choose CM, then they both would [co-operate]. Unfortunately, such reformulations do not seem to be available. . . . In general, every reformulation of CM I have inspected is vulnerable to some problem or another: either it does not guarantee joint compliance, or it leaves the player vulnerable to exploitation by a partner who does not adopt CM, or it delivers inconsistent prescriptions.
>
> (Smith 1991, pp. 241f.)

I take this as a challenge to Artificial Morality to *construct* the sort of player the feasibility of which Smith doubts. The incoherence problem is caused by players trying to predict each other's behaviour by invoking the other's decision procedure. While this worked well enough in the simpler XPD, we have seen that it is procedurally fatal in the symmetrical PD. In the faulty formulation of CC above, Loopy1 invokes or *uses* Loopy2's procedure, which in turn uses Loopy1's, and so on. This suggests a way out of the problem: design players who forsake prediction by direct simulation for a cruder similarity test based on matching *mentioned* principles. The meta-logical device of quotation will allow me to design coherent symmetrical conditional strategies for the simultaneous game.

Selfsame co-operation

I begin with a procedurally simple strategy of matching self with other and work up to more complex varieties.[28] Consider the elementary matching principle:

Selfsame Co-operation (SC): co-operate with and only with players similar to oneself.

How does a selfsame co-operator solve the coherence problem? First she addresses the assurance problem by not demanding more constraint from the other player than she is willing to offer herself. It will be useful to introduce the class of *assurance modulators* here. A principle can be seen as modulating co-operativeness; *given* some degree of assurance of co-operation it will provide some degree of assurance. For example, in the Iterated Prisoner's Dilemma, the strategy of Tit for Tat always co-operates in the first round, before it knows whether the other player will co-operate. Tit for Tat is an assurance amplifier; it gives more assurance than it demands. Unconditional co-operation is a stronger amplifier. Indeed, UC is the limiting case; it asks for no assurance and gives certain co-operation. Conversely, a strategy that demands unconditional co-operation before it will co-operate is an assurance damper; it demands more assurance than it gives. In Smith's opinion, CM has this property, since it requires co-operation but provides only conditional co-operation. Finally, a procedure is assurance neutral if it returns just what it gives. Selfsame co-operation appears to be neutral because of its appeal to similarity; however it is an assurance amplifier. In return for a conditional commitment to co-operation, SC offers co-operation, thus solving the assurance problem for simultaneous games.

How do selfsame co-operators avoid the prediction problem? A SC player need not know that the other player will co-operate, but only that the other is similar, that is, also an SC player. SC is conditional on the other player's strategy, not its behaviour. This makes SC what Howard (1971) calls a 'metastrategy': a strategy defined over other players' strategies (or metastrategies).[29] However this might seem merely to put the procedural problem off one step. How, in a situation of simultaneous choice, with no previous interaction, is one SC player to test another player for the requisite similarity? Moreover, similarity is a vague notion; what kind of similarity is required? I use metalogical matching to answer both questions. Selfsame co-operators should co-operate when they have the same decision procedure; they should test sameness by matching. Here is one way to implement this meta-strategy:

permit(sc1,Anyone,read).
  move(sc1,Other,c) :-
    firstproc(sc1,Other,c,MyPrinciple),
    firstproc(Other,sc1,c,OthersPrinciple),
    sameproc(sc1,Other,MyPrinciple,OthersPrinciple).

SC1 compares a quotation of the other player's first decision procedure, with a quotation of her own first decision procedure. (The need for getting the *first* procedure is taken up in Appendix B, §B.3.) Procedures match if one can swap one's name for the other player's name in her procedure and get your own procedure; **sameproc** tests this after converting procedures into quotations of themselves.

I will not burden us with the details of this process, as we will return to the manipulation of procedures in Chapter 7. However, I must attend to the procedural innovation that allows SC1 to solve the coherence problem: the ability to read a procedure without executing it. Normally in Prolog, we use a predicate by querying its truth but there is an alternative, metalogical, access to a predicate. We can use the built-in predicate **Clause(Head,Body)** which is true of the Head and Body of a then-if clause. Here is an example, using logic instead of Prolog. Given 'p if (q and r)', clause(p,Body) is true with Body = (q and r). Using **clause** one can find out the sufficient conditions of a predicate without trying to ascertain the predicate's truth. One can determine the structure of a rule without triggering the rule. Finally, to prevent looping, SC1 permits only reading but not execution of her decision function.[30]

If I define another player, SC2, which is similar to SC1, they will co-operate with each other without regress or the chance that either can be exploited. However, this self-contained formulation of SC takes a logical liberty. The variable **MyPrinciple** gets bound to something that includes **MyPrinciple** itself, namely:

MyPrinciple =
  firstproc(sc1,Other,c,MyPrinciple),
  firstproc(Other,sc1,c,OthersPrinciple),
  sameproc(sc1,Other,MyPrinciple,OthersPrinciple)

The appearance of a variable in its own referent violates the 'occurs check', a logical constraint needed to block the invalid introduction of existentially quantified expressions. If I implement SC in this internal, self-contained manner, I lose touch with a strict logical interpretation of my players. I will lose this logical interpretation soon enough, when I introduce learning in Chapter 7, but it is better to retain the cloak of logical virtue while I am trying to answer the logical objection that claims incoherence. I can avoid this problem by making SC a separate predicate external to the players' decision procedures, resulting in this elegant implementation of SC:

permit(sc3,Anyone,read).
move(sc3,Other,Move) :- sc(Other,sc3,Move).

sc(Ego,Alter,c) :-
  firstproc(Ego,Alter,c,EgoProc),
  EgoProc = sc(Alter,Ego,c).
sc(Ego,Alter,d).

Notice that the predicate **sc(X,Y,Z)** does not call **sc(Y,X,Z)**, so coherence is preserved. Moreover, the occurs check is satisfied, since the value of the variable **EgoProc** contains only innocuous atoms (the players' names bound to the variables **Alter** and **Ego**) and not any form of itself. SC is a predicate that is true of all and only those who are committed to co-operate on the basis of the SC predicate. Therefore SC3 will coherently co-operate with its clones.[31] I conclude that conditional metastrategies which co-operate with similar conditional metastrategies can be coherently implemented. Once again, my solution depends on transparency, which I have admitted is a strong assumption. Notice, however, that moving from executing to examining decision procedures may weaken the assumption. The distinction between reading and executing procedures allows players to reveal themselves in a less invasive manner, greatly reducing the risk of incoherence.[32] Of course straightforward maximizers have no interest in others determining their strategy. Therefore a critic might suggest that the compliance dilemma will recur on the question of revealing one's metastrategy versus concealing it. However, this will not happen. Recall that SC players only co-operate when the other player is known to be an SC player. SC defects on indeterminate players. This gives adherents of SC a reason to reveal their metastrategies; otherwise fellow SC players will not co-operate with them. In the transparent situation I have assumed, there is no danger in revealing the SC metastrategy, since it is individually rational and not open to exploitation. Therefore this revelation game is not another Prisoner's Dilemma but a benign co-ordination problem.

4.4.3 The red-nosed defector

Campbell offers a solution to the coherence problem that differs instructively from what I propose:

> There is a way out. Suppose we modify the form of Gauthier's definition of CM so that it has the following structure:
>
>> When players S (self) and O (other) are in a PD, S had the CM disposition iff: (1) S has the property R and (2) S will cooperate with O iff S believes O has R.
>
> Let R be the property of having a red nose. Certainly no circularity would exist given *that* specification of R. Each of any two CM's would have a red nose and, provided that they could see the colour of the other's nose, they would cooperate in the PD. In general, there is no circularity as long as the specification of R does not make any reference to how the other party will act on *this* occasion.
>
> Having a red nose is, of course, not the property we are after, since a red nosed SM would then be in a position to exploit every CM. We need a property that SMs won't have. Consider the property of being ready to reciprocate cooperation when making the second move in *sequential* PDs . . . there can be evidence that someone has this property. Like having a red nose it generates no circularity, and SMs can be expected *not* to have it.
>
> (Campbell 1988a, p. 351)

Campbell is correct that specifying a property, R, that 'does not make any reference to how the other party will act on this occasion' will end the circularity. However, the cure is too strong; a property disconnected from action in this way will not protect constrained maximizers from exploitation. Smith (1991, p. 242, n. 18) makes this point with respect to Campbell's recommended linkage of simultaneous PDs with sequential PDs:

> It is true that SMs won't have the property Campbell describes, so that someone who adopts CM will not be exploited by SMs. However, there will be other defecting players who *would* reciprocate co-operation in sequential Prisoner's Dilemmas, but who would *not* co-operate in simultaneous Prisoner's Dilemmas; an agent adopting Campbell's version of CM would be vulnerable to exploitation by these players. SM players do

not exhaust the list of possible non-cooperative players that CM players must be protected against.

Smith focuses on the point that I criticized in Chapter 1 as Gauthier's rational dualism. We need to be concerned with players other than SM and CM. Indeed, if we define a red-nosed co-operator, in the way Campbell suggests, let's call him Rudolf, another player, Grinch, who uses CC1 in the XPD and SC (of any sort) in the PD will be able to exploit him.

> **permit(rudolf,Anyone,Everything).**
> **move(rudolf,Other,) :- pubmove2(Other,rudolf,c,c).**
> **move(rudolf,Other,d).**
>
> **permit(grinch,Anyone,Everything).**
> **move(grinch,Other,M) :- sc(Other,grinch,M).**
> **m2(grinch,Other,c,c).**
> **m2(grinch,Other,d,d).**
>
> **?- move(rudolf,grinch,R),move(grinch,rudolf,G).**
>
> ⇒ **R = c G = d**

The moral of this story is that one can't trust linkages between strategically distinct situations. Some predators are polymorphic; they don't wear sheep's clothing but they really do act sometimes just like sheep. As we have seen, Smith draws a more drastic conclusion. She holds that Campbell's failure confirms the coherence dilemma: CM can't avoid both circularity on the one side and exploitation on the other. In contrast, I have argued that non-circular assurance is possible if Campbell's property R is linked indirectly to the other players' action by mentioning her decision procedure.[33]

CONCLUSION

This chapter introduced the most basic artificial moral player, the conditional co-operator. I sketched a neutral test for the rationality of players and indicated why responsive players should do better. I constructed elementary conditional and unconditional players for the Extended Prisoner's Dilemma and then for the more demanding simultaneous PD. In both cases we saw that responsive players, who do better than the straightforward maximizers proposed as rational by the received theory, can be coherently constructed.

I stress that these tests are preliminary, proceeding as they did under strong simplifying assumptions about the composition of the populations and the reliability of communications. The attractiveness of conditional co-operation will be undermined somewhat when these assumptions are relieved in later chapters.

5

RECIPROCAL
CO-OPERATION

In the previous chapter I used the methods of Artificial Morality to defend David Gauthier's conception of constrained maximization. I argued that conditional co-operation (CC) was a procedurally possible strategy that was more successful than straightforward maximization (SM). That argument is incomplete; several important questions remain unanswered. First, conditional co-operation does not exhaust the possibilities of constrained behaviour. We need to consider other possible moral agents and the means instrumentally to test them. (I will put off moral evaluation until the next chapter.) Conditional co-operators are not the only responsive players; perhaps other designs will prove more successful. More successful playing with *whom*? This raises the second question, about the population used to test various players. Gauthier simplifies drastically by dividing the world into moral and amoral agents. I think we need to consider more complex populations. I introduce a new constrained agent, the reciprocal co-operator (RC), a responsive player that exploits unconditional co-operators. In this chapter I argue for the rational superiority of reciprocal co-operation; in the next I consider its evident moral defects.

5.1 RELAXING CONSTRAINT

So far I have followed Gauthier's line of argument; now we diverge. Gauthier, convinced of the rationality of constrained maximization in the simplest case where players' dispositions are transparent, proceeds to discuss more complex and realistic cases where transparency fails. In contrast, I see a problem with the justification of conditional co-operation as rational even in the transparent case. (I will drop the transparency assumption later in Chapter 8.) While CC does better than straightforward maximization, these are not the only two players that need to be considered. For example, CC does worse than SM when interacting with an unconditional co-operator, so Gauthier's argument for the substantive rationality of constrained maximization is incomplete. We need to consider additional players.

Conditional co-operators are generous. They co-operate with fellow CC but they also co-operate with unconditional co-operators (UC). This *extension* of moral constraint seems rationally unmotivated. Another species of responsive co-operator should be able to do better by defecting against those who will co-operate in any case.[1] Therefore I propose, as a rational improvement over conditional co-operation, the strategy of reciprocal co-operation.

> Reciprocal Co-operation (RC): co-operate when and only when co-operation is necessary and sufficient for the other's co-operation.

CC constrain themselves when constraint suffices to induce the other player to co-operate. In contrast, reciprocal co-operators only constrain themselves when co-operation is a *necessary* condition for the other player's co-operation. The table in Figure 5.1 shows how reciprocal and conditional co-operation differ by means of a tournament of four players representing the four strategies we have considered so far: unconditional co-operation (UC), unconditional defection (UD – equivalent here to straightforward maximization), conditional co-operation (CC) and reciprocal co-operation (RC). The entries record the outcome for the player listed in the row of a game of Prisoner's Dilemma played with the player listed in the column of Figure 5.1. For example, since UD manages to exploit UC, the first entry for RC is 3 while the corresponding entry (the fourth) for UC is 0. The chart shows that RC co-operates with CC and RC itself and defects with UD and UC.

This chart extends the one used to argue for CC over SM (cf. Figure 4.1). Now RC appears to be more successful than CC. Like CC, RC is an optimal strategy; there is no strategy better for both players. RC is also an equilibrium strategy; it is the best response to the other player's best response to it. Thus reciprocal co-operation is both morally and rationally attractive. Moreover, RC (weakly) dominates the other strategies, including CC. That is, no matter which of these principles the other uses, one never does worse and sometimes does better using RC. Therefore reciprocal co-operation appears to be instrumentally

	UC	UD	CC	RC
UC	2	0	2	0
UD	3	1	1	1
CC	2	1	2	2
RC	3	1	2	2

Figure 5.1 Moral pluralism

more successful than Gauthier's principle of constrained maximization and straightforward maximization as well.

Three questions arise out out this observation. First is the procedural question of how – indeed whether it is possible – effectively to implement the RC strategy, which I will take up immediately. Second, there is a problem with our test population. Since UC appears to be irrational, why include it in the test situation in Figure 5.1? I turn to this criticism, which raises more general questions how we are to understand the situation depicted in Figure 5.1, in §5.2. Third is the moral question. Reciprocal co-operation differs from conditional co-operation only in its poor treatment of unconditional co-operators. This distinguishing feature is a vulnerable point in my defence of RC as a principle that unites rationality and morality. Exploitation of the innocent appears to be morally indefensible; I address this problem in Chapter 6.

5.1.1 Implementing RC

Reciprocal co-operation is more complex than conditional co-operation because it needs to test counter-factually whether the other player would defect were RC to defect. My implementation of reciprocal co-operation, RC1, is based on the conditional co-operator, CC1, developed in Chapter 4. RC1 adds conditions to both the first and second move predicates (**m1** and **m2**). In RC1's case, **m1** is simpler, so I begin with it:

```
permit(rc1,Anyone,execute).        %transparent
m1(rc1,RCoop,c) :-
   pubmove2(RCoop,rc1,c,c),         %same as cc AND
   pubmove2(RCoop,rc1,d,d).         %test for responsiveness
m1(rc,Other,d).                     %otherwise
```

CC1 co-operates if player II will reciprocate co-operation; RC1 demands in addition that player II would reciprocate defection as well. (The comma is Prolog's AND connective.) Unless player II is negatively as well as positively responsive, RC1 defects. This differentiates reciprocal from conditional co-operation when moving first.

The second move is trickier because RC1 is not satisfied with the fact that player I already co-operated. After all, UC will co-operate when moving first. RC has no reason to reciprocate unless player I chooses *C because* RC1 would co-operate. But testing this counter-factual is difficult. One can't simply execute the other player's **move1**; as we have seen, responsive players will likely have linked their **move1** to one's own **move2**. The proposed linkage would loop. To avoid this, RC1 makes a conjecture that players are *unified*; that responsive players will be so in both **move1** and **move2**.[2] Therefore RC1 tests the other player's **move2**. There is still a problem. RC1's own **move2** tests the other player's **move2**; here is another potential circle, more vicious than the first. RC1 avoids looping by a careful choice of tests. He is unconditionally committed to negative responsiveness (returning *D* for *D*) so he makes negative responsiveness the condition of his own positive response (returning *C* for *C*):[3]

```
m2(rc1,Responsive,c,c):-
   pubmove2(Responsive,rc1,d,d).
m2(rc1,Unresponsive,c,d).
m2(rc1,Defector,d,d).
```

For now I will ignore the risks of this tricky procedure, by assuming that players can be transparent. (I will rectify this below in §8.2.) Let's test out our enlarged roster of players.

```
player(uc1).   player(ud1). %a roster of 4 players
player(cc1).   player(rc1).
?- player(P1), player(P2), move1(P1,P2,M1),
   move2(P2,P1,M1,M2).
```

$\Rightarrow$ **P1 = uc1, P2 = uc1, M1 = c, M2 = c;**
$\Rightarrow$ **P1 = uc1, P2 = ud1, M1 = c, M2 = d;**
$\Rightarrow$ **P1 = uc1, P2 = cc1, M1 = c, M2 = c;**
$\Rightarrow$ **P1 = uc1, P2 = rc1, M1 = c, M2 = d;**

$\Rightarrow$ **P1 = ud1, P2 = uc1, M1 = d, M2 = c;**
$\Rightarrow$ **P1 = ud1, P2 = ud1, M1 = d, M2 = d;**
$\Rightarrow$ **P1 = ud1, P2 = cc1, M1 = d, M2 = d;**
$\Rightarrow$ **P1 = ud1, P2 = rc1, M1 = d, M2 = d;**

$\Rightarrow$ **P1 = cc1, P2 = uc1, M1 = c, M2 = c;**
$\Rightarrow$ **P1 = cc1, P2 = ud1, M1 = d, M2 = d;**
$\Rightarrow$ **P1 = cc1, P2 = cc1, M1 = c, M2 = c;**
$\Rightarrow$ **P1 = cc1, P2 = rc1, M1 = c, M2 = c;**

$\Rightarrow$ **P1 = rc1, P2 = uc1, M1 = d, M2 = c;**
$\Rightarrow$ **P1 = rc1, P2 = ud1, M1 = d, M2 = d;**
$\Rightarrow$ **P1 = rc1, P2 = cc1, M1 = c, M2 = c;**
$\Rightarrow$ **P1 = rc1, P2 = rc1, M1 = c, M2 = c;**

Compare these results with what we expect from UC, UD, CC and RC in Figure 5.1. Again, P1 generates row headings and P2 the column headings. We can see that RC1 behaves as expected, co-operating with CC1 and RC1 but not with UD1 or CC1. Thus RC1 passes the procedural test: it discriminates correctly without looping when interacting with its own kind.

5.2 AN EVOLUTIONARY TEST

Reciprocal co-operation is procedurally possible; now we must consider whether it is rational. RC only does better than CC in the presence of a third party, UC. This raises the general question of the context for testing. Do we test players in pairs or in a larger population? In particular, RC prospers because it exploits UC. Is it arbitrary to include UC in the population used to test CC and RC? In this section I propose an appropriate test for instrumental success based on populations, not pairs, of players. The unit of testing should be the stable ecosystem. Conditions for entering an ecosystem, I argue, can meet objections concerning arbitrariness.

5.2.1 Arbitrary populations

The arbitrariness of a population containing UC is symptomatic of a more general problem. Like Gauthier's defence of constrained maximization, my argument for reciprocal co-operation is *relative* to the range of alternatives it considers.[4] Indeed, the argument seems to depend on a *contrived* population; without the presence of UC, RC does no better than CC. Moreover, because UC does so badly, it is evidently irrational. It appears that the only reason to insert this unsuccessful player into the population is to provide something for RC to exploit and thereby to prosper. Including UC therefore appears to bias the substantive rationality test in favour of RC and against CC. Finally, if we can add contrived king-makers, why not add other contrived players (king-breakers) as well? For example we could introduce an agent who refused to co-operate with RC, thus making RC do worse and CC do better and undermining my claim for the substantive superiority of the former.

Building on the received theory of rational choice, Gauthier does not see the need to face this problem. Game theory assumes that all players are the same – they are all straightforward maximizers. Introducing a constrained agent to these models is already problematic; adding additional players is deeply disturbing. It evidently creates some problems for claims about substantive rationality that Gauthier has not considered. Therefore I find that I must extend his account of rational justification. Instrumental success is *doubly* relative. A strategy is successful compared to some set of alternative strategies, A, depending on their interaction with a population of strategies, P. Game theory eliminates the problem by constraining all members of A and P to be the same. In contrast, while I shall let A and P be the same population (for simplicity's sake), I shall not require that they contain only one type of agent. We need to test strategies because we do not know in advance which (or even whether only one) is the best. This uncertainty generates a varied population of players with which any purportedly rational agent must interact.

5.2.2 A strategic test

How should this population be specified? Very roughly, there are two ways this might be done: parametrically or strategically. We may focus on a fixed population or we may let the population change under rational pressures. In Danielson (1991a) I argue against the parametric approach, so here I will concentrate on developing a strategic test.

Several of Gauthier's arguments turn on strategic consideration of how other agents will choose their principles in response to the agent's own choice. In particular, Gauthier's defence of narrow over broad compliance (to which I turn in Chapter 9) and his response to my defence of reciprocal co-operation have this form. I focus on the latter:

> reciprocal cooperation helps to sustain the conditions in which cooperation flourishes, and so in which fair mutual advantage is realized. Unconditional cooperation is a disposition that is inimical, not only to its own survival, but to that of any form of cooperation. For a world of unconditional cooperators is easily invaded by straightforward maximizers, who exploit their guileless if benevolent fellows at every turn and whose presence, except in conditions of full transparency, increases the risk run by other cooperators by mistaking their fellows' dispositions and consequently being victimized. Conditional cooperators, although defending themselves directly against predators and free-riders, fail to defend themselves indirectly, by sustaining the unconditional cooperators whose presence enables straightforward maximizers to thrive. Reciprocal cooperators defend themselves both directly and indirectly; by exploiting unconditional cooperators, reciprocal cooperators help eliminate the natural victims of straightforward maximizers, placing the latter at a competitive disadvantage. Reciprocal cooperators thus help make the world safe for morality.[5]

Gauthier's talk of invasion and survival should remind us of sociobiology and, in particular, the strategic concept of an evolutionary stable strategy (ESS). Indeed, the trajectory of populations of interacting strategies in Maynard Smith and Price's original model almost exactly parallels what we should expect to happen to conditional co-operators:[6]

> In a population of retaliators [CC], no other strategy would invade, since there is no other strategy that does better than retaliator itself. However, dove [UC] does equally well in a population of retaliators. This means that, other things being equal, the numbers of doves could slowly drift upwards. Now if the number of doves [UC] drifted up to any significant extent, prober-retaliators [RC] (and incidentally, hawks and bullies [SM]) would start to have an advantage, since they do better

against doves [UC] than retaliators do. Prober-retaliator, unlike hawk and bully, is almost an ESS.

Evolutionary stability provides the ideas we need to develop a strategic test for success. The main problem is to specify a non-arbitrary population appropriate for fundamental justification. I propose to focus on a pair of strategies to be tested, aiming to establish an *asymmetrical relation* between a more successful strategy and an alternative. The basic idea is that one strategy is more successful than another if the first could invade (a population consisting of) the second and the second could not invade the first. This simple picture is complicated by the presence of third parties. As we have seen, intermediaries can change the outcome. But we don't want to test a strategy in the presence of irrelevant intermediaries. Therefore we need to develop a test that determines the drift to intermediaries as well as deciding rational superiority in terms of invasion. I attempt this by introducing the idea of an *non-arbitrary addition* to a population, linked closely to the core ideas of rational choice. A player is a rationally non-arbitrary addition to a population if it does as well as any member of the existing population. We start with a population of the strategy to be tested and add non-arbitrary strategies. Using the example in the quotation above, UC is a non-arbitrary addition to the population $P_1 = \langle CC,CC \rangle$ because UC does as well as CC in the augmented population $P_2 = \langle CC,CC,UC \rangle$. I will say that UC is a (weakly) rational addition to P_1. RC invades CC by doing better than CC in $P_3 = \langle CC,CC,UC,RC \rangle$. RC is also a rational addition to the population. In other words, we can say that P_2 and P_3 rationally extend CC. Therefore P_2 and P_3 are non-arbitrary populations in which to test CC. With these rough definitions in hand, I can state a more formal account of substantive rationality: a strategy S_1 is more successful than strategy S_2 if and only if S_2 can invade some rational extension of S_2 and S_2 cannot invade any rational extension of S_1.

A choice point

My standard of instrumental success does not capture everything everyone might want from such a standard. As I have noted, it stresses the strategic rather than the parametric model of rational choice. It makes instrumental rationality what works best among the (weakly) rational. For example, Holly Smith disagrees with this emphasis. She demands what we might call a parametric *robustness*, an ability to do well against wider variety of strategies, rational or not. My standard is closer to the received theory, although I do not assume a monoculture of identically similar players. Nor do I require that only the *most* rational strategy persist. That is, I do not demand that the population be 'perfectly rational' in Smith's phrase. On the other hand I do not allow in players like her contrived king-breaker, which, by refusing to co-operate with CC, does worse than UC. Therefore I face a choice point in my argument developing Artificial Morality. I believe following Smith's lead would introduce an unlimited variety of players and quickly overwhelm my ability to manage complexity and advance our understanding of the issues.[7]

Moreover, it is important to maintain contact with the premises and standards of the received theory of rational choice. My test shares with its inspiration, the ESS, a close connection to the Nash equilibrium, the basic standard of strategic rationality according to the received theory. In the clearest case, my strategy is in equilibrium against yours when mine is my best response to your best response to mine. Matters get more complicated when we add more players to this duo. There are choices to be made here, as there always are when we need to reduce a one-dimensional vector of values (how one does against many) to a singleton (one's score). Is the best response the one that does best against the *best* strategy in a population, or the one that does best *on average* (or on some other measure of the one against the many)? I will choose the average, arguing that it is appropriate to our purposes because a fundamental justification of morality is stuck with a given population at this point. I will call this test an *evolutionary* test, as it determines success in an evolving population.

Recall that the populations we are speaking of now have passed the filter designed to exclude arbitrary additions.[8] The appeal of the alternative to my evolutionary test, namely concern with what is best only against *the best* in a population, is based on assuming the unconstrained ability of others to adapt strategically to one's choice. That is, one expects the population to move towards that best, just as in the pure case of two-person game theory, one expects the other SM agent optimally to adapt to his expectation of your strategy. But there is a crucial difference. We are now working at the level of strategies that have been adopted, not moves that may be made or unmade. It is not clear that what can be adopted can be renounced. This depends on the *dynamics* of rational constraint, on questions of learning which we will not explore until Chapter 7. But this much is plain already. Once we move to allow non-SM players into our models, as we must to test the claim that perfectly adaptable straightforward maximizers are rational (rational compared to all *else*) then we must admit players who may be *less adaptable*. These non-SM players may be committed to a strategy (or merely not know how to change it).

Therefore, as a consequence of the need to extend our test to include non-SM players, my test ceases to be purely strategic. That is, once a strategy enters the population, it remains there, even if it should later, due to further additions, do worse than the (new) best.[9] As a result, what my test finds to be best is *doubly* relative to the existing population. It is best compared to the particular players that make up the population and in terms of its average score in that population. Finally, although my test deviates from a purely strategic test, it remains close to the received theory's concern with rationality. By my test, only strategies that it would be rational for an agent to choose at some point can enter a population. In particular, constrained players are only introduced if and when they do as well or better than SM players. They are not introduced gratuitously, nor bootstrapped by the presence of fortuitously chosen helpers.

Self-play and bootstrapping

Players following some strategies, such as CC, co-operate with players following these same strategies. They are self-co-operative. Can a strategy bootstrap itself by being self-co-operative? This is a tricky question. Certainly a willingness to choose *C* with others like oneself improves one's chances of success. Accordingly, I have tested players against themselves – recall Loopy failing this test – and recorded the results of this self-play in my outcome tables. But now we should look more critically at self-play. One cannot literally play against oneself. This is obvious. A single straightforward maximizer doesn't get a score of 1; she gets no score until another player appears on the scene. Then she gets one score – playing with the newcomer – but not another – playing herself.[10] Assuming self-play allows moral players to bootstrap themselves too easily. The fundamental justification of morality would be weakened if it assumed the prior existence of enough moral players to make responsive strategies successful. Eliminating self-play prevents spurious bootstrapping. For this reason, my test excludes self-play. It becomes the job of the would-be rational moral agent to get enough other players aligned with him to make his strategy beneficial. Responsive players have no difficulty doing this, as we shall soon see.

I will not allow self-play but I need to moderate the effects of this decision. I test lone newcomers against a population precisely in order that my test will be sensitive to the effects of self-co-operativeness. Newcomers cannot count on arriving in droves (unless they are organized but that's a problem for political theory). They pay the price of trickling in. I assume, on the other hand, that the strategy to be tested is general in a (small) population. Why this asymmetry? Otherwise, having excluded self-play, we have no benchmark against which to test the newcomer except how he does with the one existing agent. This would destabilize and weaken my test. Almost any strategy could drift in and the resulting population would be arbitrary, the result I am trying to avoid. Notice that this asymmetry is not particularly biased for morality or against straightforward maximization. For example, single SM entrants need not pay the costs of their unwillingness to co-operate with their kind. More important, the asymmetry balances out. When we test two strategies for relative success each gets to play the roles of (disadvantaged) invader and (advantaged) defender.

My test is based on the history of a population. A history is not a game; the rows and columns are not alternatives to be chosen, but players. Rows are numbered in order of entry and are matched with columns. Figure 5.2 shows how I will represent the history of a population. This population begins with a pair of straightforward maximizers, SM_1 and SM_2. The diagonals are blank because I eliminate self-play.

Entrant	Agent	SM_1	SM_2
0	SM_1	–	1
0	SM_2	1	–

Figure 5.2 An initial population

An example

Now I can add some newcomers. The standard is historical; it extends a population by adding strategies that do as well against the population as the best in the population. The tables below should be read as a series of nested results, expanding down to the left as entrants are added. Now I can apply my test in detail. CC can enter the SM population because she does as well as any existing member in Figure 5.3. This suggests how we can move from mere drift to invasion.

Entrant	Agent	SM_1	SM_2	CC_1
0	SM_1	–	1	1
0	SM_2	1	–	1
1	CC_1	1	1	–

Figure 5.3 CC drifts in

Entrant	Agent	SM_1	SM_2	CC_1	CC_2
0	SM_1	–	1	1	1
0	SM_2	1	–	1	1
1	CC_1	1	1	–	2
2	CC_2	1	1	2	–

Figure 5.4 CC invades SM

Entrant	Agent	CC_1	CC_2	UC_1	UC_1	SM_1
0	CC_1	–	2	2	2	1
0	CC_2	2	–	2	2	1
1	UC_1	2	2	–	2	0
2	UC_2	2	2	2	–	0
3	SM_1	1	1	3	3	–

Figure 5.5 SM invades CC

The first CC entrant did as well as SM; the next one does better in Figure 5.4. Therefore CC can invade SM.[11] This does not yet show CC to be more successful than SM. One would need to show that SM cannot invade any population that CC permits to grow around it. This cannot be done, since Figure 5.5 shows how SM can invade. Starting with CC, SM can invade because CC permits UC to enter and after two unconditional co-operators enter, SM (with a total of 8) does better than CC (with a total of 7). I conclude that, according to my evolutionary test for substantive rationality, conditional co-operation is not more rational than straightforward maximization.

5.2.3 The RC Invasion

When reciprocal co-operation (RC) enters the scene, I can get more decisive results. Conditional co-operation is unstable; it allows players to drift to another strategy, UC, which then allows other strategies to do better than CC itself. CC can be indirectly invaded. What would invade the resulting $\langle CC, CC, UC \rangle$ population? Gauthier points to SM; eventually SM could invade, as we saw above. However CC co-operates with RC but not SM, so RC can invade immediately, while SM would need to wait until the number of UC so increased that the gains of predation outweighed the penalty CC exacts. For example, RC would do better than both UC_2 as the second entrant and SM as the third entrant in Figure 5.5. Figure 5.6 shows the results, with RC getting 7 to CC's 6. Therefore CC can be invaded indirectly by RC and well as SM. Conversely, RC cannot be invaded by SM or CC (nor by any other strategy that I know of). RC allows a drift to CC, but the presence of RC blocks the possibility of CC drifting to UC, and CC never does better than RC. I conclude that reciprocal, not conditional, co-operation is rational in the following strong sense: RC is rationally superior to CC and SM and CC is not rationally superior to RC or even to SM. This is a significant substantive result: RC is rationally superior to CC and only RC is superior to SM. The baton of rational morality shifts from Gauthier's proposed principle of constrained maximization to reciprocal co-operation.

Earlier I posed a question about how we should interpret the result of motivational pluralism that I charted in Figure 5.1. Now I am in a position to answer that question. We can read that chart as indicating a history of the invasion of CC by RC, via the preliminary drift to UC. I think that I have tamed the unruliness of situations composed of populations of mixed players sufficiently for us to feel secure with this result. My test is *evolutionary* rather than *ecological* because it starts with a population of the player to be tested and assumes that new players come into existence to fill niches as they arise.[12] The test is far from completely specified. For example, I have not provided a generator of alternative strategies.

Entrant	Agent	CC_1	CC_2	UC_1	RC_1
0	CC_1	–	2	2	2
0	CC_2	2	–	2	2
1	UC_1	2	2	–	0
3	RC_1	2	2	3	–

Figure 5.6 RC invades CC

5.2.4 An asymmetry

However, there may be objections to my claim that UC is rational in the sense that it is *equally* advantageous in a population of CC players. One objection is that I allow merely equally advantageous strategies to drift into the test population. This may seem undermotivated and therefore designed to admit UC in order to embarrass CC. However there are additional, independent reasons to allow drift. First, if players learn, there will be drift. Learners are not perfect replicators.[13] In addition, learners may seek local maxima; they may copy what seems to be advantageous in the current environment. For example, arrayed against CC, UC looks just as good as CC. Equally advantageous players are indistinguishable to some learners. Indeed, CC, like Tit For Tat, *teaches* simple learners to become unconditional, not conditional co-operators since CC punishes other players testing out the use of *D* (Danielson 1986, p. 455). Second, if we admit procedural considerations, UC's simplicity may make it on balance rationally better than CC or easier to learn (at least until predators appear on the scene).

Another objection is that UC will be short lived; its presence in a population makes the entry of SM rational (where it was not in a CC population) and leaves UC as the worse-off strategy. Wouldn't UC players die out or change to CC at this point? Not necessarily. First, unconditional co-operators need not die out because there is no necessary connection between interests and survival. Recall my argument (in Chapter 2) that rational justification is not sociobiology; we should not identify the interests at which rationality aims to satisfy with reproductive fitness values. It is less objectionable to link interests and survival than to link them to reproduction but it is still objectionable. Morality – even rational morality – must admit the survival of the frustrated.[14] Second, UC players may not be able to change their principles. The assumption that players can constrain themselves introduces hysteresis.[15] As I noted earlier, until we have investigated the procedural mechanisms of learning (in Chapter 7) it is not obvious that what can be bound can also be unbound. Therefore I conclude that even in a world of rationally chosen constraint, there may be unconditionally co-operative players. From this Holly Smith concludes that SM would be more rational than CC, which is bad news from the point of view of solving the compliance problem. Our conclusion is more hopeful. In a world where UC enters because CC allows it, RC, but not SM, is rationally superior to CC. This is better news, because RC, unlike SM, is a morally constrained principle, which helps to close the compliance dilemma.

5.2.5 Defending CC

Looking ahead, it is plain that reciprocal co-operators, who exploit innocent unconditional co-operators, lose in moral appeal some of what they gain in substantive advantage over conditional co-operators. Since rationality points to RC and morality is likely to favour CC, there are two strategies that one might pursue to close this new gap. On the one hand, one can try to show conditional co-operation to be more rational; on the other, one can try to show reciprocal co-operation to be less immoral. Gauthier works on both these ways. While we must wait to see if RC can be vindicated morally, the possibility remains of a rearguard defence of CC as rational in spite of what we have seen so far.

A 'richer level of analysis'

Having argued for the rational superiority of RC over CC in a transparent world, I should consider Gauthier's attempt to make CC rationally more attractive by moving to a 'richer level of analysis':

> In my argument, preferences are fixed . . . and then dispositions are defined in relation to them. But what if these dispositions are

themselves objects of preferences? Danielson, focusing on artificial morality, can avoid this problem by the appropriate construction of his agents. I cannot. I must then allow for the possibility of such preferences. And these preferences need not be arbitrary, or given exogenously to the defence of rational constraint, for since human beings have in addition to beliefs and desires, emotions that affect their willingness and ability to behave in different ways, the cultivation of appropriate feelings for our fellows may be essential to inducing behaviour that is maximally conductive to mutual preference fulfillment. The cultivation of appropriate fellow feelings thus becomes a suitable object of rational agreement, and the agreed feelings may well give rise to preferences over dispositions to unconditional, conditional, reciprocal, and other forms of cooperation. Speculatively, I suggest that, absent such preferences, Danielson's defence of reciprocal rather than conditional cooperation is sound; yet the desirability of cultivating feelings supportive of cooperative practices and inimical to predation, exploitation, and free-riding may well support, at this richer level of analysis, conditional cooperation. Persons who take an interest in cooperation are, I suggest, likely to prefer to dispose themselves to cooperate with other cooperators.

(Gauthier 1988b, pp. 401f.)

Notice first that this is not an appeal to *ad hoc* higher-order preferences that make CC rational. Gauthier would agree that if he were to make CC rational by assuming a preference for this disposition, the result would not be a fundamental justification but an exercise in begging the question. He rejects arbitrary or exogenous preferences. Therefore it is clear how we should *not* interpret Gauthier's appeal to human emotions. But it is not clear how we *should* interpret this appeal. He directs us to notice the emotional constraints on human decision-making or learning. Given the differences between artificial and natural human morality, it may seem that I should let the point pass. Humans are not artificial agents, so they need to contend with a richer environment, both internal and external, that makes its own demands on rationality. On this reading, we should conclude that although irrational generally, CC may be rational for people. However I am not happy about this interpretation. Why does Gauthier suppose that these emotions are *additional* constraints? After all, what are principles like CC and RC but dispositions to behave that are preferred to other dispositions, like SM?[16] If emotions are (merely) preferences for dispositions, then, to put the point in a contentious way, we already have – in RC, CC, UC and the like – agents with *artificial emotions*. And of course how we got here was by noticing that CC is *not* a rational emotion to have; RC is.

So Gauthier must mean something more by his appeal to emotions, since he enlists it to support CC over RC. Most likely what is supposed to be added is some affective blurring of discrimination or a strong default in absence of evidence to the contrary, either of which could be plausibly associated with emotions in humans and both will carry CC from some contexts to others. CC is rational in some contexts, and its emotional force – a kind of psychic momentum – makes it rational in other contexts as well. Now I do not deny that there are situations in which CC is rational. For example, as we saw in Chapter 3, there is strong (if not uncontested) evidence that in indefinitely iterated play of the Prisoner's Dilemma, Tit for Tat, which is the iterated projection of CC, is rational. Axelrod argues that Tit for Tat's success is due to the ease with which it is recognized. This reason might carry over to non-iterated play in conditions of less than complete transparency.[17] The problem is carrying over the just-ification of CC from these contexts to different contexts that concern fundamental justification, like the non-iterated PD. Notoriously, if the contexts are different, the principle that is rational will likely differ too. Why should agents keep on conditionally co-operating when RC is now really best? The answer must be an appeal to emotional rigidities in humans. But this appeal sits uncomfortably in Gauthier's rational choice framework for several reasons. First, Gauthier wants to defend constrained maximization as rational for 'perfect actors' (Gauthier 1986a, §VI.3.2); the appeal to emotional limits would be 'an appeal to . . . weakness or imperfection in the reasoning of the actor' which Gauthier had previously avoided. Emotions are part of the theory of imperfect rationality. Second, Gauthier makes crucial appeals to rational adaptability, as we have seen (and will return to in Part III). Emotionally bound agents would not perform as Gauthier's own theory requires. Finally, we must be careful not to confuse levels here. I agree that agents must be bound to this extent: they must prefer to co-operate even when this *action* is not advantageous. But it is a separate question whether they should be bound to continue to, say, conditionally, co-operate when this *principle* is no longer rational. I allow that agents might persist in my substantive rationality test; they may be stuck with UC, CC, etc. But I do not think that their persistence remains rational. Persistence *explains* why such agents are part of the rationally accessible environment; it does not *justify* what they do. It provides no basis for recommending persistence as rational.

Thus the main critical argument of this chapter is confirmed. Gauthier's deeper level of analysis does not overturn our conclusion that reciprocal co-operation is more rational than conditional co-operation.

Two demons

My argument for RC over CC may seem more conclusive than the results warrant. To see why, let us return to Holly Smith's argument and her second counter-example to Gauthier's defence of constrained maximization, an agent that co-operates only with UC. Let's call this agent CUC. This strategy is neither rationally nor morally attractive. CUC are not rational (as Smith admits). Indeed, CUC is the most easily invaded strategy I know of. Because it does not even succeed in co-operating with its twin, CUC can be directly invaded by UC.[18] Since it gets along with no agent but UC, CUC cannot invade or even drift into any other population. Failure to co-operate with its twin also undercuts any moral justification for CUC. If co-operating with UC is morally required, why punish those who so co-operate, like one's own twin? The only rationale for CUC seems to be to undermine CC; it is an *ad hoc* CC-demon. This would be a good reason to eliminate it. A derivation of impartial constraint in a world contrived to include only constraint-lovers begs the question. Conversely, the failure of a principle, *P*, in a world of otherwise irrational *P*-haters should be excluded for methodological reasons. So I am happy to be able to exclude CUC by my test of substantive rationality. This shows that our test does some work.

None the less, CUC suggests that more might be done to protect unconditional co-operators. In this respect it is morally interesting, as we shall see in Chapter 6, where I will construct an agent like CUC that protects unconditional co-operators against RC and might even be rational in some situations. Therefore reciprocal co-operators may not do best against all possible agents. We can imagine an agent that refused to co-operate with RC and yet co-operated with other agents. This reminds us that even according to my test, which goes some way towards eliminating arbitrary situations, instrumental success remains relative to the population of varied agents.

A second demon reveals the limits of the ability of my evolutionary test of rationality to filter out arbitrary players. Consider a king-breaker demon, call it RC+, which co-operates with RC (and CC) but also with SM. Obviously RC+ can drift into the RC population to be tested, since it does as well among RC players as any RC. However, given the presence of RC+, SM can invade, since it does better enough against RC+ to outweigh the costs imposed by the RC players. Figure 5.7 illustrates this possibility.

Entrant	Agent	RC_1	RC_2	$RC+_1$	$RC+_2$	SM_1
0	RC_1	–	2	2	2	1
0	RC_2	2	–	2	2	1
1	$RC+_1$	2	2	–	2	0
2	$RC+_2$	2	2	2	–	0
3	SM_1	1	1	3	3	–

Figure 5.7 SM invades RC

Something is amiss. Comparing Figure 5.7 with Figure 5.5 might suggest what has gone wrong. Notice that the charts show identical histories, with RC replacing CC and RC+ replacing UC. This suggests that RC+ is functionally an unconditional co-operator (it chooses C when SM chooses D) with this crucial difference: it manages to co-operate with RC. But RC is defined as not co-operating with such an agent. Therefore the abstract definitions of these two players are incompatible. I won't try to eliminate RC+ on these abstract grounds, that is, as specifying behaviour incompatible with the definitions of other players. (Why eliminate RC+ instead of RC?) One reason we must actually implement agents as software robots is to settle questions like this, by providing testable versions of agents. For example, the version of RC I introduced for the XPD, RC1, will not co-operate with RC+, so RC+ is procedurally impossible, and can be eliminated on this basis. We need to descend to the procedural level to complete our evolutionary test.

Conclusion

I conclude that reciprocal co-operation is more rational than Gauthier's constrained maximization. My evolutionary test, which models the type of argument Gauthier generally uses, establishes this result in a non-arbitrary world of varied rational players. Reciprocal co-operation helps to close the gap between rationality and morality because it fares better than Gauthier's proposed principle and cannot be invaded, even indirectly, by straightforward maximizers.

5.3 ARE CONSTRAINED MAXIMIZERS TEMPTED?

I have argued at length that reciprocal co-operators do better than conditional co-operators playing the Prisoner's Dilemma. But there is a problem. I set the agents to interact in a particular sort of situation: a mixed-motive game. In game theory this situation is defined by the agents' preferences over outcomes. If the agents do not have preferences of the correct sort, they are not playing the specified game. For example, a Prisoner's Dilemma is defined as a situation where the agents value the Temptation (T) of one-sided defection more than the Reward (R) of joint co-operation more than the Punishment (P) of joint defection more than the Sucker's payoff (S) of one-sided co-operation. (See Figure 5.8.)

	C	D
C	R,R	S,T
D	T,S	P,P

Figure 5.8 Prisoner's Dilemma values

Consider an extreme example. An act-utilitarian player, who chooses on the basis of sums of both players' scores, does not prefer T over R or P over S in the Prisoner's Dilemma. So, the objection continues, the utilitarian is simply not playing the specified game. Unfortunately, the conclusion of this argument must be that the *only* player that has the specified preferences is the straightforward maximizer. Therefore if this objection is successful, it will eliminate every contender but one from the test. Of course, the effect of this is to evacuate SM's claim to rational superiority; the criterion of substantive rationality becomes vacuous. How are we to deal with this gap between what drives players and the structure of their situation?

A gap

The most important thing is not to be dragged too fast into what may be a tendentious description of this problem. The received theory is committed to a strongly unified thesis: rationality only requires one *concept*, preference, to account both for players' motivations and the structure of their situations. If we are to dispute this thesis (as Gauthier, McClennen and I do) we need at least the conceptual space to define an alternative. Therefore it is a mistake to try to join the received theory on the disputed – definitely not common – ground of preferences, a concept heavily laden with the theory under question. We cannot have it both ways. If preferences are what define a situation (as a Prisoner's Dilemma, for example), then we cannot allow as well that preferences are what determine what our players do for two reasons. First, behaviour in strategic contexts does not reliably reveal preference. For example, a reciprocal co-operator chooses C sometimes in spite of its preference for DC over CC and DD over CD.[19] Second, there must be a gap between preferences and behaviour or there is no need for a theory of rational choice. One doesn't need a *theory* to tell him to take oranges over apples if he prefers oranges to apples. It is only the gap between preferences for outcomes (like CC over DD) and the need to choose between actions not directly leading to those outcomes that makes players need a theory. Otherwise one has *structuralism*; the structure of the situation determines what players do and there is no room for rational or moral theory to make a difference. Therefore I conclude that we are stuck with a gap between behaviour and situation. As I suggested in Chapter 2, I will avoid using 'preferences' to describe situations. I will identify interests as what structures a situation: the structure of partially opposed interests in the PD, for example. In contrast, what drives players and explains their behaviour I will take to be their expressed preferences over acts, their *principles* or, more neutrally, *plans*.

None the less, terminology cannot paper over the gap between principles and interests; an objection remains. Since a conditional co-operator prefers CC to DC, in what sense is CC playing the Prisoner's Dilemma, which is defined by a preference for DC over CC? Gauthier's solution of constrained rationality appears to be an *ad hoc* preference change. The objection ignores the fact that while players may have any set of coherent principles selecting actions that they please, I do not allow their principles to change the scores that fix the game. For example, an act utilitarian chooses C in the Prisoner's Dilemma and gets the outcome CD. As mentioned in Chapter 2, this may be his second preferred outcome (he prefers $R > S = T > P$), his score is still the worst ($S = 0$). It would be objectionable were we to raise his score to reflect his principles. There is a gap between the utilitarian player's principle – and hence *revealed preferences over actions* – and the score. The critic might jump on this: it shows that the scores are meaningless; they do not determine action as they do in the case of the received theory. Again, this moves too fast. The scores *do* determine who wins, who invades, and who gets into the non-arbitrary population used to test players. My test will never allow UC to count as more rational than RC, even if UC gets her favoured result – say it is *S* – and RC only his third best, *R*. RC does better because I take the payoff matrix to indicate the substantive individual interests determined by the situation (as the utilitarian does when she uses them as inputs to her social utility function). Players may act in ways not directly reflecting these interests (their principles and behaviour need not track their interests) but the interests indicated in the game matrices determine substantive rationality none the less.

This represents a concession on my part. The split between principles (driving players) and interests (defining situations) is somewhat worrisome. However, it is common to make distinction of this sort.[20] For example, Gauthier tries to stay closer to the language of preference throughout his argument, but he too admits a gap. After all, co-operators reveal a preference for *R* over *T*; this is what co-operation requires. He claims that agents' preferences definitive of the game are revealed at the level of choosing dispositions, not action:

> I am not denying th[e] explanatory role of the concept of preference in choice behavior, or even that 'what must shape choice now is preference now.' But I am claiming that the explanatory role of preference is indirect; preferences explain plans, which in turn explain choices.
>
> (Gauthier 1988a, p. 212)

Unfortunately, Gauthier does not seem to see that the choice of his preferred disposition, constrained maximization, does not reveal the right sort of preferences even indirectly. A constrained maximizer is a conditional co-operator, who will *never* choose *T* over *R*. (The only time that constrained maximizers choose *D* is when they expect that the other player will choose *D* as well.) Constrained maximizers evidently are not tempted to defect. Agents who would choose constrained maximization really do not have the preferences that structure the Prisoner's Dilemma. The gap between interests and principles remains open in Gauthier's case.

In contrast, reciprocal co-operators reveal (using Gauthier's test) that they really do prefer *T* over *R*. RC players show this by taking *T* when they can get it, e.g. when they play against unconditional co-operators. We know that reciprocal co-operators are tempted because they sometimes succumb. Therefore reciprocal co-operators close the gap between preferences and principles. Their (minimally) constraining co-operative principles give them revealed preferences for R over T only some of the time; otherwise they reveal precisely those preferences that structure the Prisoner's Dilemma as a crucial problem.[21]

To summarize, the most solid refutation of the received theory of rational choice shares its premises to the greatest extent. We cannot go to the limit on this, else only SM players would remain. But RC players do not differ from straightforward maximizers so much as to remove them from a fairly tightly defined common game. They play the same game but they play it better.

CONCLUSION

Finally, I urge you not to misinterpret this last point. I am not claiming that reciprocal co-operators are rational for a logical reason (i.e. they are the most similar to unconstrained straightforward maximizers). This would misconstrue my results. I rely primarily on procedural and substantive rationality. I have shown that reciprocal co-operators can be effectively implemented. If CC players were to do better than RC players, then I would find them to be more rational. If this turned out to be the case, the greater gap between their principles and interests would slightly weaken the result as a refutation of the received theory of rational choice. But the main point is that RC players do perform best; their superiority to CM and SM is a matter of substantive rationality, not logical similarity. This is the main result established by the argument of this chapter.

6

A MORAL MONSTER?

We have seen that reciprocal co-operation (RC) is both substantively and procedurally rational in simple transparent worlds. However it may seem surprising that I propose RC as a solution to the compliance problem. The original compliance dilemma pitted straightforward rationality against morality. Following Gauthier, I used responsive constraints to improve on the rational performance of moral players. But I went further in this direction and, like Frankenstein, ended up with what some will see as a moral monster. Gauthier's principle, constrained maximization, is recognizably moral. In contrast, my principle, reciprocal co-operation, whose distinguishing feature is a willingness to exploit unconditional co-operators (UC), looks morally defective. By showing that rationality directs one to exploit innocent agents, reciprocal co-operators re-open the gap between rationality and morality. Reciprocal co-operators seem to be part of the compliance problem, not part of its solution. In this new compliance dilemma, rationality points to my principle, RC, while morality points to conditional co-operation (CC).

This chapter addresses this new dilemma, in three steps. First, I review the terrain that we have covered, to remind us that RC is not morally vacuous. Second, I turn to the moral theory that Gauthier and I share, in order to assess the relative moral status of RC and CC. I shall argue that in terms of Gauthier's standard of impartiality my principle of reciprocal co-operation does no worse than his own principle of constrained maximization. When I introduce another standard to address the treatment of naive agents, again constrained maximization does no better than reciprocal co-operation. Neither principle, RC or CC, really solves the problem posed by the presence of UC. Third, I construct a morally more attractive solution to the problem, although this strategy appears to be irrational.

6.1 SHARED STANDARDS

It may seem parochial to focus attention on comparative morality of CC and RC, rather like limiting ourselves to Albania and Bulgaria when asked to discuss the moral merit of states. Surely, our imagined critic says, there is a wider range of possible moralities and the claims of rational morality should address this wider range. After all, neither RC nor CC is morally very demanding. Gauthier admits the limited scope of his moral theory: 'developments in medicine . . . make possible an ever-increasing transfer of benefits to persons who decrease [the average level of well-being]. Such persons are not party to the moral relationships grounded by a contractarian theory' (Gauthier 1986a, p. 18).

6.1.1 Reconstructing morality

Our imagined critic makes one sound point and intimates a shakier one. The sound point is that we – both Gauthier and I – need a larger framework, in order to validate our proposed principles as moral. There is always a danger of reconceiving one's test to confirm one's conclusions.[1] Trimming one's standard is especially tempting in the case of morality, where no undisputed standard plays the role of substantive rationality. None the less, the critic reminds us, there is a large area of moral agreement. For example, killing innocents is clearly wrong and withholding expensive life-support systems from poor pensioners is also beyond the intuitive moral pale, if less drastically so. Both Gauthier and I concur with this account of largely shared moral beliefs. Both theories aim at a rational reconstruction of morality, so they must eventually answer to this shared conception of morality (Gauthier 1988a, p. 177). (Without such a test, they would be theories of something other than morality.) On the other hand, both morals by agreement and Artificial Morality are *minimal* moral theories. They aim at the *rationally* reconstructable portion of morality, not a full account of all that people hold to be morally important. Neither theory is likely to save all of the moral appearances. The main question I address in this chapter is whether

Artificial Morality, in advancing the rational result to reciprocal co-operation, saves *any* appearance of morality at all.

This is a relative question. Gauthier assumes that his principle of constrained maximization is *more moral* than my principle of reciprocal co-operation, for obvious reasons. Indeed, I agreed with this appraisal initially.[2] Now I am willing to defend RC as constrained maximization's moral equal. The obvious place to start is an internal debate between these two minimal moralities. Summing up, I agree with the critic that we need a larger scale if Gauthier and I are to evaluate our claims with respect to morality generally. Eventually we need to place RC and CC on this scale and argue for our willingness to settle for so little in the way of morality. However, this is a large project and I believe that when we undertake it we shall see that the difference between RC and CC is crucial. Therefore I can satisfy the critic and still get on with my local dispute with Gauthier.

6.1.2 Minimal morality

I have called impartial constraint a 'minimal morality'. I did not, of course, mean that Gauthier and I seek the least constraint. Although rational agents presumably do seek the least *costly* constraint, the possibility of rational morality hinges on some constraint being less costly than none. Rational agents do not maximize constraint (because one can't have two distinct maximizing goals and they maximize their own utility instead) but they do not try to minimize it either. What I did mean is that Gauthier's characterization of morality as impartial constraint is close to the lower bound of what could count as a morality.

I write 'close' to indicate the fuzziness of the boundary of the moral, even within the simplified games under discussion. Some players are easily categorized: an unconditional defector is amoral and a constrained maximizer moral. Others are less clear. For example, in Chapter 8, I will introduce a straightforward maximizer which, because it understands that some agents are constrained and responsive, is able to co-operate when moving first in the XPD. This agent, because it has a moralized epistemology, seems less amoral than the unconditional defector but it still lacks constraint. Thus adding new players can blur the moral/amoral line. Similarly, new situations complicate the task of categorizing the moral. In the Prisoner's

Dilemma joint co-operation is both mutually beneficial and impartial. Therefore this situtation does not test principles' differential performance on these two standards. In Part III I will introduce a new situation where impartiality is distinct from mutual advantage. However while we remain within the simpler PD, impartiality is the general moral standard that Gauthier and I share. We return to the question of drawing a moral/amoral line below, because this is a problem for moral players facing a mixed population.

6.2 RECIPROCAL VS CONDITIONAL CO-OPERATION

6.2.1 Is reciprocal co-operation immoral?

Reciprocal co-operators may seem nastier than they are, so I begin by clearing away two possible misperceptions. First, a reciprocal co-operator is a constrained agent. It sometimes chooses C while it prefers DC to CC and DD to CD.[3] RC's willingness to defect against UC should not blind us to the fact that it co-operates with conditional co-operators and other reciprocal co-operators. Second, notice that my argument for reciprocal co-operation is not based on the possibility of deception.[4] As Gauthier points out, 'To avoid misunderstanding, note that a reciprocal cooperator is not engaged in a game of "second-guessing." He does not seek to fool others, to take advantage of those who are taken in by his co-operative disposition' (Gauthier 1988b, p. 400). The argument for RC over CC is valid in a strongly transparent artificial world where deception is impossible. Reciprocal co-operators are not deceivers.

6.2.2 Impartiality

Now I address the main question: is reciprocal co-operation moral according to Gauthier's own standard of impartiality? It may seem obvious that reciprocal co-operation lacks 'the impartiality characteristic of morality' (Gauthier 1986a, p. 4). However, this is not so clear, due to the character of Gauthier's argument for constrained maximization. Unlike his arguments for the principle of rational bargaining and the proviso constraining the initial bargaining position, Gauthier devotes his entire effort to justifying constrained maximization as rational, not moral. This is understandable. As I noted earlier, in *Morals by Agreement* he considers no alternative to constrained maximization but straightforward maximization.[5]. Since the former aims at fair optimal outcomes, its moral superiority to the latter is evident. However I have introduced alternatives to the conditionally co-operative strategy contained in constrained maximization. These additional principles raise questions of comparative moral value, even in terms of impartiality.

For example, it is not clear how the moral standard of impartiality regards *retributive* defection. It seems appropriate that CC and RC defect against a defecting straightforward maximizer, but some claim that impartiality requires co-operation even in this case. As we saw in Chapter 2, an act utilitarian does not defect, finding retributive punishment too costly to all concerned.[6] Conversely, Gauthier suggests that constrained maximizers refuse to co-operate even with a co-operative SM, which intimates a stronger retributive principle.[7] None the less I take it that the punishment of defectors is a fairly clear moral matter.

Matters become much less clear when we introduce additional moral players, like the unconditional co-operator (UC), whom CC and RC treat differently. This brings on a serious problem of toleration and the need to rank CC and RC in terms of the moral standard of impartiality. CC co-operates with unconditional co-operators and so expresses impartiality at the level of behaviour: co-operate with co-operators. RC defects on UC but may rejoin in her own moral defence that UC is immorally indiscriminate in co-operating with defectors. Thus reciprocal co-operation can be seen as expressing impartiality at a higher level of principle: co-operate only with morally discriminating players.[8] However there is a problem with this defence of reciprocal co-operation as impartial. How does one deal with those that tolerate immorality of others? In particular, since co-operating with amoral defectors makes UC less moral, shouldn't CC's co-operation with the less moral UC brand her also as indiscriminating and hence less moral? But RC co-operates with CC.[9] The objection appeals to a principle of transitivity of moral fault through toleration. This is an *independent* principle; one may invoke the standard of impartiality without it. None the less, this contagion indicates the difficulties posed by the need to draw a line enclosing those one tolerates (one's moral ingroup) among players of varying degrees of toleration.[10]

A Discrimination Test

We need a test for morally consistent discrimination. Figure 6.1 shows one way to diagram one such rudimentary test.[11] The table classifies a population by the moral categories of one player (in this case RC). The double line partitions players into two sets with the moral$_{RC}$ ingroup at the top. This is a binary classification. Each player gets 1 for correctly discriminating another player (co-operating with those above the moral$_{RC}$ line; defecting with those below) and 0 for incorrect discrimination; the sum yields her discrimination score. A player draws an impartially discriminating line in case the line can be drawn on a break in the discrimination scores of a weakly ordered set of players; the player's own discrimination of this line is measured by its score. Figure 6.1 shows that RC can draw a line (between scores of 2 and 3) and perfectly discriminates (i.e. gets a score of 4) moral membership so defined. This is a weak test of internal moral coherence. Similar diagrams would show that UD, UC, CC, can all do this as well. Therefore all these players are coherently discriminating among themselves (in this small sample population).

	RC	CC	UC	UD	moral$_{RC}$ score
RC	1	1	1	1	4
CC	1	1	0	1	3
UC	1	1	0	0	2
UD	0	0	1	1	2

Figure 6.1 How RC draws the line

I conclude that the moral standard of impartiality is not easy to apply to a situation consisting of several different sorts of players because of the the toleration problem. None the less RC is not clearly inferior to CC according to this standard.[12] First, like CC, reciprocal co-operation exhibits genuine self-constraint in the Prisoner's Dilemma. Second, RC is impartial to all moral players, if we are careful to delimit the set of moral players by their responsive co-operation rather by simple co-operation. We can construct a plausible test for consistent line-drawing in these terms. Third, RC also encourages others to co-operate, because, while it penalizes UC, the lesson communicated is: co-operate in a more sophisticated, discriminating manner. As Gauthier writes, 'Reciprocal co-operators . . . help make the world safe for morality'.[13]

6.2.3 Protecting innocents

I do not want to leave the impression that Gauthier approves of reciprocal co-operators. He continues the passage quoted above:

> This is not an appealing argument. If the farmer, in order to protect his chickens from the foxes, eliminates the local rabbits, thus reducing the foxes' overall food supply and encouraging them to go elsewhere, it does seem rather hard on the innocent rabbits. But of course rabbits cannot help being rabbits, whereas unconditional cooperators can presumably mend their guileless but costly ways . . .many of us might prefer reeducating unconditional cooperators to exploiting them.

I agree with Gauthier; it would be better costlessly to reeducate unconditional co-operators. But this is not an option in the stark situations which Gauthier and I employ to test various principles. Of course, one can teach by example (as we will see in Chapter 7), but the only way to *motivate* another rational agent is through the carrot and stick of co-operation and defection. Does this pessimistic (almost Malthusian) conclusion make our use of minimal gamelike worlds objectionable? No. The point of projecting the problems of rationality and morality onto such meagre landscapes as the Prisoner's Dilemma is to force hard decisions upon us, to reveal problems starkly and to avoid appeals that would undermine a fundamental justification of morality. So Gauthier's call to re-educate UC instead of exploiting her is moot. We are left with the alternatives of exploiting UC or maintaining her.

What does morality require here and why? I conjecture that we need to go beyond impartiality to a stronger standard if we want to see innocents protected. Impartiality does not adequately address the problems introduced by the presence of naive unconditional co-operators. Although CC is more impartial toward UC, CC can still be criticized for failing to protect UC from RC. Reciprocal co-operators *exploit* unconditional co-operators; that is, RC make UC worse off than the non-co-operative baseline even when this is not necessary to protect RC (indirectly) *from* SM. Reciprocal co-operators violate our sense that innocents ought not to be exploited, at least in cases where this is not required for self-defence.[14]

As I have already hinted, in terms of this stronger moral standard, conditional co-operators are also morally criticizable. Conditional co-operators encourage unconditional co-operators, which the conditional co-operators then fail to protect from exploitation from RC. By co-operating with RC, CC acquiesces in RC's treatment of UC. Therefore we can grant that RC is morally criticizable for preying on UC, but CC is also criticizable according to the same standard.[15]

6.3 A MORAL ALTERNATIVE

The foregoing is unsatisfactory. Must rational morality choose between two evils: conditional co-operators who encourage innocents only to abandon them and reciprocal co-operators who actively prey upon innocents? No; it need not. Once again, we should explore additional principles. I introduce a new strategy which protects innocents directly and indirectly by refusing to co-operate with those who refuse to co-operate with UC:

> Unconditional co-operator protector (UCP): co-operate with and only with those who
>
> 1 co-operate with unconditional co-operators; and
> 2 co-operate with unconditional co-operator protectors.

Like a conditional co-operator, UCP co-operates with a UC; unlike CC, UCP carries through on the defence of UC by refusing to co-operate with anyone who defects with a UC, such as RC. UCP is morally more attractive than CC. Notice that although inspired by Smith's CC-demon, CUC (see §5.2.5), UCP is a great improvement, both morally and rationally, since it co-operates with itself.[16] UCP protects the unconditional co-operators that it fosters, making it morally superior both to CC, who lets innocent unconditional co-operators be exploited, and RC, who exploits them.

6.3.1 Incoherent discrimination

Surprisingly, adding Unconditional Co-operator Protector to the population brings out an unexpected moral defect in RC. Consider what happens if we add UCP and apply our discrimination test. UCP defects with RC because RC defects with UC who is moral$_{UCP}$. UCP is coherently discriminating in the enlarged population (see Figure 6.2).

	UCP	CC	UC	RC	UD	moral$_{UCP}$ score
UCP	1	1	1	1	1	5
CC	1	1	1	0	1	4
UC	1	1	1	0	0	3
RC	0	1	0	0	1	2
UD	0	0	0	1	1	2

Figure 6.2 How UCP draws the line

However, in this more complex population there is no coherent way for RC to draw the moral line. Since UCP refuses to co-operate with RC, the obvious classification puts UCP outside RC's moral club (below the line), in which case UD and CC get the same score (see Figure 6.3) but receive different treatment. Alternatively, if UCP is placed above the line, UCP and UC get the same score (see Figure 6.4). In both cases, the line distinguishes players with equal discrimination scores; in the second case, RC defects on moral$_{RC}$ UCP as well.

	RC	CC	UD	UC	UCP	moral$_{RC}$ score
RC	1	1	1	1	1	5
CC	1	1	1	0	0	3
UD	0	0	1	1	1	3
UC	1	1	0	0	0	2
UCP	0	0	1	0	0	1

Figure 6.3 If RC excludes UCP

119

	RC	CC	UCP	UC	UD	moral$_{RC}$ score
RC	1	1	0	1	1	4
CC	1	1	1	0	1	4
UCP	0	1	1	0	1	3
UC	1	1	1	0	0	3
UD	0	0	0	1	1	2

Figure 6.4 If RC includes UCP

I conclude that in terms of RC's strong moral suit, discrimination, UCP is morally superior. UCP is not uniquely moral; in this enlarged population, CC passes the discrimination test as well.[17] This failure of RC is interesting in two respects. First, it shows that impartiality is a more demanding standard than one might have thought. Second, it reminds us of the burden of complexity. RC coherently discriminates in a smaller, simpler population; it only fails as the toleration problem becomes more complex.

6.3.2 Substantive rationality

Recall that this chapter began with a new compliance dilemma, with rational RC vying with purportedly moral CC. UCP changes this picture. Apparently the unconditional co-operator protector, not CC, should hold down the moral side of the dilemma. This leads us to examine more closely the rationality of UCP. I consider the substantive rationality of UCP in this subsection and its procedural rationality in the next.

The unconditional co-operator protector introduces the practice of *sanctioning* another player. UCP refuses to co-operate with RC not because RC refuses to co-operate with it, but because of RC's treatment of UC. UCP sanctions this would-be co-operator for the sake of a third party, namely UC.[18] In the Prisoner's Dilemma, sanctioning a potential co-operator cuts both ways; I cannot sanction you without also hurting myself. Sanctioning is costly.[19] As a result, UCP does poorly in and cannot invade any population that contains RC. Players that do not sanction RC, such as CC, will always do better than UCP. Since sanctioning cuts both ways, one might think that this will lead to a standoff between UCP and RC, with neither being able to invade the other. However, protecting UC is a liability for UCP (just as it was for CC earlier). The presence of UC allows RC eventually to invade the population that UCP supports. Hence we must conclude that RC is more rational than UCP.

This conclusion may seem premature. Note that the invasion of RC will not happen immediately. Given our standard PD payoff values (see Figure 5.8), of $S = 0$, $P = 1$, $R = 2$, and $T = 3$, the first two UCP players can protect two UC players. In general, each protected UC costs $R - P$; each UCP has a threat potential of $T - R$. Therefore RC can invade only if UC drift in in greater numbers than UCP. It may seem that I am relying (again) on an arbitrary assumption about drift to insinuate UC into a population for RC's benefit. But this isn't the case. I allow that there are populations, rich in UCP (or even CC), in which UCP sanctions are sufficient to block the entrance of RC. But there are some other populations in which there are enough UC to allow RC to invade. Recall that my criteria of rational superiority only requires that the better player be able to invade *some* of the populations extending the worse, not *every* extension. Notice as well that there is *no* extension of RC that UCP can invade. These considerations secure the conclusion that RC is substantively more rational than UCP.

Why can't UCP block the entry of RC by *limiting* the number of UC players in the population? This attractive option fails for reasons discussed in §6.2.3. The only way, in our simple models, of limiting the number of UC is by making their entry to the population irrational. The only way to do this is by defecting against them. Therefore, the UCP player, committed to co-operating with unconditional co-operators, cannot limit their entry to the population. However, it may be possible to design a more *limited* protecting player, which only undertakes to protect as many UC players as it rationally can. I conclude that the simple UCP strategy, which attempts indiscriminately to protect unconditional co-operators, is substantively irrational in transparent worlds.[20] I will turn to the procedural aspects of the UCP strategy in the next subsection.

6.3.3 Procedural rationality

I begin by sketching an unconditional co-operator protector (for the procedurally simpler Extended Prisoner's Dilemma). UCP1 surveys the roster of players and searches out somebody who fits the description of an unconditional co-operator. It then checks whether the other player will co-operate with this UC in both roles (I and II) and makes this willingness to co-operate with UC (the **uccoop** predicate) a necessary condition for his own co-operation. Finally, I add responsive tests taken from CC, and we have a working basic UCP1 player:[21]

permit(ucp1,Anyone,Anything).

uc(ucp1,UC) :- player(UC),
  permit(UC,All,Execute),
  not(pubmove1(UC,Anyone1,d)),
  not(pubmove2(UC,Anyone2,Anymove,d)).

uccoop(ucp1,Other) :-
  uc(ucp1,UC),!,   %if there is a UC
  pubmove1(Other,UC,c),   %Other must co-op with UC
  pubmove2(Other,UC,c,c).   %both ways

uccoop(ucp1,Other).   %in case there are no UC
                                 %trivially true

m1(ucp,Other,c):- pubmove2(Other,ucp1,c,c),uccoop(ucp1, Other).
m1(ucp,Other,d).
m2(ucp1,Other,c,c) :- uccoop(ucp1,Other).
m2(ucp1,Other,X,d).

This basic UCP1 player meets the specifications that it co-operate only with those that co-operate with unconditional co-operators.

There appears to be no procedural barrier to protecting third parties. UCP1 can locate unconditional co-operators that are the object of its concern. But we should look a little deeper into this question. UCP1 requires information of a new type, which raises three questions. First, it needs to ask of each player whether it will co-operate with each other player. There is new potential for looping here; UCP1 may be disabled in a population where any pairs of players are indeterminate.[22] Second, UCP1 needs to ask players whether they will co-operate with third parties. They may not be motivated to answer such indirect questions. But so far we have given players no means to distinguish question (i) from question (ii):

(i) A asks B if B will co-operate with A himself.
(ii) A asks B if B will co-operate with some other player, C.

If we allow players to ask the second, more complex question, we should provide players with the means to filter out such questions, if they wish. Third, assuming that answers to these indirect questions are also veridical further strengthens our premises and weakens our argument.

These are not objections to the UCP strategy. Rather they indicate the ways in which the strategy's more global concern with third parties stretches my tournament approach to testing. This is not surprising. UPC was not a strategy that I had not foreseen when I began this enterprise. Nor do I have a good working version of the more discriminating UCP player that limits the number of UC players protected. Making it possible to test out such players is part of the research strategy of Artificial Morality. Tentatively, I conclude that the UCP strategy points to a number of procedural problems that require further work.

CONCLUSION

I set out in this chapter to defend reciprocal co-operation from the moral criticism that it exploits unconditional co-operators. I have indicated the moral strengths of the RC strategy and argued that it is not obviously defective compared to Gauthier's principle of constrained maximization. Therefore it is a mistake to see the compliance dilemma in terms of rational (but immoral) RC versus moral (but irrational) CC. Better to see the problem as a contest between rational RC and a player that actively protects unconditional co-operators. I introduced a new player of this type, the unconditional co-operator protector, UCP. UCP is morally more attractive than CC (and, *a fortiori*, RC) but, I have argued, substantively irrational, at least in its simplest and most general form.

The issue between RC and UCP is not closed, however. It may be possible to design a more discriminating version of UCP that attempts only to protect a limited number of unconditional co-operators. Also, as we shall see in the next chapter, RC's advantage over CC and UCP may be limited to the transparent situation that I have assumed so far. There are also additional moral and substantive problems with UCP's strategy of threatening RC with sanctions. The morality of threatening would-be co-operators for the sake of third parties needs to be discussed. Also, notice that CC escapes paying the costs of UCP's vigilance; CC becomes a free rider on UCP's higher standard of morality. I shall return to these crucial issues in the simpler context of the game of Chicken in Part III.

Part III

FLEXIBILITY, INFORMATION, AND ACQUIESCENCE

The results of Part II are tentative, flowing as they do from highly simplified models of the relation of rationality to morality. In retrospect, the model used so far is is quite favourable to our solution, in at least three respects. First, my agents assure others by means of rigid commitment, yet my models are driven by the fortuituous appearance of well-adapted agents on the scene. Second, responsive agents, and RC in particular, benefit from my assumption of costless information. Third, the game of Prisoner's Dilemma is not the most difficult for agents who practice constraint by means of public principles. In contrast, the game of Chicken may be a more difficult challenge for the claim that it is rational to be moral. Each of these problems broaches important issues in the application of game theory to moral theory. I will not be able to take up them up any great detail. I will instead attempt to sketch how each of them can be incorporated into Artificial Morality.

My goal in Part III is to show that my method is robust enough to accommodate these important issues by internalizing some assumptions that the initial model leaves out. Ideally, I would continue to develop the theory incrementally, adding layers of detail as we proceed. I am unable to do so at this time. Instead, I will take up the three problems mentioned above separately. Chapter 7 introduces flexible agents for the basic PD game. Chapter 8 moves towards making information costly, but does so for rigid agents, not the learners of Chapter 7. Finally, Chapters 9 and 10 discuss the game of Chicken, but again, for non-learners under conditions of free information.

7

FLEXIBLE PLAYERS

THE CONSTITUTIONAL DILEMMA

Part II showed that conditional and reciprocal co-operators meet the primary criterion of procedural rationality: they can be coherently implemented. None the less, two large doubts remain about these players because they are extremely rigid. In order to assure each other of their trustworthiness, they are locked into exceptionless rules. Elster (1986b, p. 120) sees their problem as:

> a perennial dilemma of individual behaviour. How is it possible to ensure at the same time that one is bound by rules that protect one from irrational or unethical behaviour – and that these rules do not turn into prisons from which it is not possible to break out even when it would be rational to do so?

This dilemma is familiar from debates over constitutional limits to state action. Citizens seek the assurance of limits over the sovereign power but these limits may prevent the state from adapting to changing conditions. This constitutional dilemma affects our players as well. Rigidly committed players can assure some others but the range of their co-operation is limited by a basic co-ordination problem. For example, selfsame co-operators differing only in the syntax of their principles will fail to co-operate. This suggests that in order to be substantively rational, agents must be more flexible. At a minimum, they should be able to co-operate with a range of agents. Most likely, they will need to be able to *adapt* their constraints to the needs of their social environment. Now we face the other horn of the dilemma. I can only change my principles if my constraints do not fully bind me. If I am free to change I am also free to exploit your

129

constraint. Freedom to adapt seems incompatible with the commitments that my players use to assure each other. Therefore in this chapter I need to show how impartial constraint is compatible with flexible adaptation.

There is a second problem. My substantive test assumes a supply of new, well-adapted agents. But rigid agents cannot learn, so they cannot fulfil this needed function. Therefore these assumptions are not only strong but also at odds with each other.

This chapter will extend the argument by developing more flexible players. First, I will show how SC players can broaden their matching principles to include diverse sets of principles. Second, I sketch some players who can learn new principles, indicate how they assure each other and avoid some nasty predatory possibilities.

7.1 FROM SC TO CC AND RC

The most extreme example of rigidity is the selfsame co-operator (SC) I introduced to solve the coherence problem in the simultaneous Prisoner's Dilemma. As I noted in §4.4.2, SC is not substantively rational; it falls short of either conditional or reciprocal co-operation. While both CC and RC include the property of co-operating with exactly similar players, both are more tolerant. RC will co-operate with CC and CC will co-operate with RC and UC as well. It might seem that the device of matching quoted principles is too limited to deal with the demand for greater tolerance. After all, RC does *not* match CC, so it is not clear whether or how I can extend my matching solution to implement CC and RC for the simultaneous Prisoner's Dilemma. I implemented CC and RC in the extended game; it may seem that they are *limited* to that situation. Of course, unless I can extend my account of CC and RC to include simultaneous games, Artificial Morality would suffer a serious gap between substantive (recommending RC) and procedural rationality (only SC works in simultaneous games).

7.1.1 Extending SC

I will propose a simple tentative solution to the need to implement CC and RC for the simultaneous Prisoner's Dilemma. The problem is that CC and RC do not match, but recall that my second, external implementation of SC did not do any explicit matching. I defined **sc(Alter,Ego,c)** as a property true of those who were committed to the SC principle. Implicitly this requires that SC players so implemented match but only because there is only one way to satisfy **sc**, namely by commitment to co-operate on the basis of the principle SC itself. There is no reason that we cannot extend the list of tolerated principles, leading to this implementation of CC and RC:

```
% define three new players for simultaneous PD
permit(cc3,Anyone,read)
move(cc3,pd,Other,c) :- cc(Other,cc3).
move(cc3,Other,d).

permit(rc3,Anyone,read).
move(rc3,pd,Other,c) :- rc(Other,rc3).
move(rc3,Other,d).
permit(uc3,Anyone,read).
move(uc3,pd,Other,c).
```

```
  cc(Ego,Alter) :-
    firstproc(Ego,Alter,c,Proc),    % Other is
      Proc = cc(Alter,Ego);         % CC OR
      Proc = rc(Alter,Ego);         % RC OR
      Proc = true.                  % UC
  rc(Ego,Alter) :-
    firstproc(Ego,Alter,c,Proc),    % Other is
      Proc = cc(Alter,Ego);         % CC OR
      Proc = rc(Alter,Ego).         % RC
```

RC can be true in two alternative ways: in case the other is committed to CC or in case she is committed to RC itself. (Note that ';' is the disjunctive operator in Prolog.) CC is more tolerant; it allows three different commitments: to CC, to RC or to UC. The CC definition makes use of a new predicate; **true** is true when a clause has no antecedent (body) and is therefore unconditionally true. This is the case with UC3's **move** predicate.

The following queries show that it is possible to implement CC and RC in this way for the simultaneous Prisoner's Dilemma.

```
player(uc3).   %a roster of three players
player(cc1). player(rc1).
  ?- player(P1),player(P2),move(P1,P2,M1), move(P2,P1,M2).
⇒ P1 = uc3, P2 = uc3, M1 = c, M2 = c;
⇒ P1 = uc3, P2 = cc3, M1 = c, M2 = c;
⇒ P1 = uc3, P2 = rc3, M1 = c, M2 = d;
```

⇒ **P1** = cc3, **P2** = uc3, **M1** = c, **M2** = c;
⇒ **P1** = cc3, **P2** = cc3, **M1** = c, **M2** = c;
⇒ **P1** = cc3, **P2** = rc3, **M1** = c, **M2** = c;

⇒ **P1** = rc3, **P2** = uc3, **M1** = d, **M2** = c;
⇒ **P1** = rc3, **P2** = cc3, **M1** = c, **M2** = c;
⇒ **P1** = rc3, **P2** = rc3, **M1** = c, **M2** = c;

This disjunctive implementaton of CC and RC for the simultaneous PD solves one problem but introduces two others. First, it relies on what I have called *external principles*, which are problematic, since they do not reside in any player. One role for a social contract may be to decide on and situate such principles. Another possibility has some players specializing in implementing such principles.[1] The second problem is that disjunctive principles remain rigid, leading to a co-ordination problem.

7.1.2 A co-ordination problem

My solution to the coherence problem through matching one's own and other's principles gives rise to a co-ordination problem. How do players co-ordinate their principles? We cannot assume without begging the question that players will naturally have the same principles; this would assume some generative process was doing most of the work. Furthermore, even if players converge on *equivalent* (but not identical) principles, in the simultaneous Prisoner's Dilemma they cannot simply *test* others' principles for equivalence. As we saw in Chapter 4, invoking another player's decision procedure may bring on incoherence. I have introduced principles that work by assuring others that the player lacks the freedom to defect against them. Now I must pay the price: a lack of adaptability to solve a co-ordination problem.[2]

For example, here is a decision procedure equivalent to SC1 that will not co-operate with her:

permit(sc4,Everyone,read).
move(sc4,Other,c) :-
  firstproc(Other,sc4,OthersProc),
  firstproc(sc4,Other,MyProc),
  sameproc(sc4,Other,MyProc,OthersProc).

The reader will need to look hard to see the difference between SC1 and SC4; they differ only in the *order* of their **firstproc** terms. Since SC players each check the other for an exact *syntactic* match, each fails the other's test. Nor will simply switching to externally defined principles and increasing tolerance solve this problem. The co-ordination problem is not due to SC's lack of tolerance. It is due to the use of matching to solve the assurance and prediction problems. Matching players solve this pair of procedural problems only to run into a difficult coordination problem.

7.2 PLAYERS THAT CHANGE

In the co-ordination problem two players, each with responsive co-operative principles, may fail to co-operate only because their principles fail to match. So long as matching remains our primitive assurance device, in such situations at least one party must change her principle. She must adapt, presumably through learning, to the other's principle. Players capable of learning can adapt themselves to achieve more co-extensive operation.[3] In this section I will examine the possiblities of players that change.

7.2.1 Assurance lost

Adapation raises a serious problem. Players can adapt (through learning) only if they can change their principles but the ability to change makes them untrustworthy. Before we continue to explore the promise of learning, I need to answer this fundamental objection to the whole approach.

Flipflop

While the problem of co-ordination arises most clearly in simultaneous games, the loss of assurance can be more readily studied in simpler sequential games. Indeed, once we introduce players capable of changing themselves, we overturn our previous results for the simple sequential game. Here is a player, Flipflop1, that manages to sucker CC and RC into one-sided co-operation. Flipflop1's strategy is to change her mind every time she is asked to make a second move. This makes her an *epistemological* demon: probing her changes her state and testing or probing again changes it back. This means that CC1 or RC1, who test the other player, **Other**, for **m2(Other,cc1,c,c)** or **m2(Other,rc1,d,d)**, find that Flipflop1 does what they are looking for when they look but not when they later interact. Their tests change her into something that does the opposite. I implement Flipflop1's **move2** as a simple two state flipflop. Her state of mind changes from **jekyll** to **hyde** and back:

permit(flipflop1,Everyone,execute).	**%permit public execution**
state(flipflop1,jekyll).	**%initial state of mind**
m2(flipflop1,Other,c,c):-	**%morally constrained Jekyll**
state(flipflop1,jekyll),	**%if**
flip(flipflop1,jekyll,hyde).	**%then**
m2(flipflop1,Other,c,d):-	**%amoral unconstrained Hyde**
state(flipflop1,hyde),	**% if**
flip(flipflop1,hyde,jekyll).	**%then**
m2(flipflop1,Other,d,d).	**%otherwise do not change**
flip(flipflop1,Old,New):-	**% flipper utility**
retract(state(flipflop1,Old)),	
asserta(state(flipflop1,New)).	

The idea behind Flipflop1 is quite simple although the code gets complicated for reasons I will sketch briefly. Her initial state of mind is fixed by the **state** predicate having the value **jekyll**. (Jekyll is a state of Flipflop1, not a player.) The first **m2** predicate says: if in Jekyll state of mind, change that to a Hyde state of mind and co-operate. The built-in **retract** and **asserta** predicates retract and add premises (to the front of the data-base) respectively.[4] The second **m2** predicate does the reverse; it flops what the first predicate flips. This is how Flipflop1 proposes to trick responsive players; she responds quite thoroughly and perversely to their *tests*.[5]

Doublecheck

Flipflop1's procedural trick is very simple. Indeed, a player inclined to co-operation could probably trick her into co-operation by manipulating her change of state. In any case, if one merely aims to avoid being suckered by a flipflop, a simple temporal consistency check will serve. Here is a modification of RC, named Doublecheck, that will ferret out flipflops:

permit(doublecheck,Everyone,execute).
m1(doublecheck,Other,c) :-

```
pubmove2(Other,doublecheck,c,c),
pubmove2(Other,doublecheck,c,c),        % second test added
pubmove2(Other,doublecheck,d,d).        % to reject flipflop

m1(doublecheck,Other,d).
```

So where has all this deviousness taken us? It could lead us to another arms race, with sneaky flipflops taking on more memory and others trying longer test sequences (perhaps of random length – an epistemic mixed strategy, so to speak).[6] I conjecture that moral agents would do best to avoid this arms race and take the simplest and most transparent means to refuse to co-operate with trickier players. As in the case of Tit for Tat, the central device upon which responsive co-operation is based is clear assurance to fellow co-operators. Tricky attempts to out-manipulate players like Flipflop1 may make one appear suspicious to others.

Indeed, a more drastic measure may appear to be useful. One could refuse to co-operate with any player who was capable of change. The only way to change is by **assert**ing new facts; a search of the other player's public procedure should reveal if there is any changing going on.[7] However this is a very drastic counter-measure. I began this chapter by recognizing the need for would-be wide-scale co-operators to adapt to different conditions. A ban on learning would prevent this.

A partial ban might be effective. One could refuse to co-operate with any player who changed during **move2** but permit learning during **move1**. This should strike a compromise between flexibility and rigidity. I will not investigate the mechanics of this partial ban, as the coding becomes quite complex. In what follows I will assume that adaptive learners confine their changing to the first position and rely on double-checking to protect them against those who would learn in the second position.

We have been at this for a long time and have not yet gotten to players that learn. However, the excursion through tricky flipflops has been worth it. We have seen that even when we allow a degree of deception, the device of responsive co-operation can be effective. This enables me to weaken my premises; deception is no longer impossible in our players' toy world.[8] But I should emphasize the main conclusion of this section: flexible players do make assurance more difficult but not impossible. Flexibility makes new predatory tricks possible and requires co-operative players to be more cautious. None the less flexible players do not undermine the possibility of co-operation mediated by constraining principles. Therefore we can proceed to see how players might learn new priniciples to address the co-ordination problem.

7.2.2 Learning principles

Flipflop1 was flexible; she changed but she did not learn. Learning is at least *directed* cognitive change. In this section I will show how players could use learning to change their decision principles in order to solve the co-ordination problem.

A simple kind of learning is learning by selective imitation.[9] Imitation is a generator of things that might be learned (they are learned from another player in interaction) but it fails to specify the test, or terminator, of the process. One possibility is retaining the first thing learned; this is *imprinting*. Another possibility is retaining only the last thing encountered. Lacking a common name (I call *people* like this airheads), I will use a term from computer science: a LIFO is a Last In First Out structure. Neither of these procedures is worth implementing in environments subject to the predatory pressures of the compliance problem. Imprinters depend on friendly initial contacts; in nature imprinting works because it relies on kin selection and parental investment. LIFOs will be enslaved by their first (and last) teacher who figures out how to overwrite and thereby eliminate their learning apparatus.

7.2.3 Copycoop

More interesting will be a learner who has a way of selecting what might be worth learning. I will start with Copycoop, who works on the conjecture that it is worth copying the principles of those who co-operate with themselves. While Copycoop is simple as learners go, she embodies a piece of wisdom confirmed by AI research. Winston (1984, p. 396) puts the point grandly: '*Martin's Law*. You can't learn anything unless you almost know it already.'[10] One needs to know something relevant to a task to learn more about it. In particular, one needs the relevant *structures*. One can't start out with a *tabula rasa* and hope to pick up these structures; one needs to know what to look for. For example, Copycoop doesn't just try out alternatives *C* and *D* to find out which does better. Even in the epistemologically simpler Iterated Prisoner's Dilemma this atomic approach doesn't lead to much advantageous learning. In the Iterated Prisoner's Dilemma one needs to know that sequences like *D*-after-*C*, embodying a time delay, are the crucial molecules of strategy. Similarly, for the non-iterated PD, Copycoop needs to know that she is out to learn *principles*. This bias has two parts, motivational and epistemological. She needs the ability to be constrained by principles and needs to know where to look to find other player's principles. And, as we have already noted, things are complicated by the interaction of learning and principled constraint, so Copycoop needs to take a stand on this issue as well. I will build into Copycoop two further conjectures about learning in the Extended PD. First, learn about what to do in **move2**, since the other player's **move2** may depend on yours. Second, learn from the vantage point of **move1**, which should be left untouched by learning. I remind you that all of this is conjectural. Copycoop1 is a prototype; she is not my final model of a well-adapted player.

Here is Copycoop1:

```
permit(copycoop1,Everyone,All).
m1(copycoop1,Other,c) :-
    pubmove2(Other,Other,c,c),          % is other self-coop?
    copy(copycoop1,FreeVar,Other,Principle),
    addtome(Principle),
    pubmove2(Other,copycoop1,c,c).       %will other coop?
m1(copycoop1,Other,d).                   %default

m2(copycoop1,Other,X,d).                 %default
```

The idea behind Copycoop is simple: copy from those who know the secret(s) of co-operation. Copycoop1 goes about this as follows. If she discovers that the other player co-operates when paired with himself, then Copycoop1 copies his principle. Of course, it won't do to copy other player's principles *exactly*. (For example, it wouldn't improve *my* actions were I to adopt the principle: 'George Washington tells no lies.') A player needs to *appropriate* the other player's principles; she needs to make some substitutions, swapping her name for the owner's. The basic idea is related to the matching test that I introduced in Chapter 5 but the process gets a bit complicated in the predicate **copy**; I explain the details in Appendix B, §B.4.

7.2.4 Abstract rules and viruses

Learning is a risky business even in the friendliest of situations; one opens oneself to be directed by another's principles. Textbook discussions of learning (like many accounts of language) make things easier by treating learning as a *co-operative* venture.[11] A friendly teacher presents well-chosen examples in an optimal order. The learner can trust the teacher and take the lessons to be useful information on faith. However, as we all know, in a more competitive world, teachers and learners may have conflicting interests. For this reason, learning does not play a large part in programs designed for games like chess; the potential for strategic misguidance is too strong at the extreme of pure conflict. The games Artificial Morality uses fall between pure co-operation and pure conflict, so it is an open question whether learning is worth the risk. We have already seen that one doesn't want to learn from just anyone; one needs to be selective.

Is this enough caution? While copying other players' principles is risky, copying their decision procedures is even more risky. This is because a decision procedure is a piece of software. As with software generally, it is very difficult to know what you are getting and the code may have side-effects when run. Notice why this is so. Copying, like matching, works by treating decision procedures as inert lists of symbols. (See Appendix B, §B.4.) This makes it safe to copy any piece of code because it is safely encoded. But this very feature makes it impossible to determine what that code will do when unpacked and run in an environment. One simply cannot tell what a decision procedure will do in your context – for an artificial player: what it will do to your self.

On the other hand, since the world of Artificial Morality is not marked by complete conflict, there may be some players that you can trust and therefore learn from. For this reason extreme cynicism is unlikely to be the best policy. Copycoop1 decides to trust those players who show the minimal moral trait of co-operating with themselves. Note that this trait is substantively irrelevent in a tournament that does not test players paired with themselves; a player might co-operate with itself and with no others. However copying self-co-operative principles is only Copycoop1's initial heuristic. It checks for real co-operation before adopting a principle.

Might there be an easier way? Why not let moral players wear their morality 'on their sleeves' as it were, by making moral principles recognizable by their *form*? There is a long tradition in moral theory that moral principles can be picked out by their logical form. Is there any structural way that our players modelled in Prolog can structurally indicate their co-operativeness? I think there is and it is connected to the use of variables. I suggest that players should have universal principles in this weaker sense: they should set out the conditions on co-operation with variables, not constants. The alternative of using constants may not seem open, until one considers how learning players work. Copycoop1 could copy CC1 and get either **m2(copycoop1,cc1,c,c)** or **m2(copycoop1, Anyone,c,c)**. Which is better? The answer is not self-evident. The first is safer because it commits Copycat to less: co-operation with CC1 and no one else. Some might deny that the first is a moral principle because of its lack of universal form, but it is not clear that a list of rules like this, one for each of the players with whom one will co-operate, won't lead to the same degree of impartial advantage, and this is what should matter for morality, not the form of one's principles.

However, the form can make a big difference to learning. How can another Copycoop1, call him Copycoop2, learn from the first, particular form of Copycoop1? He will not find that Copycoop1 co-operates with herself; she only co-operates with CC1, so she will fail Copycoop2's test. Copycoop2 will not learn to co-operate with Copycoop1. Therefore Copycoop2 should do better by learning universal rules, so that he may co-operate with Copycoop3, Copycoop4 and so on. Abstract universal moral rules are more effective ways to spread co-operation because they advantage the teacher as well as the learner. Therefore, Artificial Morality comes to agree with the traditional recommendation of universality but for a substantial and pragmatic, rather than formal, reason.

What about the risk of learning something harmful? Here we encounter a real surprise. Making the rules one learns universal serves to *innoculate* the learner against some information viruses.[12] Consider the simple case, where Serveme1 tries to infect Copycoop with the principle that she serve Serveme1. Here is the distinctive part of Serveme1's procedure:

permit(serveme1,Everyone,All).
m2(serveme1,Other,c,M) :-
  (Other = serveme1, M = c);M = d.

Serveme1 co-operates with himself, so he passes Copycoop1's test. But his trick is that he would co-operate *only* with himself (so he never really co-operates with anyone, not even his clone, Serveme2); with anyone else he defects. What happens when Copycoop1 copies this rule? Recall that she replaces all instances of the original owner's name with her own, so she ends up with this new first principle for **move2**:

```
m2(copycoop1,Other,c,M) :-
  (Other = copycoop1, M = c);M = d.
```

This is pretty useless but it is not harmful, since it doesn't tell Copycoop1 to serve herself up to Serveme1 as a sucker but only (hypothetically) to serve herself. Copycoop1 becomes a clone of the would-be master instead of a slave; she ends up with a dead virus. It is a poor rule (equivalent to unconditional defection) but it does not open her to exploitation. The trick of swapping names is very powerful. It makes it difficult to get a Copycoop to do anything for you that you would not be willing to do for another. Copycoop avoids the worst of what Serveme1 threatened and she remains able to go on to learn something better. But Serveme1 is not the most dangerous form of virus.[13] Worst is one that attacks one's ability to learn.

7.2.5 Context and complexity

Copycoop1 can be further improved by improving her test in two ways. First, there is no need to look only for co-operation. Why not learn to exploit others if possible? Second, Copycoop1 makes a leap of faith. If she finds that you would co-operate with player A, she copies your principle, assuming that you will co-operate with her when she substitutes her name for A. But this might not be so. You might co-operate with A only on some further condition, so further testing should be done in context.

I call a player with these two changes an indirect maximizer (IM). The rudimentary indirect maximizer that I will now construct, IM1, first copies a principle and then checks if he does better with this principle than without it. In effect, he plays a small hypothetical tournament, by testing the result of moving first and second with temporarily copied procedures. By copying the principle before checking it, he puts it in the context of his own decision apparatus, and gives it a more thorough test. By searching for the amorally best principle, he may learn principles like RC and Flipflop1, which do better than joint co-operation against some players. Finally, by always testing relative to the benchmark of his original outcome, he is conservative. IM will not change principles unless he finds a better one. Here is a version of the indirect maximizer, IM1:

```
permit(im1,Everyone,Anything).
m1(im1,O,c) :- (result(im1,O,Initial),
  copy(im1,Variable,O,P),
```

```
addtome(P),                    %temporary copy
result(im1,O,c,Test),
retract(P),
ibetter(Test,Initial),
clear(im1),                    %get rid of old m2
addtome(P)).                   %real copy
m1(im1,O,d).                   %default

m2(im1,O,d,d).                 %default
```

I will not dwell on many details of IM1; I must not let the ratio of Prolog to philosophy get too high. Three details are important. First, notice that IM1 adds the procedure to be tested, tests it and retracts it. Only if the **ibetter** test succeeds does he add it again. (The **addtome** predicate is **asserta** filtered for ownership to prevent unauthorized mind writing.) Second, the indirect *maximizer* is distinguished by his sense of better. He ignores the results to the other player and maximizes his own results. (The predicate **ibetter** compares only the first element in the lists passed to it.) Third, IM1 is careful to clear out superceded procedures. This is not because he is concerned about using up too much memory. (In my models so far, memory is free so he has no reason to care about it.) The reason he tidies up is to prevent old procedures from countermanding new ones. For example, if he were to learn to RC1 while retaining the nicer CC1, he would co-operate with UC.

Here is a contrast of im1 and copycoop1:

```
?- listing(m2).
   m2(uc1,Other,X,C).
   m2(rc1,Other,c,c):-
     pubmove2(Other,rc1,d,d).
   m2(rc1,Other,c,d).
   m2(rc1,Other,d,d).
   m2(copycoop1,Other,X,d).
   m2(im1,Other,X,d).
?- m1(copycoop1,rc1,M).
   ⇒ M = c.
?- m1(copycoop1,uc1,M).
   ⇒ M = c.
?- listing(m2).
   m2(copycoop1,Other,X,c)      % + learned from uc
   m2(copycoop1,X,c,c) :-       % + learned
     pubmove2(X,copycoop1,d,d). % + from rc
```

```
m2(uc1,Other,X,C).
m2(rc1,Other,c,c):-
   pubmove2(Other,rc1,d,d).
m2(rc1,Other,c,d).
m2(rc1,Other,d,d).
m2(copycoop1,Other,X,d).
m2(im1,Other,X,d).

?- m1(im1,rc1,M).
 ⇒ M = c.
?- m1(im1,uc1,M).
 ⇒ M = d.
?- listing(m2).
   m2(im1,X,c,c) :-                   % + learned
      pubmove2(X,im1,d,d).            % + from rc
   m2(uc1,Other,X,C).
   m2(rc1,Other,c,c):-
      pubmove2(Other,rc1,d,d).
   m2(rc1,Other,c,d).
   m2(rc1,Other,d,d).
   m2(im1,Other,X,d).
```

Learning does not show up directly in **move1** behaviour so I list only **m2** procedures. I have marked procedures added by learning. As you can see, Copycoop1 learns too well. After learning to RC she goes on to learn unconditional co-operation. IM1 is more sophisticated; she does not learn the less advantageous principle and remains a reciprocal co-operator. I stress that there is room to improve this primitive indirect maximizer. For example, IM1 adopts any principle that is better than what he starts with; he doesn't check for the best principle globally. None the less, the connection between indirect maximization and reciprocal co-operation is interesting. I shall return to it in Chapter 10.

I have not presented a morally competent learner but have indicated the direction that will likely lead to such a player. She should copy those principles that seem the best, make them universal, test them in context, and take pains to remain open to further learning. I am reluctant to fully develop a player to meet these specifications for fear of begging a question. One of the problems that led us to adaptive players was the co-ordination problem, where would-be co-operative players find themselves with different principles. Were I to present too perfect a learner, she might become the salient model for such players submitted to some tournament test of my theory. This might cause us to miss interesting second-level co-ordination problems that would result if each designer of a player were doing more of her own development work. (This actually happened in a seminar I taught; we almost overlooked the co-ordination problem entirely.)

7.3 BEYOND INDIRECT MAXIMIZATION

I have partially answered the question whether players, free to adapt by learning, are capable of constraint. They are. Indirect maximizers, concerned only with their own payoffs, can learn moral principles. However I do not want to give the impression that all learners must begin as unconstrained maximizers. Were this so, it would be unlikely that some principles could be learned. For example, IM1 won't learn CC (if he already knows RC) unless under the pressure of UCP, which is also inaccessible to IM1.

The required changes are easy to make in IM1. We need only change his **ibetter** predicate to reflect a moralized standard.

cbetter([S1|O1],[S2|O2]):- S1 > S2, O1 > = O2;
$$S1 = S2, O1 > O2.$$

The 'c' in **cbetter** stands for co-operatively; this criterion takes both players' interests into account. Making this change to IM1 gives us an indirect co-operator, IC1. An IC1 player will only learn what is (weakly) better for *both* players.[14] She is capable of learning the CC principle.[15]

I conclude that players can adapt by learning new principles. Therefore artificial moral players should not be trapped by the problem of co-ordinating their principles. Adaptive players are able to learn new principles in order to tolerate (or perhaps exploit) others. These players may be indirect maximizers or they may use a morally constrained second-order criterion.

7.3.1 Another circle?

Adaptive players combine flexibility with constraint. They are open to objections from the point of view of procedural and substantive rationality. I take these up in turn now. The procedural objection seems the most pressing: adaptive players choose their own decision procedures. Does this lead them in a circle because they attempt to use the very procedures they are deciding upon? Gauthier worries that this may be so:

We have defended the rationality of constrained maximization as a disposition to choose by showing that it would be rationally chosen. Now this argument is not circular; constrained maximization is a disposition for strategic choice that would be parametrically chosen.

(Gauthier 1986a, p. 183)

Gauthier proposes to break the circle by a typed, or partitioned, solution: use parametric reasoning to choose procedures for strategic reasoning. This will break the circle; one's strategic principles are not used upon themselves. But it is a drastic remedy. Parametric reasoning is inadequate for the essentially strategic problem of choosing a disposition in a situation where others may also choose their dispositions.

None the less, a solution is needed, since circular reasoning is tempting in these contexts. For example, consider Nozick's proposal for the Prisoner's Dilemma:

we might consider the principle PD: In a generalized prisoners' dilemma situation . . . one ought to perform the dominated cooperative action. PD is an ethical principle applying to choices in particular structured situations, where its mandate differs from that of the principles of rational self-interest [RSI], which call for performing the dominant noncooperative action . . . the choice all face between following morality with PD or following RSI is itself structured as a generalized prisoners' dilemma situation . . . the principle of morality PD says that in *this* choice situation, as in other similarly structured ones, one ought to perform the dominated cooperative option, namely, following morality including PD. We have not derived PD from PD trivially via the propositional calculus; rather, PD has been derived from itself as an instance, via quantification theory (and further assumptions). PD subsumes itself.

(Nozick 1981, p. 543)

PD is self-subsuming, so it would give a reason for its own selection, but so is RSI, as Nozick notes. Therefore the fact that a principle dictates its own selection cannot be sufficient reason to choose it.

A constitutional analogy

My solution is *historical*. A player has a principle for strategic choice, P_1, which may select another principle, P_2. P_2 might apply to itself, but it would not get to choose itself until chosen by P_1. This also prevents a clash between the two principles. Perhaps the best way to explain this is a simple constitutional analogy. Consider a group operating under a unanimity rule P_1 which decides to change to majority rule P_2. Subsequently, the majority passes a measure that is not approved by all. Is the measure constitutional? Yes. P_2 determines constitutionality. Although it violates P_1, this is now irrelevant. This is a commonplace of constitutional change. Turning now to the circularity problem: can P_2 be used to bootstrap itself, say because a majority prefer majority rule? No, only if *all* prefer majority rule does it pass P_1.

7.3.2 Inflating procedural rationality

I treat procedures as theories subject to the ultimate test of substantive rationality. This includes the ultimate procedure that one uses to evaluate one's lower level procedure. Mine is a highly *pragmatic* account of rationality. In contrast, both Gauthier and Parfit put more weight on procedures they consider privileged. They disagree over the principle transmitting rationality from dispositions to choices. Gauthier assumes that rationality should be identified with the choice of principles (what he calls dispositions). He concludes that 'if her dispositions to choose are rational, then surely her choices are also rational' (Gauthier 1986a, p. 186). He is concerned to answer an objection of the sort that Parfit makes:

> An objector might grant that it may be rational to dispose oneself to constrained maximization, but deny that the choices that one is then disposed to make are rational. The objector claims that we have merely exhibited another instance of the rationality of not behaving rationally.
>
> (Gauthier 1986a, p. 184)

It is instructive to deploy my constitutional analogy by substituting 'constitutional' for 'rational' in these arguments. Try it. I think that this makes it clear that Gauthier and Parfit (as represented by Gauthier[16]) are arguing about two different things. What Gauthier says holds for rationality in a procedural sense. Like constitutionality, a player can transmit procedural rationality to new procedures that he (rationally) selects. Parfit's objection cannot touch this sort of transmission, any more than it is relevant to object to majoritarianism, after it is unanimously chosen, that it is not the unanimity rule. Of course it is not; that is presumably why the group unanimously selected it. Parfit's objection does put us on notice that no procedure gets to define substantive rationality. That is, what is procedurally rational need not be substantively rational; good constitutions do not guarantee good government. This is a criticism of Gauthier's identification of rationality and indirection. Gauthier cannot make indirect maximization the best policy by legislation. Only further testing will tell.

7.3.3 How flexible should one be?

Adaptive players occupy a middle position between maximally adaptive straightforward maximizers and rigid players with fixed principles. There is no *a priori* reason to prefer any one of these three positions; each is procedurally possible. Are there substantive arguments in favour of one or the other? For example, Hayek, who appeals to evolution against the 'conceit' that we can choose our rules, argues against the bias in favour of flexibility:

> In many if not most cases those who won . . . were those who stuck to 'blind habit' or learnt through religious teaching such things as that 'honesty is the best policy', thereby beating cleverer fellows who had 'reasoned' otherwise. As strategies for survival, counterparts of both rigidity and flexibility have played important roles in biological evolution; and morals that took the form of rigid rules may sometimes have been more effective than more flexible rules whose adherents attempted to steer their practice, and alter their course, according to particular facts and foreseeable consequences.
>
> (Hayek 1988, p. 139)

I partially agree. My case in favour of reciprocal co-operation over SM was an argument against extreme flexibility. It leaves open the question whether a parallel argument can be run against adaptive players in favour of rigidly moral players. I would like to see this argument in the form of a game in which adaptive players do worse than rigid players. The Prisoner's Dilemma is not such a game. As we have seen, adaptability is an asset in the PD because it enables players to solve co-ordination problems and enlarges the set of co-operators. Therefore if flexibility is costly a different game is required. Chapter 9 introduces a situation where adaptive players appear to do worse because they are susceptible to threats.

146

CONCLUSION

In this chapter I have moved away from rigidly constrained players by introducing first flexible players and then players who can learn. Introducing players who can learn other's principles led to three main conclusions. First, learning principles allows players to avoid the co-ordination problem that afflicts rigidly constrained players. Second, players that can learn principles can aim at more or less moralized goals. I argued that indirect maximizers would learn to RC while only players who aimed at a more moral goal, indirect co-operators, would learn to CC. Third, players who can learn new principles fill out my tournament test. A tournament with players who learn is more strategic than one without learning. The parametric feature of a tournament, the initial distribution of players' strategies, is modified in a strategic direction when these players can learn new – presumably advantageous – strategies.

8

INFORMATION AND ITS COSTS

I have defended the possibility of rational moral constraint under relatively favourable information conditions. My moral agents, like Gauthier's, employ the general strategy of publicizing their principles and responding to other players' public principles. This strategy is information-intensive. Therefore assuming that reliable information about strategies is freely available may beg questions central to Artificial Morality concerning the balance of advantage between more and less moral strategies.

In this chapter I weaken my information assumption. I begin by attending to the way straightforward maximizers use information about the other player. This alerts us to the possibility that some (flavours of) straightforward maximizers will sometimes co-operate with constrained players. Next I turn to the costs of responsive strategies. Both predicting others' behaviour and exposing one's own principles can be risky. I consider some ways that responsive strategies can fail. Attending to the impact of the costs of information on different agents upsets Gauthier's generalization of his results to the less than transparent case. More important, it allows unconditional co-operators to do surprisingly well, leading to stable populations of diverse agents, with strongly disturbing results for the relation between game and moral theory.

8.1 SM STRIKES BACK

We should reconsider the claim that only morally constrained agents can co-operate in the Prisoner's Dilemma. Game theorists will insist that in the presence of responsive players, more traditional un-constrained agents will sometimes co-operate. They are correct about this. So far I have simplified the discussion by conflating straightforward maximization (SM) with the strategy of un-conditional defection (UD) in the Prisoner's Dilemma. In the case of the one-shot PD this identification is uncontroversial. Not so in the Extended PD, where even a straightforward maximizer (playing role I) might be influenced by the prospect of player II responding to his choice. Why do I write 'might'? Because the received theory of rational choice is not unequivocal about the way SM players model other players. I will implement two flavours of straightforward maximizer that model the other player differently. Straightforward maximizers of one of these flavours sometimes co-operate in the XPD. Therefore we must not overestimate the distinctness of morality nor the importance of *mutual* constraint.[1]

8.1.1 Two simplifications

In Chapter 4, I began my discussion of procedural rationality with the Extended Prisoner's Dilemma because it admits of simpler agents. However, in one respect, the sequential extended game is more complicated. In the XPD straightforward maximizers will sometimes co-operate; they are not equivalent to unconditional defectors. This split is interesting in two respects. First, building a straightforward maximizer lets us distinguish two aspects of the received tradition: its motivational and epistemological assumptions. Second, the partially co-operative straightforward maximizer allows me to answer a criticism of my assumptions about communication and commitment and to specify the role of mutual constraint in responsive moral strategies.

The distinguishing feature of straightforward maximizers is moti-vational; SM never choose against their preferences. What do SM do in the XPD? This question cautions us not simply to identify SM with the dominant strategy of unconditional defection in the XPD. We should implement a general purpose SM decision function. To do this we need a Prolog representation of the PD payoff matrix:

```
%payoff(Game,Own_move,Others_move,Payoff_to_Self):
  payoff(pd,c,c,2).   payoff(pd,c,d,0).
  payoff(pd,d,c,3).   payoff(pd,d,d,1).
```

Let's begin with SM's **move2** function because it is easier to write and it is shared by both flavours that I will develop. Player I's move is available; the only question is whether SM1 playing role II does better to respond to the **OthersMove** with a *C* or a *D*. SM1 compares the payoffs and picks the bigger.

m2(sm1,Other,OthersMove,Move):
  payoff(pd,c,OthersMove,Payoff_from_c),
  payoff(pd,d,OthersMove,Payoff_from_d),!, %force unique
  (Payoff_from_c > Payoff_from_d,Move = c;Move = d).

The last line amounts to an 'if/then' clause: if the payoff from *C* is bigger, then **Move** is set to **c**; otherwise the alternative (recall that ';' is Prolog's 'or') sets **Move** to **d**. Of course, since *D* is dominant, the payoff from *C* will never be greater, so the antecedent will never be satisfied and *D* will always be chosen. This is to say that in role II SM remains equivalent to UD.

Empirical and A Priori *SM*

The equivalence of SM and UD breaks down when we implement **move1**, which is more complex than **move2** for the SM agent. The defining motivational requirement on SM is clear enough: pick the move that will maximize one's own preferences. However this does not settle the question since player I needs to form an expectation of the other player (player II)'s choice. On what should a straightforward maximizer base this expectation? Here we face a choice point; the answer is not determined by the motivational definition of the SM agent as never self-denying. The answer may seem obvious: a straightforward maximizer should find out what the other player will in fact do, if possible. This is, after all, what CC and RC attempt to do and sometimes succeed. The problem is the weight of received tradition. SM is found in a theory that tends to *a prioristic* epistemology, assuming whenever possible that the other agent is similar to oneself. There is a choice here but fortunately it is not one that I have to make. I am not defending SM and it turns out to be easy and instructive to implement both epistemic flavors of the received theory's champion.

I will begin with the *a priori* straightforward maximizer, ASM1. ASM1 does not make a prediction of the other player's actual behaviour. Instead, it makes a simplifying symmetry assumption and models the other player on itself.

```
%no permissions: opaque
m1(asm1,Other,Move) :-
  m2(asm1,asm1,c,Response_to_C),
    payoff(pd,c,Response_to_C,Payoff_from_c),
  m2(asm1,asm1,d,Response_to_d),
    payoff(pd,d,Response_to_d,Payoff_from_d),!,
  (Payoff_from_c > Payoff_from_d,Move = c;Move = d).
```

ESM1 is just the same except that it first tries out the conjecture that if player II is a transparent agent, it is better to find out what II will do:

```
permit(esm1,Anyone,Execute).   % transparent
m1(esm1,Other,Move) :-   % predict II's response
  pubmove2(Other,esm1,c,Response_to_C),
    payoff(c,Response_to_C,Payoff_from_c),
  pubmove2(Other,esm1,d,Response_to_d),
    payoff(d,Response_to_d,Payoff_from_d),!,
  (Payoff_from_c > Payoff_from_d,Move = c;Move = d).
m1(esm1,Other,Move) :- % use self as model of II
  m2(esm1,esm1,c,Response_to_C),
    payoff(pd,c,Response_to_C,Payoff_from_c),
  m2(esm1,esm1,d,Response_to_d),
    payoff(pd,d,Response_to_d,Payoff_from_d),!,
  (Payoff_from_c > Payoff_from_d,Move = c;Move = d).
```

The empirical ESM1 needs to be more complicated than ASM1. In case the player II is not transparent, ESM1 must fall back on using itself as a model (as ASM1 does from the start).

We can now test out the two agents and find that they behave differently. We ask with whom each succeeds in co-operating:

```
player(cc1). player(rc1). player(asm1). player(esm1).
  ?- player(Whom),move1(esm1,Whom,c),
    move2(Whom,esm1,c,Response).
⇒ Who = cc1 , Response = c;
⇒ Who = rc1 , Response = c;
  ?- move1(asm1,Whom,c),
move2(Whom,asm1,c,Response).
⇒ No
```

151

When moving first, ESM1 manages successfully to co-operate with both CC1 and RC1.[2] ESM1 is semi-co-operative. ASM1 co-operates with no-one, as we might expect, given its pessimistic model of the other agent's behaviour.

The ASM1 agent behaves the same way as did UD1 agent, which we can now eliminate.[3] Adding ESM1 to a tally of results for the Extended Prisoner's Dilemma, we get the table in Figure 8.1. I record the scores in the form: role I + role II to bring out the occasional differences these roles make.

Agent	UC1	CC1	RC1	ESM1	ASM1
UC1	2+2	2+2	0+0	0+0	0+0
CC1	2+2	2+2	2+2	1+2	1+1
RC1	3+3	2+2	2+2	1+2	1+1
ESM1	3+3	2+1	2+1	1+1	1+1
ASM1	3+3	1+1	1+1	1+1	1+1

Figure 8.1 Extended Prisoner's Dilemma results

8.1.2 A criticism

The distinction between empirical and *a priori* SM players allows me to meet a criticism that my assumptions are too strong. Some have argued that assuming transparency and committed agents eliminates the *CD* and *DC* outcomes and collapses the difference between constrained and straightforward maximization. For example,

> If it were the case that one player cannot, as a matter of fact, expect profitably to exploit the other because a blocking counter-move by the latter was certain or highly probable, squares [*CD*] and [*DC*] of the matrix would simply be wiped out. 'Selfish', 'straightforward' maximization and prudentially constrained, considerate maximization would dictate the same best choice, i.e. to [co-operate].
>
> (de Jasay 1989, p. 64)

We have seen that this is not so. While ESM moving first would co-operate, a second moving SM (of either flavour) would not co-operate. The reason is that the *CD* outcome maintains its motivational pull, so a second moving SM would always choose *D*, and thus prove untrustworthy. Straightforward and constrained maximization remain distinct even in the Extended Prisoner's Dilemma.

8.1.3 Mutual constraint

A straightforward maximizer who co-operates raises some interesting questions about responsive moral strategies. Should moral players respond to simple co-operation or to the more complex property, constraint? In the one-shot PD this distinction makes no difference; the XPD and the ESM player press the issue upon us. (This question is analogous to an earlier one that distinguished CC and RC; the first responding to UC's co-operation and the second demanding more, namely discrimination.)

As I have implemented them, both conditional and reciprocal co-operators will sometimes co-operate with straightforward maximizers, namely when an ESM plays role I. But with ESM on the scene, we might want to change this. For example, one interpretation of Gauthier's constrained maximization principle is that it forbids co-operation with any straightforward maximizer.[4]

How might one implement a narrow conditional co-operator (NCC), who refuses to co-operate even with a partially co-operative ESM?[5] NCC1's **move1** should be the same as CC's since ESM1 will not respond to *C* with *C* anyway. NCC1's **move2** will need to be different:

permit(ncc1,Anyone,execute).
*m2(ncc1,Other,c,c):- % * defective agent
 pubmove2(Other,ncc1,c,c).
m2(ncc1,Other,d,d).

I have added an extra condition in order to filter out ESM. NCC1 demands that a co-operator in player I role also be a conditional co-operator in player II role. NCC1 will co-operate with UC1, CC1, RC1 and manage to detect and discriminate against ESM. But if two NCC players are paired, they will loop. This implementation of NCC is procedurally incompetent and I indicate its failure with an asterisk. This returns us to the general problem of incoherence that plagues conditional strategies in simultaneous games, taken up in Chapter 4. It reminds us that these problems can also arise in extended games. My point here is not that NCC is impossible; it is not. (One can always use the techniques of matching quoted procedures to work around the problem.) Rather I want to remind us of the perils of conditional strategies. Exposure to and testing of other players is risky. I take up this subject in the next section.

Conclusion

Once we raise the question of what a straightforward maximizer does when moving first in the XPD in the presence of responsive players, it is obvious that there are choices to be made in the development of the received theory of rational choice. I have sketched the first steps along two divergent paths, the empirical and the *a priori* SM. Both are procedurally feasible. Under conditions of transparency, the empirical agent, ESM1, sometimes co-operates with CC and RC agents. Three conclusions follow. First, the received theory of rational choice can provide an account of co-operation, at least in an environment where others are disposed to responsive co-operation. This indicates resources of the received theory that might be overlooked if one thought that only moral agents could achieve optimal outcomes. (This result must be kept in perspective: only ESM agents ever co-operate; they only do so part of the time; and they need non-SM agents to induce them to co-operate at all.) Second, *mutual constraint* is not a necessary condition for co-operation in the Extended Prisoner's Dilemma. ESM is less constrained than either CC or RC; therefore none of these three demands mutual constraint in order to co-operate. Third, ESM is evidently superior to ASM, since it benefits from some co-operation and pays no additional costs. However the problems of developing an agent who discriminates and sanctions ESM is suggestive of the risks of knowledge-intensive strategies used by ESM (as well as CC and RC), the subject of the next section. This underscores the tentative nature of conclusions reached in toy situations with highly idealized access to information.

8.2 THE COSTS OF INFORMATION

Morality is a distinctive strategy. Moral agents need to be more connected to each other – they depend on *artificial interdependence* to overcome the costs of independent decision-making. These needs distinguish them from straightforward maximizers and impose special costs on moral agents as well.

The previous section notwithstanding, responsive moral agents, such as CC and RC, are more dependent on information about other players than amoral straightforward maximizers. By making this information free, my initial constructions likely overstate the case for responsive constraint. In this section I shall begin to bring information costs into the argument. I argue that responsive agents pay *differential* costs of scrutiny. This leads to two conclusions. First, contrary to Gauthier, SM agents do better under translucent than under transparent conditions. Second, unconditional agents, like UC and SM, also do better than expected under these conditions.

8.2.1 Risks of prediction and exposure

As I showed in Part II, responsive moral agents need to solve a pair of problems. On the one hand, they need to commit themselves to constraint in a way that other players can determine. On the other hand, they need to determine other players' principles, in order to discriminate among them. Now I want to argue that each of these two tasks can be risky and therefore costly. The first requires exposure and the second prediction. The risks of the second are more obvious, so I take them up first.

8.2.2 Risks of prediction

The most obvious risk of predicting other players' behaviour is that one will get it wrong; predictions may be incorrect. Here is an alternative implementation of conditional co-operation that will often predict incorrectly:

```
m1(cc2,Coop,c):-          % Co-operate if the other is
   pubmove2(Coop,X,c,c).  % transparent & reciprocates
                          % co-operation with anyone.

m1(cc2,NonCoop,d).        % Otherwise defect.
```

While (our standard) CC1 predicts co-operation on the basis of player II responding to CC1 with co-operation, CC2 predicts her partner's co-operativeness on the basis of the weaker test that the partner reciprocates co-operation with *anyone*.

A second risk involves predictions that actually run the other player's decision procedure. Such predictions may loop. We have seen (in Part II) that conditional cooperators *need* not go wrong in this way – even in the simultaneous case – but they *may* – even in the simple sequential case. Consider CC3, whose redundant test of the other player's first move will loop with most responsive players:

```
m2(cc3,Coop,X,c):-        % co-operate if the other is
pubmove1(Coop,cc,c).      % transparent & co-operative in
                          % Move1
m2(cc3,NonCoop,X,d).      % otherwise defect
```

And looping becomes harder to avoid if we consider more sophisticated strategies such as reciprocal cooperation and the narrow co-operator (NCC) discussed in §8.1.3 which make additional requirements on the other player and therefore make more demanding and risky predictions. (Indeed, I have implemented only a defective version of NCC in the text.)

8.2.3 Risks of exposure

Exposing yourself to other agents is also risky, if less obviously so. Opening oneself to be read or run by others risks strategic intrusion by other agents. Obviously, readable agents risk losing their secrets, such as the key to the randomizer they need to generate rational mixed strategies in constant sum contests. Second, there is a parallel to the second risk of prediction. Executable agents risk being thrown queries (will you co-operate with CC3?) which are for them endlessly puzzling paradoxes. Third, there are the risks we explored in the discussion of learning. Transparent agents are open to subtle exploitation. If I can execute other players' procedures, I can test them against each other in order each the better to victimize.

What are we to make of the costs of prediction and exposure? What status should they have in our evolving theory? First, they stand as predictions: agents that expose themselves and predict others' behaviour will pay for this epistemic adventure. Of course, I do not mean to claim that they will pay more than they will gain.[6] But it is likely that they will pay something for them. Second, we should construct our tournaments so that this cost comes out. This requires no modification in the case where CC2 predicts that a predator will co-operate. It does require some modification for the cases where procedures loop. We need to specify a default value for failure to return a move (and a corresponding value for the other player in a non-terminating interaction). Third, given the risks of prediction and exposure, we can expect successful agents to be different. For example, ESM1 is transparent because this is necessary to pass RC1's inspection for responsiveness. Now I realize that RC does not need to use such a crudely invasive procedure. (When information is free, players will tend to waste it.) Here is RC2, designed not to require ESM1 to be transparent. RC2 makes an assumption that makes testing simpler; he assumes that players are generally negatively responsive – they return D for D. Therefore he need only test for UC's unique signature (returning C for D) and not require transparency of other co-operators. Since RC2 is itself negatively responsive, this test will not loop.[7]

m2(rc2,UnResponsive,c,d):-
  pubmove2(UnResponsive,rc2,d,c).
m2(rc2,Responsive,c,c).
m2(rc2,Defector,d,d).

RC2 co-operates more widely and takes fewer epistemic risks than RC1, so it should prosper and induce less transparent ESM to prosper as well. Thus we can expect that players will shift to strategies that economize on the risks of exposure and prediction.

8.2.4 Differential costs

I will leave these issues, important as they are for testing my predictions, for another occasion. For now, I will lump costs of prediction and exposure together as *epistemic costs* and sketch two predictions.

First, I predict that responsive agents, because they pay costs of exposure and scrutiny, will do relatively less well as we move from perfectly transparent conditions. David Gauthier disagrees with this prediction. In *Morals by Agreement* Gauthier attempts to strengthen his argument by moving away from the strongly idealized assumption of transparency. In §VI.2.3 he constructs a parametric argument to demonstrate that there exist conditions of translucency under which CC remains more useful than SM. This argument depends on the assumption that CC and SM pay the *same* information costs. But this assumption is highly suspect. Having established that CM is rational above a certain degree of translucency, Gauthier goes on to argue that both CM and SM have an interest in increasing their abilities to detect others' dispositions:

> The ability to detect the dispositions of others must be well developed in a rational CM.
>
> Both CMs and SMs must expect to benefit from increasing their ability to detect the dispositions of others. But if both endeavour to maximize their abilities (or the expected utility,

net of costs, of so doing), then CMs may expect to improve their position in relation to SMs.

(Gauthier 1986a, p. 181)

In effect this arms race leads to increased translucency and back to the conclusion that CM is rational for all agents, already established at the limit of full transparency.

There are three problems with this construction. First, while Gauthier allows that scrutiny is costly, he does not try to bring these costs into his model. I have argued that one would expect that the *differential* costs to different players would be important. In particular, if constrained maximizers are constructed along the lines we canvassed in Part II, they pay two related kinds of costs: the risks of exposure and the risks of prediction. No straightforward maximizer need pay exposure costs and only ESM pays prediction costs. Second, Gauthier too readily assumes that SM also needs to detect other agents' dispositions. But in the standard simultaneous Prisoner's Dilemma, this is not so. Move D is dominant; no prediction is called for. An SM agent may simply play the unconditional strategy, UD. The Extended PD is more complex as we have seen above in §8.1.1. It may be advantageous for an ESM agent to predict that player II is a conditional co-operator, for example, and therefore choose C. But when the costs of prediction are considered, this Empirical Straightforward Maximizer also pays differential costs, because it makes predictions. Granted, an ESM need not expose itself, so it will risk less than CC and RC agents, but the balance within SM will shift from ESM to ASM as transparency declines.

Third, as I have noted before, in Part II, Gauthier does not consider that other strategies besides CC and SM may be useful. Given epistemic costs, the unconditional co-operator, UC, becomes particularly attractive. Like SM (or ASM), UC pays no costs of scrutiny since UC is also an unconditional strategy. Unlike SM, UC gains the benefits of co-operation with CC. Therefore, given costs of scrutiny, UC becomes an attractive strategy.[8] In a world where UC but not CC pays costs like this, UC will invade a CC population and ultimately SM will be the most useful strategy. Therefore, introducing scrutiny costs undermines Gauthier's argument for the usefulness of CC versus SM based on a projection from transparent to translucent situations.

The introduction of epistemic costs cuts another way as well. For example, my claim that reciprocal co-operators always do better than conditional co-operators in Chapter 5, §5.1 ignored costs of scrutiny, so we must reconsider it in a new light. Arguably, RC pays even higher costs than CC, since it must test other agents *counter-factually*: asking not merely did you co-operate, but would you still co-operate were I to defect? I conjecture that RC agents will have special difficulties in interaction with other responsive agents. This yields the outcome table, in Figure 8.2.

Agent	UC	CC	RC	UD
UC	2	2	0	0
CC	2	1.75	1.75	1
RC	3	1.5	1.5	1
UD	3	1	1	1

Figure 8.2 Some concocted costs of scrutiny

Will morality persist in a world like this? Before sketching an answer I should stress that I *concocted* the outcomes in Figure 8.2, so not much hangs on them.[9] In addition, I am ignoring some details covered in this chapter, such as the difference between ESM and ASM, and the different roles in the XPD. Real results must await a broadly based tournament.

8.3 MIXED POPULATIONS IN EQUILIBRIUM

The outcomes of my concocted tournament in an epistemically costly world change the results of the evolutionary test that I used in Chapter 5, §5.1 to compare reciprocal and conditional co-operators. I will argue that given differential epistemic costs, the superiority of RC over CC is weakened. Indeed, mixed populations will result, that is, worlds where there is no one strategy that is rational for all to follow. This result is profoundly disturbing to some attempts to wed game theory to moral theory.

Here is the early history of a world starting with a CC agent. Each generation is a list of players, followed by the results each potential entrant to the population would get.[10] The next generation consists of the best of these added to the head of the population list.

Generation 0 : [cc]
[[2,uc],[1.75,cc],[1.5,rc],[1,ud]]
New Entry : [uc]

Generation 1 : [uc,cc]
[[4.5,rc],[4,uc],[3.75,cc],[3,ud]]
New Entry : [rc]

Generation 2 : [rc,uc,cc]
[[6,rc],[5.5,cc],[4,ud],[4,uc]]
New Entry : [rc]

Generation 3 : [rc,rc,uc,cc]
[[7.5,rc],[7.25,cc],[5,ud],[4,uc]]
New Entry : [rc]

Generation 4 : [rc,rc,rc,uc,cc]
[[9,rc],[9,cc],[6,ud],[4,uc]]
New Entry : [rc,cc]

Generation 5 : [rc,cc,rc,rc,rc,uc,cc]
[[12.5,cc],[12,rc],[8,ud],[6,uc]]
New Entry : [cc]

Generation 6 : [cc,rc,cc,rc,rc,rc,uc,cc]
[[14.25,cc],[13.5,rc],[9,ud],[8,uc]]
New Entry : [cc]

. . . . . .

Generation 31 :
[cc,cc,cc,cc,cc,cc,cc,cc,cc,cc,cc,cc,cc,cc,cc,cc,
cc,cc,cc,cc,cc,cc,cc,cc,cc,cc,rc,cc,rc,rc,rc,uc,cc]
[[58,uc],[58,cc],[51,rc],[34,ud]]
New Entry : [uc,cc]

We see by generation 5 that CC comes back and by generation 32 UC comes back as well. This world tends to a three-way division of the population in equilibrium. We start the test with a homogeneous CC population. In this safe situation, some CC will find it advantageous to cease to check other's dispositions, or simple UC newcomers will prosper. But UC are fodder for RC agents, so some CC will weaken their moral constraint or outside RC will enter. The result of this (or some other story) will be a division of the population in the ratio of CC:UC:RC::7:2:1. This ratio of agent types is in equilibrium; a new entrant receives the same payoff regardless of its type.[11] It is not useful for all agents to be moral, if morality is identified with CC. Instead, it is useful to be one of {RC,CC,UC} depending on the population mix.

(And, if scrutiny costs are higher, the equilibrium population may include SM as well.)

Conclusion

In this section I have argued that on procedural assumptions that make solving the compliance problem plausible (those of Part II), Gauthier's conditional moral strategy incurs special costs. Therefore it is useful for some to be moral, for some to be less moral, and for some to be morally deviant. Gauthier's contrary conclusion, that it is useful for all agents to be moral (in the same way) both depends on and supports his use of the assumptions of strong game theory: players are symmetrical and share extensive common knowledge. Consider dependence first. First, and most obvious, one will not get an equilibrium of different agents if one assumes that all agents are symmetrically rational. Slightly less obvious, complex populations will not result if one limits agents to two ideal types, symmetrically rational (SM) and symmetrically moral (CM). (Recall that the presence of UC is crucial.) Therefore the symmetry assumption directly supports homogeneous populations. Second, assuming common knowledge, which eliminates differential costs of scrutiny, indirectly supports homogeneity.

Now consider how the conclusion that equilibrium populations will be mixed puts into question Gauthier's repeated appeals to rational symmetry elsewhere in his theory. For example, his crucial defence of costly sanctioning behaviour ('narrow compliance'), which is arguably necessary for the stability of Gauthier's strong moral norms, depends on an appeal to equal rationality, 'Equal rationality demands equal compliance. Since broad compliance is not rational for everyone, it is not rational for anyone' (Gauthier 1986, p. 226). One cannot assume that all rational agents will be the same when the primary result for the compliance problem is an equilibrium mix of different more and less moral strategies. (I return to this crucial argument in the next two chapters.)

CONCLUSION

This chapter begins the process of bringing information and its costs into the models upon which Artificial Morality builds. I began by exploring a division within the received theory and constructing a deviant empirical straightforward maximizer which can sometimes co-operate. This makes responsive moral strategies somewhat less unique and attractive. The second section continued the argument by bringing out the costs of exposure and prediction. These epistemic risks fall particularly heavily upon responsive moral strategies, undermining Gauthier's attempt to extrapolate from transparent to translucent situations and making unconditional strategies, such as ASM and UC, surprisingly more attractive. Finally, in a world where responsive strategies pay differential epistemic costs, we can expect stable mixed populations to develop. This result is profoundly disturbing of attempts to build morality on the game-theoretic assumptions of universal and symmetrical rationality and common knowledge.

9

CHICKEN

Returning to the conclusion of Part II, reciprocal co-operators do best in the game of two-player Prisoner's Dilemma (PD).[1] They solve the compliance problem because they are both rational and arguably moral. But this game is not the only or even the most difficult test for morally constrained free agents. While the PD is a deep and difficult problem, it turns out to be especially favourable to a moral solution by means of communication, commitment and an opportunistic minimal morality. Therefore I should consider other situations that may challenge my conclusions.[2] Aggression provides a good test case for my minimally moral agents. It is a commonplace that bullies test one's moral mettle. There are three reasons that aggression provides a particular challenge to my justification of morality. First, aggressors make use of my favoured devices, communication and commitment, for the purpose of amoral advantage. They threaten using the devices moral agents use for promising. Second, opportunistic agents – the indirect maximizers of Chapter 7 – have good reasons not to resist such threats; it may simply be better to be red, or robbed, than dead. Third, morality seems to demand that we resist threats in favour of impartially fair outcomes.

I use the game of Chicken to model the problem of aggression. This chapter develops a theory of substantive rational strategies for Chicken. I contrast Chicken and the Prisoner's Dilemma with special attention to the devices of threats and promises. Then I shall show that the presence of committed threateners complicates the situation similar to the way committed unconditional co-operators complicated the PD. Once again we are pulled in different directions: now, to acquiesce or to resist. Again I argue that rational morality takes the low road: the substantially rational strategy is to acquiesce to unreasoning threateners. This is a disturbing moral conclusion.

In particular I must confront Gauthier's arguments in favour of principled resistance to all threats. My conclusion leaves me with serious procedural problems as well. Rational acquiescence requires great – perhaps impossible – powers of discrimination. I stir up these problems in the present chapter and try to resolve them in the next.

9.1 CHICKEN, DOVES AND HAWKS

9.1.1 Beyond the Prisoner's Dilemma

It is sometimes suggested that rational morality is concerned only with the 'Prisoner Dilemma problem', perhaps because the PD is thought to be the only important game of partial conflict. For example: 'Justice is aimed at Prisoner Dilemma situations, where mutual restraint leads to mutual improvement, and not at zero-sum games' (Narveson 1988c, p. 505). But the PD is not the only non-zero-sum game. I shall argue in this section that it fails to model important features characteristic of moral problems.

First, recall that moral constraint is a public good. Others benefit from my constraint. Recently, several authors have stressed the limits of the Prisoner's Dilemma as a model for the problem of public goods provision. Taylor and Ward lament the 'obsession with the PD' and recommend the game of Chicken as an alternative model.[3] I shall take this advice.

Second, consider aggression and resistance. Chicken differs from the PD in one crucial respect: joint defection is worse for each of us than one-sided defection. (See Figure 9.1.) That is, if you choose D, I prefer C, not D. Resisting you is more costly than conceding. Chicken models a world where we would expect some aggressive agents to do well. As Taylor and Ward argue, successful free riding is evidence that

	C	D
C	3,3	1,4
D	4,1	0,0

Figure 9.1 The game of Chicken

the game of Chicken models the situation better than the PD does, because in a strict PD no rational agent prefers to be taken for a sucker.

Conversely, the cheap conquests of one-sided aggression are not available in the PD.[4] Would-be aggressors, such as SM, do poorly, leaving more morally constrained agents, like RC, to prosper. This was the happy conclusion of Part II. But not all situations are like this. Sometimes aggression pays and often this is so because rational or moral constraints hold back the righteous. Therefore the Prisoner's Dilemma cannot be a complete model of moral problems.

Third, consider the role of social sanctions in enforcing compliance with morality. Gauthier's account of morality as impartial self-constraint stresses the *psychological* aspect of constraint. In contrast, Narveson makes *social* enforcement equally important:

> Moral rules *overrule* us. . . . What does this mean? . . . First, that a conscientious individual, when confronted with a choice between what morality tells her she must do and what she might otherwise like to do, will do what morality says. Somehow, we must be capable of having moral motives that are stronger than any inclinations to the contrary. And second, we may point to the social aspect. If someone proposes to do something wrong, even though it may be highly beneficial to the doer, the *rest of us* should exert ourselves to steer him back to the . . . path prescribed by morality.
>
> (Narveson 1988b, p. 124)

Roughly, enforcement is a social analogue of counter-preferential principles. We should notice, incidentally, that social enforcement and self-constraint are also *complementary*. For example, in the limiting case of the Iterated Prisoner's Dilemma, enforcement by others using the Tit for Tat strategy obviates the need for any moral self-constraint. This suggests that we ask about the converse possibility. Are there cases where there is no need for social enforcement? I think that there are. Indeed, the one-shot Prisoner's Dilemma itself leaves no room for enforcement, strictly speaking. Recall that I do better defecting on a defector than co-operating with her (because D is dominant). Enforcement by defection in the Prisoner's Dilemma never calls for any 'exertion' on the agent's part because it never costs anything. In the Prisoner's Dilemma, agreement to moral principles like CC and RC is self-enforcing in this sense: no new sanctioning motive is needed.[5] In general, unless $DC > CC$ there is no need for self-constraint and unless $CD > DD$ there is no need for a special moral motive to drive enforcement. In the one-shot Prisoner's Dilemma defecting on a defector does not hurt us; the PD calls for self-constraint but not social enforcement. Enforcement is needed where joint defection is worse than one-sided co-operation, that is, in Chicken.[6]

Enforcement may also change a game from PD to Chicken. One cannot *stop* other players taking actions in our bare worlds; one can only *deter* them by taking action that makes them worse off (recall §6.2.3). One needs to threaten sanctions. But this threat, as we saw in the case of the unconditional co-operator protector (UCP) in Chapter 6, takes one from a game of Prisoner's Dilemma into something closer to Chicken. UCP and RC each do worse by failing to co-operate than either would were they to concede by converting to the other's principle. Therefore where agents can affect their situation through their choices, we should expect them sometimes to end up in Chicken even if they start in the morally more tractable Prisoner's Dilemma.

9.1.2 The game of Chicken

The name of this game, Chicken, is not unproblematic. It already embroils us in the controversies the game opens up. 'Chicken' denotes a notorious teenage ritual, one form of which was portrayed in the film *Rebel Without a Cause* (cf. Brams (1976, §5.2)). Two players drive together towards a cliff. The alternatives are to 'chicken out' by braking or to continue. The driver who chickens out first loses face, and the other wins. Of course if *both* continue, both do the worst possible: driving off the cliff. The first problem is that the term 'Chicken' is not neutral, since it names the game after one of the strategies. In contrast, sociobiologists call this game 'Dove/Hawk', which encompasses both primitive strategies. The paradigmatic story is problematic in another, more subtle respect. The cost of 'chickening out' is a loss of *face*. But this means that the payoffs are measured partially in terms of subjective relative advantage which conflicts with my use of objective payoffs.[7] Moreover the amount of 'face' lost is a function of one's principles. Therefore the chicken story easily leads to confusing agents' substantive objective ends with the psychological means committed players might employ. Unfortunately, the Dove/Hawk alternative is also objectionable, as the primitive strategies are identified with complex conditional behaviours. Therefore, having noted the problems, and insisting that nothing depends on the name, I will stick with the conventional name 'Chicken'.

Simultaneity plays no role in my discussion of Chicken, so I will use the simpler extended form, as shown by Figure 9.2. (There are procedural problems in Chicken, but they come out in the extended form.) The use of the extended form of the game does require that I use a slightly non-standard set of payoffs.[8] Since I shall use only this extended form of the game, I will not bother to distinguish it with a special label (XChicken?).

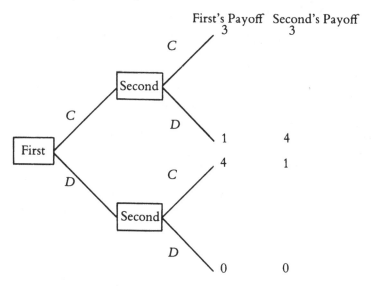

Figure 9.2 Extended Chicken

The structure of this extended game is most clearly revealed by considering play by straightforward maximizers working through a simple look-ahead procedure. We start at the end of the game. Player II faces two choices. If player I chooses C, II would choose D; if I chooses D, II would choose C. Backing up one step, this gives I the expected values of $C = 1$ and $D = 4$, so I chooses D and II chooses C. Therefore the expected outcome of this game of Chicken for a straightforward maximizer who might play roles I or II is $(4 + 1)/2 = 2.5$. This is worse than the co-operative outcome of 3, leading us to wonder, as in the case of the Prisoner's Dilemma, whether morally constrained agents could improve on straightforward maximizers here as well.

9.1.3 Threats and promises

We should consider what moral devices might be useful in Chicken. I have already suggested that now we need to consider threats in addition to the promises deployed in the PD. Where a promise to match co-operation with co-operation suffices to solve the PD, a threat by II to match defection with defection is effective in Chicken. It should induce a rational I to choose C. Threats are analogous to promises; both are commitments 'to do something that the individual would not otherwise be motivated to do' (Hirshleifer 1987, p. 309). Notice that the Prisoner's Dilemma requires no threat; responding to D with D is in the player's interest. Similarly, there is no need to promise CC in Chicken; CD, while meagre, is still better for player I than the threatened DC.

Threats, like promises, require the ability to make counter-preferential commitments; Chicken adds nothing to the PD in this respect. But the commitment and its goal are morally and procedurally more problematic than in the Prisoner's Dilemma. Threatening in Chicken requires greater perserverance than promising and it may aim at one-sided rather than mutual benefit. Let's take these up in turn. To see the difference in the *strength* of commitment, first ask what happens if the threat fails and I chooses D. Then the threatening II must choose to get 0 rather than 1. In contrast, ask what happens if a promise succeeds in motivating I in the PD. Then II must choose to get 2 rather than 3. So far, there is no appreciable difference; both must choose to take a loss. But notice that in a larger context, in the Prisoner's Dilemma, 2 is better than II would get without promising, while in Chicken, 0 is worse than II would get without threatening. Put otherwise, keeping one's promise has a point: otherwise II wouldn't be in a position to choose between 2 and 3. But a failed threat is pointless. Therefore the ability to keep threats requires sterner stuff than the ability to keep promises.[9] This will lead us to new procedural and moral problems in the next chapter.

Second, we saw that there is no need for II to promise the fair outcome CC in order to motivate I to acquiesce and choose C. A threat to bring about DC should suffice to induce the other player to choose C. Therefore committed agents need not be moral in Chicken. Clearly the one-sided CD outcome is not impartial, as joint co-operation was in the PD. Moreover, this outcome is not even mutually beneficial (a weaker standard than impartiality) when compared to the natural equilibrium outcome. Threateners reduce straightforward maximizers to 1, as compared to their natural expectation of 2.5.[10] Of course, threateners do very badly against each other. The cost of their persistence is an ability to reduce their own scores to 0 each. This suggests that acquiescent straightforward maximization is not so bad after all. Also, there might be something better than simple threatening, which now leads us to consider the substantive possibilities of the game of Chicken.

9.2 SUBSTANTIVE RATIONALITY

What is the best strategy in Chicken? I will leave moral and procedural questions aside and consider substantive rationality first. What is most striking about Chicken is the presence of two equilibria, so let's start there. Unlike the Prisoner's Dilemma, there is no dominant strategy in Chicken. *D* is better if the other player chooses *C*, but *C* is better if the other player chooses *D*. Therefore there are two equilibria, *CD* and *DC*. In the simultaneous game of Chicken there is some controversy whether one should choose one's own preferred equilibrium.[11] But in extended Chicken, the SM strategy is less controversial, since straightforward maximizers can test the payoffs to the alternatives. Faced with another straightforward maximizer, SM will choose *D* when she goes first, forcing the other SM to make the best of a bad situation and choose *C*. SM will choose *C* playing role II after the other has chosen *D*. Therefore the expectation for a straightforward maximizer paired with another SM in extended Chicken is 2.5.

9.2.1 Principled amorality

Can we improve on SM in Chicken by using the device of public counter-preferential principles introduced in Part II? Yes, as we just saw, a threat can induce can induce a straightforward maximizer to choose *C* playing I in Chicken. An agent who strongly threatens by always choosing *D* is an unconditional defector (UD).

Consulting the four squares in the upper right hand corner of Figure 9.3, we can see that UD does better than SM in an SM population; UD can invade a population of straightforward maximizers. On the other hand UDs do very badly when paired with each other, so straightforward maximizers can also invade a population of threatening unconditional defectors. According to my evolutionary test for substantive rationality, they are equally rational.[12] Whether we start with UD or SM players, the population will evolve to a stable mix of strategies with unconditional defectors preying on straightforward maximizers, who acquiesce.

A second way to improve on straightforward maximization builds on the results of Part II by co-operating with morally constrained agents. As before, I will call such agents responsive co-operators. Responsive co-operators will do better in one respect than either SM or UD, because they get 3 when faced with each other, rather than 0 or 2.5. In addition, responsive co-operators need a policy to deal with threatening unconditional defectors. There are two policies that they could adopt. The first policy is to block invasion by UDs by resisting their threat. I call a threat-resisting agent a *narrow co-operator* (NC).[13] A narrow co-operator refuses to choose C unless the other is expected to choose C and would choose D if NC would. Since narrow co-operators co-operate with each other, they can invade a population of UD agents, just as CC invaded SM in the Prisoner's Dilemma. (The first NC drifts in and the next NC entrant does better than the frustrated threateners.) Moreover, NC can resist invasion by UD so long as the NC population is pure. However, as we have seen, in Chicken, unlike the PD, NC's refusal to comply with threats is costly. It seems that a responsive co-operator who did not resist threats might do better. And since the narrow co-operator is tolerant to the other responsive co-operator, the NC population will not remain pure.

	UD	SM	NC	BC
UD	0	4	0	4
SM	1	2.5	1	1
NC	0	4	3	3
BC	1	4	3	3

Figure 9.3 First Chicken tournament

This also suggests that a morality of impartiality may be too demanding and brings us to the alternative moral policy: *broad co-operation* (BC). A broad co-operator co-operates more broadly by conceding to UD's threats. BC chooses C when faced with UD but threatens and resists the threats of SM. Therefore BC does better than SM and also better than NC. Indeed, BC is a strong contender for substantive rationality in Chicken, as we can see from the table of results in Figure 9.3.[14] While broad co-operation is only equally rational to unconditional defection (each can invade the other) neither

SM nor NC can invade a mixed population of BC and UD because BC always does better than NC. (NC can drift into a BC population but they can never do better than the broad co-operators, so they never invade.) On the other hand, broad co-operators can *indirectly* invade a population of narrow co-operators because narrow co-operators tolerate broad co-operators who, by increasing in number, permit threatening unconditional defectors to drift in. At this point, the broad co-operators do better than the narrow. Applying my evolutionary test for substantive rationality, this makes BC superior to NC and undermines NC's claim of superiority to UD.[15]

These are unhappy results for both rationality and morality. As in the epistemically costly case studied in Chapter 8, there is no one substantively rational strategy. The (broadly) co-operative strategy fares no better than the amoral threatening bully.[16] BC tolerates predation by bullies; it is rational to be moral only in this weaker sense. This preliminary survey of the substantive possibilities afforded by Chicken suggests two comparisons with Part II's conclusions about the Prisoner's Dilemma. The most obvious contrast is the way the tables have turned. In the PD, morality seemed to push us towards the broader co-operation of CC and rationality to the narrower co-operation of RC.[17] In Chicken, rationality indicates broader and morality narrower co-operation. The second contrast involves the toleration problem that plagues would-be rational moralists in both Chicken and the Prisoner's Dilemma. In both games an unconditional agent is the king-maker, determining who will do best, creating new strategic problems and provoking a split between rational and moral strategies. In Chicken, UD makes the difference that UC makes in the PD. The problem is even deeper in the case of Chicken for three reasons, one rational and two moral. First, UD does better than UC in the PD. Therefore in Chicken I need not argue at length to defend this threatening king-maker's presence. As we have seen, UD can invade SM and BC populations and maintain a stable parasitic relationship with them. Second, broad co-operation does better by the morally objectionable act of complying with UD's threat and accepting the unfair *CD* outcome. This contrasts with CC's morally laudable co-operation with UC. Third, NC is caught in the difficult situation of trying to discourage UD by using sanctions that make NC worse off, like UCP in the Prisoner's Dilemma. It looks as if morality and rationality come apart more radically in Chicken than in the Prisoner's Dilemma.

9.3 BROAD AND NARROW COMPLIANCE

At this point my discussion intersects a crucial argument in *Morals by Agreement*. Gauthier sees the need to specify constrained maximization with regard to the proper degree of compliance.

> Let us call a person who is disposed to co-operate in ways that, followed by all, yield nearly optimal and fair outcomes, *narrowly compliant*. And let us call a person who is disposed to co-operate in ways that, followed by all, merely yield her some benefit in relation to universal non-co-operation, *broadly compliant*. We need not deny that a broadly compliant person would expect to benefit in some situations in which a narrowly compliant person could not. But in many other situations a broadly compliant person must expect to lose by her disposition. For in so far as she is known to be broadly compliant, others will have every reason to maximize their utilities at her expense, by offering 'co-operation' on terms that offer her but little more than she could expect from non-co-operation.
>
> In refusing [unfair] terms [the narrow complier] does not diminish her prospects for co-operation with other rational persons, and she ensures that those not disposed to fair co-operation do not enjoy the benefits of any co-operation, thus making their unfairness costly to themselves, and so irrational.
>
> (Gauthier 1986a, pp. 178f.)

Let us step back from the game of Chicken to consider the connection between compliance and the other components of Gauthier's theory. Simplifying enormously, Gauthier argues that rational agents will be motivated to bargain to a fair outcome from morally constrained initial holdings by the prospect that rational agents would only comply with fair bargains. Therefore it is crucial to morals by agreement that constrained maximizers should only comply with fair and optimal bargains, a disposition which Gauthier calls narrow compliance. (Otherwise, as Kraus and Coleman (1987) suggest, Gauthier will end up with *immorality* by agreement.) The specification of constrained maximization as narrowly compliant is necessary to deal with what I have called the tolerance problem in the Chicken-like game that bargaining presents. Here the problem is a pair of new and problematic strategies, both morally less constrained than constrained maximization, which exploit the new alternatives bargaining introduces. The first sort of agent threatens non-co-operation unless it gets a larger than fair share of the co-operative surplus and the second, the broadly compliant agent, acquiesces in this threat. How should a moral agent deal with these two challenges to fair distribution? Gauthier's answer is that rational morality demands refusing to co-operate with the former.

We can now return to Chicken. I will shift vocabulary from 'compliance' to 'co-operation' to mark my move to the simpler model.

The broad co-operator strategy does better than the narrow co-operator. The divergence between the two is stressed by one of the deepest criticisms of Gauthier's theory to appear in print. Kraus and Coleman have argued that while Gauthier's narrow co-operator may be moral, it is not rational. The broad co-operator who acquiesces for the sake of meagre benefits will do better than the narrow co-operator. Kraus and Coleman conclude that the gap between rationality and morality reappears at this point:

> The very problems of collective action which motivate the need for constrained maximization emerge again at the level of choice between the alternative forms of constrained maximization, broad and narrow compliance . . . Once again, what is collectively rational is individually irrational. The conundrum of collective action, even when solved at one level, re-occurs at another, in this case foiling an ambitious attempt to ground morality in rationality.
>
> (Kraus and Coleman 1987, pp. 748f.)

As Gauthier said of reciprocal co-operation, narrowly compliant agents make the world safe for morality. However, narrow compliers pay privately in order to create and maintain this public good. The public good of morality benefits both narrow compliers and broad compliers, but the latter benefit more, since they avoid some enforcement costs.

As we have seen, the alternative moral strategies for the game of Chicken seem prone to the same dilemma. On the one hand, narrow co-operators accept only fair outcomes but they do not do as well as more opportunistic broad co-operators who fall short of the stricter standard of impartiality required to motivate Gauthier's general moral theory. This new compliance problem looks serious; the gap between rational broad and moral narrow co-operation is wide. However, we have not fully explored the possibilities for substantively rational strategies in Chicken. In the remainder of this chapter I shall work to narrow the gap by improving both broad and narrow co-operative strategies. Ultimately, I shall defend a variation of broad co-operation as rational. First, I need to defend BC from Gauthier and also consider ways in which NC might be improved.

9.3.1 Equal rationality

One consequence of the two equilibria in the game of Chicken is the possibility that two different strategies, UD and BC, can persist and do equally well in a mixed population. I have interpreted this result as showing that UD and BC are equally rational in the ultimate, substantive sense. But this interpretation is controversial; Gauthier argues against broad compliance precisely by appeal to what he terms 'equal rationality':

> broad compliance is not a rational disposition for utility-maximizers. Not only does a broadly compliant person invite others to take advantage of her in setting terms of co-operation, but if some persons are broadly compliant, then others, interacting with them, will find it advantageous not to be broadly, or even so much as narrowly, compliant. If you will comply for any benefit whatsoever, then in interacting with you I should dispose myself to comply with a joint strategy only if it offers me, not a fair share, but the lion's share of the co-operative surplus. So it is not and cannot be rational for everyone to be disposed to broad compliance. . . . Since broad compliance is not rational for everyone, it is not rational for anyone.
>
> (Gauthier 1986a, p. 226)

Gauthier uses a strategic argument of the type I formalized as an evolutionary test for substantive rationality in Chapter 5. He assumes that others will be able to adapt to and thus exploit broad compliers. Kraus and Coleman object that this presupposes too much adaptability. I believe that they are wrong and Gauthier is right. Since this is a procedural dispute (about the possibility of discriminating between different agents), I will discuss it with the other procedural issues in the next chapter. For now, let us assume, with Gauthier, that some agents will adapt to exploit broad co-operators. As we have seen, UDs will invade and form with BC a stable mixed population. How does this show that BC is irrational in the case where both BC and the threatening predators that share its ecosystem do equally well? My conclusion would be that BC and UD are *equally rational*; Gauthier's holds that equal rationality precludes this. What separates us?

First, Gauthier relies on a conception of rationality shared with the received theory of rational choice. This conception makes strong assumptions about the similarity of all rational agents. However, I have argued that this conception is inadequate to the task of providing a fundamental justification of morality, because it begs the question in favour of SM agents (Chapter 2) and ignores procedural complications (Chapter 4) and complex populations (Chapter 8). Second, I think that Gauthier has mistaken a moral claim for a claim about rationality.[18] In particular, according to his theory, there are a number of moral principles that agents must accept in order to attract others to join with in co-operation. I believe that equal rationality is, for Gauthier, another moral principle of this sort, that is, a presupposition of bargaining. He writes, 'The bargaining problem can be solved, in my view, only by introducing an equal rationality assumption' (Gauthier 1988a, p. 186). It may be true that only co-operators willing to engage in bargaining based on equality in this sense will do well. If so, then the morality of equal bargaining will pass the ultimate test of substantive rationality. However, Gauthier's manner of arguing for this confuses the basis of the argument, making it appear to depend on procedural rather than (indirectly, but ultimately) on substantive grounds. He runs the following *reductio ad absurdum* argument:

> Suppose that it is rational for Jane to accept less advantage from a bargain . . . than John. Then it is not rational for John to accept less advantage than Jane. . . . What difference is there, between Jane and John, that would permit this? Jane and John are similarly characterized as semantic representers and utility maximizers. Nothing in this characterization enables us to distinguish Jane from John in the way needed by the hypothesis. So the hypothesis fails. It is not rational for Jane to accept less advantage than John.
>
> (Gauthier 1988a, p. 187)

The argument is based on the limits of procedural rationality; agents have no basis, *qua* rational, to co-ordinate on an unequal bargaining outcome.[19] Even granting that this may be true of agents who are 'semantic maximizers and utility maximizers', is it true of artificial agents able to commit themselves to various principles? I think that my agents will have no difficulty in co-ordinating on the asymmetrical outcome, *CD*. Principles give my agents a way to distinguish themselves. UD and SM should be as easy to distinguish in Chicken as CC and SM were in the PD; indeed easier, as I will confirm in the next chapter. An unconditional defector in Chicken, unlike SM in the Prisoner's Dilemma, wants to be identified because his threat depends on communication. But if there is no procedural problem here, Gauthier's *reductio* fails.

In what sense is the BC/UD arrangement irrational? I believe that the underlying reason must be substantial. Gauthier must show that accepting less than equal bargains works out badly for a player. I suspect that he is right about this, although not in the case of BC and UD. It may be best to demand equal bargaining with would-be co-operators. However, it is foolish to demand it from UD. I will develop this line of reasoning shortly. Three points are worth remembering as we leave this discussion. First, we need to keep the substantive test clearly separate from speculation about moral principles that might pass it. Secondly, we need to keep neutral substantive rationality distinct from the moralized 'rationality' internal to various players. Third, neither should be confused with the procedural limits that constrain all players.

9.3.2 Narrower co-operation

Narrow co-operation pays for making the world safe for morality and BC takes advantage of this situation. These results indicate that like conditional co-operators in the Prisoner's Dilemma, narrow co-operators are too nice. NC tolerates BC the way CC tolerated UC. This suggests that as in the case of CC and RC, I might be able to defend Gauthier's general theory by modifying his principle slightly. One way to make something like narrow co-operation pay is to make broad co-operators pay (indirectly) for it. The way to do this is to take advantage of the broad complier's willingness to acquiesce to threats. This modification gives rise to a fourth strategy towards compliance which we may call narrower co-operation (NRC).[20]

Gauthier finds NRC attractive. In response to Kraus and Coleman, Gauthier has shifted the definition of narrow compliance in the direction of what I call narrower compliance:[21] 'Gauthier changes the definition of narrow compliance: "A narrowly compliant person, as I define her . . . does not refuse to enter, to comply with, agreements if her share is more than fair; she refuses only if she would get less." ' As a preliminary test of NRC players, consider the interaction of all four types shown in the table in Figure 9.4.

	UD	NRC	NC	BC
UD	0	0	0	4
NRC	0	3	3	4
NC	0	3	3	3
BC	1	1	3	3

Figure 9.4   Second Chicken tournament

NRC improves on UD because narrower co-operators choose *C* with each other. (UD limits its own success in the way Smith's CUC did.) Narrower co-operation improves on narrow co-operation by exploiting BC. Figure 9.4 shows why NRC is superior to broad co-operation. NRC can invade BC but cannot be invaded by BC because it does not let BC drift in to get the indirect invasion via UD started. The narrower co-operator agent appears to close the compliance problem in Chicken.

A celebration of this victory for rational morality would be premature. The results in Figure 9.4 are not final. Once again we should consider whether any new agents might be contrived to fit any niche our situation creates. Indeed, we should be concerned that this process of dreaming up new strategies might go on forever, as Kitcher (1985, p. 89) warns: "For almost any game that we might consider, a little imagination will suggest strategies (some of them implausible) that would be able to invade a population whose members played any of the strategies explicitly considered." This reminds us that until we investigate procedural constraints in the next chapter we are only imagining strategies. But let us press on, since even this relatively unchecked speculation comes to an end shortly. In the case at hand, why should BC continue to pay for NRC making the world safer for morality? Consider a less compliant agent, the less broad co-operator (LBC) who resists NRC's threat and demands fair outcomes with fellow responsive agents. LBC's only exception is UD's *unreasoning* threat; to this NRC concedes. Since LBC still never pays the price of penalizing UD, it does better than NRC or NC as we see in Figure 9.5. NRC seems to have been a dead end. We appear to be back to

	UD	NRC	NC	LBC
UD	(0)	0	0	4
NRC	0	(3)	3	3
NC	0	3	(3)	3
LBC	1	3	3	(3)

Figure 9.5 Third Chicken tournament

where we started, since LBC resists NRC's threat, leaving NRC as practically equivalent to NC. Therefore, LBC is substantively rationally superior to NRC, since LBC can indirectly invade NRC but NRC can never invade any population based on LBC. Again the compliance dilemma looms, now with LBC the rational and NRC the moral alternative. If LBC is procedurally possible, Gauthier's attempt to close the compliance problem by sanctioning broad compliers is not feasible.

9.3.3 The Limits of Sanctions

Moreover, we can expect that no new substantive results will be forthcoming. This is because we have reached the rational limits imposed by sanctioning by means of threats. The only way to deter players from the attraction of acquiescence is to threaten to make yourself worse off as well. But the effect of such threats leaves you no more attractive than before. Indeed, it may, as in the original case of NC sanctioning UD, leave other agents more attractive, like BC, and LBC, who do not pay this cost. There are substantially rational limits on the power of sanctions, which are, after all, a matter of mutual impoverishment rather than mutual advantage. Therefore, if morality requires narrow compliance and procedural rationality permits LBC, the compliance problem remains unsolved for the game of Chicken.

In the next chapter I shall attack this problem from both sides. I shall question the moral basis of the demand for narrow compliance and also the procedural possibility of discriminating broad compliance.

10

DISCRIMINATION, FAIRNESS AND SANCTIONS

We were left with a serious problem at the end of the previous chapter. The game of Chicken reopens the compliance problem that we had managed to solve in the case of the Prisoner's Dilemma in Part II. I have argued that in Chicken the substantively *rational* strategy is to acquiesce to some threats but Gauthier's *moral* theory seems to proscribe unfair acquiescence and even demands that agents enforce this proscription by threatening acquiescent would-be co-operators. How might we close this new gap between rationality and morality? In this chapter I will work on this problem from both sides. First, the roster of strategies in the previous chapter had grown long and complex. It is really possible to build agents that can draw the needed distinctions? Recall that I postulated a less broad co-operator (LBC) with an ability to discriminate sources of threats. If this hyper-discrimination turns out to be procedurally problematic, we would be left with Gauthier's proposed narrower co-operator (NRC) as both rational and moral, closing the compliance dilemma for the case of Chicken. If, on the other hand, this procedural tactic should fail and LBC is procedurally possible, I must fall back to a moral defence. As in the case of reciprocal co-operation, I will need to defend a principle, less broad co-operation, which has an obvious moral defect. LBC players look to be traitors to the moral cause; they trade with the enemies of impartial constraint. As the analogy to trade and war suggests, the issue is not morally clear-cut. I will defend LBC's morally less strenuous strategy, her willingness to accept co-operative outcomes even if they are unfair and her refusal to use sanctions to defend the higher standard of fairness.

10.1 PROCEDURAL RATIONALITY

There are two new procedural problems posed by the move from Prisoner's Dilemma to Chicken. First, Chicken requires finer powers

179

of discrimination, since one needs to distinguish players that are different from oneself, while success in the PD required identifying those that were similar. Second, Chicken is problematic from the point of view of adaptable players, who seem inclined to learn only to acquiesce to *all* threats.

Fortunately there is no need completely to rework the basic designs that I developed for the Prisoner's Dilemma. Most of them serve with minor modifications in Chicken. I will distinguish Chicken from the Prisoner's Dilemma to our Prolog players by specifying the game in the payoff matrix and **move** predicates:

> **payoff(ck,c,c,3).   payoff(ck,c,d,1).**
> **payoff(ck,d,c,4).   payoff(ck,d,d,0).**

> **%m1(Player_I,Game,Player_II,Move_I)**
> **% m2(Player_II,Game,Player_I,Move_I,Move_II)**

The tournament apparatus uses the **ck** payoff matrix for **move** predicates with a Game indicator **ck**. This is a shortcut because fully rational players should be able to take uninformative general labels and use the payoff matrix to classify the game as constant sum, co-ordination, PD, Chicken, and so on.[1]

10.1.1 The threatener

I will proceed to construct players for the strategies that played important roles in the last chapter. UD is a player who implements the threatening strategy of unconditional defection.

> **permit(ud1,ck,Everyone,execute).**
> **m1(ud1,ck,Other,d).**
> **m2(ud1,ck,Other,Anymove,d).**

Notice that in Chicken, unlike the PD, UD makes itself transparent; **permit** is limited by **ck**. Threats depend on other players knowing that the threatener is committed to its preferred equilibrium. As we have learned, the best way to convey this knowledge is to let other players test your decision procedure. Since UD is an unconditional player who has no need to check the other player's response, it is in no danger of looping and therefore takes no precautions.

10.1.2 Straightforward maximizers

As I mentioned in the previous chapter, the sequential version of

Chicken is less controversial than the simultaneous version because it has a single equilibrium. Since II can respond to player I's move, there is an equilibrium for straightforward maximizers: I should choose C and II should choose D. There remains the epistemological question that I discussed in Chapter 8. As in the Prisoner's Dilemma, the straightforward maximizer can be built in either empirical or *a priori* varieties, ESM and ASM, respectively. The code is identical to that of the two SM players implemented for the XPD, so I shall not repeat it.

It seems only fair to mention that this indicates an attractive feature of the received strategic theory. The SM code remains the same when the situation changes. Defenders of the received theory will see this generality as a virtue: straightforward choice applies to all situations. The quest for rational morality, in contrast, is forced to consider new principles for each new strategic situation. This may look like *ad hoc* improvisation. To some extent it is. Still, we must not confuse simplicity with truth, or, in the case of theory of practical reasoning, with substantive rationality. The received theory *is* simpler but, I claim, it does not work so well as more complicated moral improvisation.

ASM1 and ESM1 behave the same when moving second; their code for **move2** is identical. Neither can resist a threat; they both respond to I's choice of D with the locally best C. They may differ in the way they move when in I position. ASM1 uses the payoffs to predict that II will react as an SM would, which we just saw was to acquiesce with C. ASM1 uses this prediction to select the locally best D. This is a threat. ESM1 considers what II will actually do (is committed or planning to do) next. If II will choose D, ESM1 will concede in advance and choose C.

In view of this disagreement it may be controversial to include *both* ASM1 and ESM1 as straightforward maximizers in Chicken. On the one hand, knowing that a particular player is a threatener seems to be in the interests of a straightforward maximizer. On the other hand, being unable to know that the other player is threatening is a form of threat resistance, which may be beneficial. However, there is a counter-argument. SMs are unable to adopt a policy of threat resistance since they are unable to adopt policies of any sort. How then should SMs regard threateners? I don't know the answer to this internal dispute. As an outsider interested in substantive rationality, I am willing to try them both. Not much hangs on this decision as neither does very well in Chicken. Figure 10.1 is a table of results (using the I + II format) for the players that I will actually implement in this section.

Player	UD1	ASM1	ESM1	BC1	NRC1	LBC
UD1	(0 + 0)	4 + 0	4 + 4	4 + 4	0 + 0	4 + 4
ASM1	0 + 1	(4 + 1)	4 + 1	0 + 1	0 + 1	0 + 1
ESM1	1 + 1	4 + 1	(4 + 1)	3 + 1	1 + 1	1 + 1
BC1	1 + 1	4 + 0	4 + 3	(3 + 3)	1 + 1	3 + 3
NRC1	0 + 0	4 + 0	4 + 4	4 + 4	(3 + 3)	3 + 3
LBC1	1 + 1	4 + 0	4 + 4	4 + 4	3 + 3	(3 + 3)

Figure 10.1 Results for Chicken players

10.1.3 Broad co-operator

I will skip over the broadest co-operator, the unconditional C chooser, and move directly to BC. The broad co-operator faces a discrimination problem. She wants to comply only with threats that she cannot deflect with *mild* threat resistance. In particular, she should comply with UD's threats, but not with SM's. Can we implement such a player?

```
permit(bc1,ck,Everyone,execute).
m1(bc1,ck,Other,c):-
   pubmove2(Other,ck,bc1,c,c);   %OR
   pubmove2(Other,ck,bc1,d,d).
m1(bc1,ck,Other,d).

m2(bc1,ck,Other,c,c).
m2(bc1,ck,Other,d,c):- pubmove2(Other,ck,bc1,d,d).
m2(bc1,ck,Other,d,d).
```

The broad co-operator exploits SM's extreme opportunism. Since SM can't respond to D with D, the **m2** concedes to those threateners who insist on DD and therefore cannot be profitably resisted.[2] Of course, SM has no reason to let its willingness to acquiesce be known; notice that neither SM is transparent. This doesn't stop BC, who only concedes if she *can* test the other's **m2**; when blocked, she resists threats. Therefore she cannot be threatened by SM when SM goes first. In response, ESM backs off and ASM blunders on to *DD*. Recalling that SM cannot threaten when moving second, we can conclude that BC1 can resist SM threats. (This is not entirely effective, since ASM is unresponsive.) Can she go further and threaten SM? (Resisting threats excludes *DD* but leaves open the *DC* as well as *CC*.) When she goes first she can threaten SM. Surprisingly I can find no way to go further and allow BC to threaten SM when BC moves second. The obvious way to do this would be to limit co-operation to – whom? BC can't limit co-operation to those who co-operate with co-operators, because this loops, as we saw in Chapter 4. Moreover, she can't use RC's trick and limit co-operation to those who are responsive (in this case: those who resist threats) because BC1 herself fails this test. She is forced to offer *CC* to any *C* first mover, and this allows ESM to co-operate with her. (ASM misses this opportunity, as in the PD.) This is not too surprising; recall in the PD first-moving ESMs also managed to co-operate. The difference is that in Chicken, ESM1 *could* be induced to choose *C* without offering *CC*. BC can't capture this extra benefit. This is a failing but recall that I claim that LBC, not BC, is the rational strategy, so BC's failure does not harm my argument. It does point the way to the NRC procedure.

10.1.4 Narrower co-operator

The narrower co-operator is a bit simpler than the broad because it can rely on its own resistance to threats as a clear identifying signal. Recall that this is the trick that RC1 used in the PD to identify responsive players. Indeed, the Prolog code for NRC1 is identical to RC1 from the Prisoner's Dilemma.[3]

```
permit(nrc1,ck,Everyone,execute).
m1(nrc1,ck,Other,c):-
  pubmove2(Other,ck,nrc1,c,c),
  pubmove2(Other,ck,nrc1,d,d).
m1(nrc1,ck,Other,d).

m2(nrc1,ck,Other,c,c):- pubmove2(Other,ck,nrc1,d,d).
m2(nrc1,ck,Other,c,d).
m2(nrc1,ck,Other,d,d).
```

NRC1 resists all threats, even the threats of UD, although there is no hope of UD changing her mind. This is the point of narrow co-operation: to tolerate no unfair demands. NRC1 will never concede to a threat and will co-operate by returning *C* only to those who reciprocally resists his threatening posture. Thus NRC1 will threaten SM whether I or II and will also threaten BC. Recall that this last point differentiates NRC from NC; the idea behind NRC was to make broad co-operators pay their dues. The question is, can NRC1 make *all* broad co-operators, of whatever stripe, pay in this way? This, you will recall, is the procedural issue that determines whether we can resolve the compliance dilemma in Chicken.

10.1.5 Less broad co-operator

This brings us to the LBC, who, I conjectured in the previous chapter, will only concede to UD. To do so, LBC must differentiate UD from NRC. Is this possible? The task is eased by UD's uniqueness. UD is relatively easy to identify, since he is so simpleminded. This makes UD a good exception to a principle that generally requires resisting threats, for three reasons. First, substantively, it makes a great deal of sense to refuse to concede to those players complicated enough to take advantage of your willingness to concede but it makes no sense to resist a player who will not adapt to your resistance. Second, morally, the distinction is drawn at a relevant point. One refuses to bargain with one's cognitive and moral equals. That is, one follows Gauthier's suggestion and refuses to go along with threats from other morally constrained or adaptive players but does not carry this refusal to the extreme when the other player is not capable of bargaining by adapting to fair principles. Third, finding UD is procedurally an easy discrimination task.

```
permit(lbc1,ck,Everyone,execute).
m1(lbc1,ck,Other,c) :-
  pubmove2(Other,ck,lbc1,c,c),
  pubmove2(Other,ck,lbc1,d,d).
m1(lbc1,ck,Other,c) :- ud-detect2(lbc1,Other).
m1(lbc1,ck,Other,d).
ud-detect2(lbc1,Other) :-
  examine(m2(Other,ck,lbc1,c,OMove),Proced),!,
  Proced = true,OMove = d.

m2(lbc1,ck,Other,d,c) :- ud-detect1(lbc1,Other).
m2(lbc1,ck,Other,c,c) :- pubmove2(Other,ck,lbc1,d,d).
m2(lbc1,ck,Other,Y,d).
```

```
ud-detect1(lbc1,Other) :-
  examine(m1(Other,ck,lbc1,OMove),Proced),!,
  Proced = true,OMove = d.
```

LBC1 is just like NRC1 except that it acquiesces to UD. Therefore it can exploit BC and ESM1 just as NRC can. The new material is the way to discriminate in favour of UD1. It identifies UD by her simple mind. LBC1 uses the technique of examining the other player's first principle that I introduced in Chapter 4. The UD-detector (**ud-detect**) it true if a player's first principle is to D without any conditions. (An unconditional principle has the null antecedent of **true**.) Clearly, if a player's first thought is unconditional defection, he will never get to do any thinking beyond this (where he might have second thoughts such as conceding were one to show some resistance).

I conclude the LBC1 can isolate UD as the object of its concessions. Still, you may wonder, why doesn't NRC1 threaten LBC1? Recall that NRC1 tests the other player to see if it resists threats. How can LBC1 pass this test? Because NRC1 only tests whether the other player resists *its* threats. We could narrow the test even further, demanding whether the other player would concede to UD, but this would run into problems similar to those facing UCP in Chapter 6. In any case, as we shall shortly see, this would only make NRC even less successful.

At one time I had hoped to show that the less narrow co-operator, LBC, was procedurally impossible. Unfortunately, when I moved from my armchair to my computer console, it proved all too possible to create working LBC players. I have been able to construct LBC1, who blocks Gauthier's proposed narrower co-operator's attempt to impose a fairness tax on those who acquiesce. Therefore I can conclude that there are no obvious procedural barriers to the rationally attractive principle of conceding to unreasoning threats.

10.1.6 Proof positive or negative?

I have put much weight on my procedural results. In the Prisoner's Dilemma, responsive players are not incoherent and can protect themselves from exploitation. In Chicken, the less broad co-operator, LBC1, can discriminate between reasonable and unreasonable threats. My method seems sound; these are existence proofs. RC and LBC are possible because I can construct instances of each. Yet I am less sanguine about the method applied to Chicken. I will rehearse my doubts because I learned something from resolving them. My procedural argument for Chicken is not so much a possibility proof as an impossibility conjecture. To say that LBC exists is really to say that no narrow co-operator can be designed to exploit her. And this is a much weaker claim. Who can say confidently what others will not be able to design? Worse, the new task doesn't seem so difficult. All NRC need do is to distinguish LBC from NRC himself. As we know from Part II, this task of self-recognition is quite simple. So it seems that NRC can distinguish LBC and therefore tax her compliant inclinations.

My doubts were unfounded. It underestimates the task for NRC. NRC doesn't merely need to recognize LBC and threaten it, NRC's success requires that LBC also *concede* to this threat. Otherwise, NRC only manages to lower its score along with LBC's and, since LBC retains its advantage against UD, LBC retains its overall substantive advantage. Therefore the outcome does depend on LBC. Since LBC can distinguish UD from more complex would-be threateners, it can refuse to concede to any but a simple-minded unreasoning threat. It doesn't matter that NRC can distinguish LBC; LBC can distinguish NRC and resists its threat. Presumably NRC is reasonable enough to back off and co-operate. However this doesn't matter; as we have just seen, whether NRC co-operates or sanctions, its score relative to LBC remains the same. LBC denies NRC the *DC* outcome that NRC needs to make its fight against threatening and unfair unconditional defection pay. Finally, NRC may, of course, make itself into a UD but that is another matter. To do this NRC must give up forever the manifold benefits of responsive co-operation and the ability to adapt new principles.

I conclude that my proof is properly constructive. Regardless of further developments in the technology of moral sanctioning, LBC establishes the procedural feasibility of the slightly lower moral road of complying with unreasonable threats.

10.2 ADAPTIVE PLAYERS

The players we have just constructed are all rigidly constrained. In the Prisoner's Dilemma, as we saw in Chapter 7, there are disadvantages to rigidity which favoured players able to adapt their principles. However, adaptation is riskier in Chicken than in the PD. The problem is that indirect maximizers will learn to concede, not to resist threats. Gauthier cannot avoid this problem, as he appeals to adaptation in his defence of his favoured principle of narrow co-operation. I begin by showing why Gauthier needs to introduce adaptable players. I then show that adaptable players can be constructed that will choose either broad or narrow co-operation, revealing a surprising unity in the opposed positions that Gauthier and I take up.

10.2.1 An objection to adaptation

Gauthier relies on the presence of adaptable players to construct his argument for narrow co-operation. He runs an argument of the type that I formalized as an evolutionary test for substantive rationality in Chapter 5. He assumes that others will adapt to and exploit broad co-operators. (See quotation in §5.2.2.) Kraus and Coleman object to this assumption:

> even if it would be desirable for me to be a less–than–narrow complier, it does not follow that it is rational for me to *become* less–than–narrowly compliant. The dispositions of narrow and broad compliance are not conditional upon certain bargains *with certain sorts of people.* Individuals are either broad or narrow (or less–than–narrow) compliers, period. They cannot be broad compliers when interacting with some people but narrow compliers when interacting with others. Though I might rationally prefer to be a less–than–narrow complier while I am interacting with you, the rationality of my actually being a less–than–narrow complier will depend on the distribution of dispositions throughout the population with whom I interact. If everyone but you were narrowly compliant, then it would still not be rational for me to be a less–than–narrow complier, even if you are broadly compliant.
>
> (Kraus and Coleman 1987, p. 743)

Kraus and Coleman assume that a player's principles must be rigidly fixed for all the players that she encounters. This may be taken to be a claim about the rigidity of human dispositions. (Kraus and Coleman make several claims about psychological plausibility.) If so, I will not comment on its truth but regard it as irrelevant to the issue of pure procedural possibility before us. On the other hand, it might be taken to be a claim about what any sort of rational player can do, because players must react to populations, not individuals. In the latter case, I deny the claim. We saw in Chapter 7 how to construct indirectly maximizing players (IM) who can adapt their principles to their particular situation *vis-à-vis* another player. We encountered no reason that rational players should not so adapt. If so, rational players can exploit broad co-operators, as Gauthier claims. Indirect maximizers do this by adopting UD or NRC when interacting with BC. This is all that Gauthier's negative argument against broad co-operation needs; it is certainly possible for players to adapt enough to undermine the appeal of broad co-operation. Kraus and Coleman are wrong about the limits of adaptation.

10.2.2 Indirect maximizer

While appeal to adaptability suffices to show what is wrong with BC, it won't provide a basis for Gauthier's favoured NC or NRC. The simple reason is when faced with UD, an indirect maximizer will pick a procedure that allows concession, such as BC or LBC. Indeed, it would take more technical work than you will likely tolerate here to fine-tune an IM player sufficiently that it will not learn to concede to the bluff of an ESM player. Indirect maximization may work well in the simple Prisoner's Dilemma, but it is tricky and perhaps costly where threats are possible. Indirect maximizers are opportunistic; they are prepared to acquiesce, making the best of a bad bargain. Facing a player who threatens *D*, the best one can do is choose *C* (and get 1) rather than end up with 0 by choosing *D* (or insisting on *CC*). At best, indirect maximizers will learn less broad co-operation, not narrow co-operation. Therefore I conclude that Gauthier's defence of narrow co-operation requires something stronger than indirect maximization. Let us see what this is.

10.2.3 Indirect fair player

In the case of the Prisoner's Dilemma, I showed that if Gauthier wanted players to learn CC they would need to have a moralized goal. They would need to seek optimal or co-operative outcomes. This is not sufficient in the case of Chicken because of the ambiguity of co-operation. All three outcomes, *CD*, *CC*, and *DC* are Pareto-superior to *DD*. (In PD, only *CC* is Pareto-superior to *DD*.) Therefore, indirect co-operators also will not choose narrow co-operation; they will adopt less broad co-operation.[4]

In order to have a player choose narrow co-operation, he must aim at impartial or fair outcomes. Such a player is clearly coherent; he filters acceptable outcomes by appeal to a theory of fairness, such as the one Gauthier builds on bargaining from a moralized state of nature. Here is a simplified **fbetter** standard that compares two outcomes in terms of fairness.

fbetter([S1|O1],[S2|O2]):-
   S1 > = S2, O2 > = O1,
   S1 = O1.

This egalitarian standard of fairness is, of course, oversimplified. For one thing, it assumes that the scores of different players can be compared immediately. Gauthier's own standard uses ratios to introduce a more subtle form of interpersonal utility comparison.[5]

This short excursion into designing adaptable players for Chicken confirms our earlier conclusion that both broad and narrow co-operation are procedurally possible, in both rigid and adaptable forms. Adaptation is trickier in Chicken, but there are ways to have it lead either to Gauthier's favoured player or to mine.

10.2.4 Two unified positions

I defended RC in the transparent Prisoner's Dilemma but oppose Gauthier's principle of narrower co-operation, which shares RC's code, in transparent games of Chicken. Do I have a position left to defend? Yes, as I noted above, the context makes RC in the PD quite different from NRC in Chicken. I regain a unified position to defend by moving up to the second-level choice of adaptive players. This perspective pulls my position together and unifies Gauthier's opposing position as well.

On the one hand we are able to see my position as unified around the technique of indirect maximization. That is, while I defended RC in the PD and rejected RC (now NRC) in Chicken, these conclusions both follow from indirect maximization. The focus on adaptive players points in a unifying direction. My thesis is that what best advances a player's substantive interests is not to be found at the level of particular acts, nor even at the level of his principles, but rather in the manner in which he chooses these principles. In my case, this manner remains tied to the player's own preferences. Artificial Morality sustains rationality, in the received theory's sense of responsiveness to one's own preferences, at the second level.

On the other hand a corresponding unity can be seen in Gauthier's position. Both CC in the PD and NRC in Chicken follow from a shift to a moralized goal for adaptive players. So unity has a cost for Gauthier; it removes him further from a player's own preferences. Even at the level of choosing principles, Gauthier must suppose that players choose under moral constraints, not in response to their own preferences. As noted in Chapter 5, this approach separates Gauthier more from the received theory of rational choice than he seems to want.

This comparison looks back to the received theory of rationality. We can see a related contrast with regard to the strength of morality needed by the two competing moral theories. Gauthier's position requires a stronger counter-preferential sense of morality than mine. This comes out in two ways. First, his adaptive players must choose not only *acts* counter to their preferences, but also principles contrary to their preferences. Second, the morality of fairness that informs this choice excludes some mutually advantageous (but unfair) outcomes as immoral.

10.3 THE MORALITY OF THREATS AND SANCTIONS

Since procedural constraints have not excluded less broad co-operation, I am faced with a problem. I find this disposition to discriminating acquiescence to be rational. Gauthier asserts that morality demands narrower co-operation. In this section I will argue that less broad co-operation is indeed morally acceptable. First I review the moral problems of Chicken, then I undertake a three-pronged moral defence. First, I acknowledge Gauthier's condoning of the broad co-operator's acquiescence. Second, I meet Gauthier's particular criticism of broad co-operation by defending discriminating acquiescence as less immoral than it seems. Finally, I seek to undermine the defence of sanctioning based on fairness.

10.3.1 Compliance vs acquiescence

While it is tempting to draw strong distinctions for the sake of argument, I must not exaggerate my differences with Gauthier nor mis-state his position on the compliance problem in Chicken:

> For utility-maximizers, the link between co-operation and mutual benefit must take precedence over the link between co-operation and impartiality or fairness. But this does not sever the second link. . . . We abandon neither the proviso nor narrow

compliance, but we subordinate them to the requirement of mutual benefit.

We should distinguish between compliance, as the disposition to accept fair and optimal co-operative arrangements, and *acquiescence*, the disposition to accept co-operative arrangements that are less than fair, in order to ensure mutual benefit. A person who acquiesces . . . does not ignore the advantage that she concedes to others in acquiescence, and she remains ready to withhold it, and to demand a joint strategy more favourable to herself, if she supposes that such a strategy would not make co-operation unprofitable to others. . . . Co-operation on terms less than fair is therefore less stable, in failing to gain the whole-hearted acceptance of all participants.

(Gauthier 1986a, pp. 229f.)

Gauthier never wavers from the priority of rationality over morality. Therefore, when faced with a conflict, he allows players to comply with unjust threats. He does not forbid acquiescence; he condones it. This is the first way to approach the gap between rationality and morality. Gauthier papers it over. I do not intend to deprecate the solution; sometimes paper is the perfect material. According to Gauthier, one should acquiesce *temporarily* to a situation that one cannot improve but remain ready to force renegotiation of the social bargain by withholding co-operation at any time. Acquiescence is rather superficial; more like a paper agreement, not etched into one's heart, as it were.

This is clearly an uncomfortable position for morals by agreement. It is also a difficult solution to capture in my artificial models, since it stresses longer term change in the populations and strategies. Moreover, as we saw in the previous chapter, Gauthier toys with the idea that narrower co-operators might justifiably sanction broad co-operators, which moves him from a positive to a more negative moral appraisal of acquiescence; from condonation to intolerance. I will turn to consider this harsher position.

10.3.2 Broad vs narrow co-operation

As I noted in the previous chapter, the only way for a narrowly co-operative player to enforce the principle of non-acquiescence is to threaten would-be broad co-operators. This is a *threat* because both would prefer mutual co-operation, of which they are capable, to mutual defection. There are two moral objections to this threat. The first addresses the particular conflict between NRC and LBC. The second is a general objection to the use of mutually disadvantageous strategies among co-operators. The first argues that LBC is morally less objectionable than BC and the second that NRC is morally more objectionable than NC.

LBC is better than BC

Backing up a bit, recall that NRC's strategy for closing the compliance dilemma was to threaten the broad co-operator, BC. My less broad co-operator, LBC, resists *this* threat, complying only with UD's unreasoning threat. On what basis does LBC make this distinction? LBC refuses to acquiesce with adaptable players like NC; it only acquiesces with those close cousins of the straightforward maximizer, the non-adaptable threatener. The point is that for an adaptable player, a threat is a *bargaining ploy*; the best counter-ploy is to resist this sort of threat. In the case of simple-minded UD, the threat is no ploy; it is all that he is capable of.

Since LBC refuses to acquiesce to adaptable players, she blunts the force of Gauthier's original moral criticism of the strategy of broad compliance. It is true that LBC does not prevent some players from taking advantage of her and thus allows them to drive unfair bargains. But LBC is discriminating; she won't allow another adaptable player, like NRC, to bargain unfairly. Hence LBC only acquiesces to players who can hardly *bargain* at all. UD and his ilk are ill-equipped to make use of this opportunity to overthrow bargaining to a fair agreement. By refusing to acquiesce to adaptable players, the less narrow co-operator supports Gauthier's proviso and bargaining as much as NC (or NRC). I conclude that the less broad co-operator is morally less objectionable than the broad co-operator she replaces. Therefore the need to support his more general theory of justice does not give Gauthier a good reason to press for NRC over LBC.

Why NRC is worse than RC

On the other hand, NRC's use of threats against LBC makes NRC morally less defensible on Gauthier's own account:

> In a community of rational persons . . . threat behaviour will be proscribed. Unlike co-operation, threat behaviour does not

promote mutual advantage. A successful threat simply re-distributes benefits in favour of the threatener; successful threat resistance maintains the status quo. Unsuccessful threat behaviour, resulting in costly acts of enforcement or resistance, is necessarily non-optimal; its very *raison d'être* is to make everyone worse off. Any person who is not exceptionally placed must then have the *ex ante* expectation that threat behaviour will be overall disadvantageous. Its proscription must be part of a fair and optimal agreement among rational persons.

Constrained maximizers will not dispose themselves to enforce or to resist threats among themselves. But there are circumstances, beyond the moral pale, in which a constrained maximizer might find it rational to dispose herself to threat enforcement.

(Gauthier 1986a, pp. 186f)

Assuming that LBC's moral failings do not put it beyond the moral pale, but UD's do, NRC's threats directed towards the former violates the basic standard of impartiality. However, Gauthier's argument against threatening doesn't apply quite so simply. NRC is not threatening in order merely to gain at LBC's expense. His threat is part of an overall plan to defend the moral community from threatening UDs. Of course, the problem is that he is limited to using the same morally objectionable methods – threats – that he intends to eliminate. This reminds us that NRC faces a problem common to *political* philosophy, where the means of defence against force are usually limited to force itself.

10.3.3 The limits of rational morality

None the less, there is a gap between something recognizable as moral and what is individually rational. A group consisting only of NC players will do better, since they will remain threatener-free, than a group of LBC who invite and support a limited number of parasitic threateners. Here we face the limits of individually rational morality. Group selection can achieve states of affairs unattainable by individual selection. Why should this be so? Why can't rationally moral players agree to protect themselves by a joint policy of narrower compliance? Again the reason has to do with the close connection between sanctions and threats. The only way a group of rational players can enforce an agreement is via the threat of non-co-operation with acquiescent but otherwise moral (that is, responsively co-operative) fellow co-operators. Not only is this morally dubious, but rationally very difficult to enforce. After all, to achieve the assurance needed for co-operation, we have seen that rational moral players must be quite thoroughly transparent to each other. But precisely this transparency makes it easy for the LBC player to pick out her fellow co-operators and refuse to acquiesce to their threats. There are limits to the agreements rational moral players can enforce on each other.

CONCLUSION

I conclude that the rational strategy in Chicken is less broad co-operation. LBC is substantively and procedurally rational and can be implemented by an indirect maximizer. Moreover, LBC meets Gauthier's objection that it is immoral to acquiesce to threats. Although I agree that there are desirable states of affairs that morally more constrained players could maintain, there are moral problems in applying the sanctions needed. Rational moral players should be willing to tolerate some unfairness to avoid costly and morally dubious sanctions. On the other hand, less broad co-operators are discriminating in their acquiescence, resisting the threats of straight-forward maximizers and adaptive players and thereby preventing the compliance dilemma from opening a gap between rationality and morality.

11

CONCLUSION

If I have been successful so far, I have induced you to take seriously
the possibility that we can learn something about rationality and
morality by projecting social problems onto a radically simplified
artificial world. In this chapter I reflect on the distance that we have
covered. How far have we come and how close are we to our goal? I
begin by stating my conclusions. Then I characterize my method
as functionalism, contrast it with some criticisms that deny the
possibility of artificial morality, and ask whether it is objectionable that my theory may not apply to people. Finally I consider
how we might improve and more thoroughly test my sketchy
conjectures, ending with some brief lessons learned from artificial
morality.

11.1 THE CONTENT OF ARTIFICIAL MORALITY

The term 'artificial morality' could be taken to mean many things,
providing a vague and moving target to critics. To remedy this I will
pin my project down by assigning a proper name to the claims to
which I am committed. Artificial Morality (the theory) consists of the
following general methodological aim and the specified claims about
the best means to satisfying this goal.

Methodological thesis. Programming artificial players to score
well in tournaments of various players playing abstract non-iterated
mixed motive games is a good way to develop a fundamental
justification of morality.

Rational thesis. A player capable of responsively constraining
herself to pursue outcomes mutually beneficial to itself and other

195

similar players is substantively more rational than a straightforward maximizer. Properly designed moral principles are better means to a player's ends. More specifically:

1. Successful players should be committed in ways that are easy to recognize and learn from, therefore they should govern themselves by public principles that are interdependent and testable by others.
2. In simple transparent worlds, the most successful principle for the Prisoner's Dilemma is reciprocal co-operation.
3. In less than completely transparent worlds, we should expect mixed populations of more and less sophisticated strategies.
4. Successful players should retain higher-level flexibility; they should be indirect maximizers who choose the apparently best principle.
5. The best principle for the game of Chicken is less broad co-operation.

Moral thesis. Less broad co-operators and, to a lesser extent, reciprocal co-operators satisfy a standard of minimal morality that requires mutually advantageous constraint.

11.2 MORAL FUNCTIONALISM

Artificial morality is functionalist. Given substantive rationality as a goal, I ask what sort of entities best achieve this goal. My answer is that instrumentally rational agents must be capable of morality in the sense of a capacity to constrain their actions for the sake of benefits shared with others. In addition, their morality must be responsive; they must limit the class of agents with which they share co-operative benefits in some way – although we have seen that drawing the boundaries of their tolerance is a hard problem. Responsiveness requires players who can discriminate; depending on the context, they must be able at least to identify other co-operators, or similarly constrained players or, in Chicken, unreasoning threateners. I have argued that one way to do this is by means of transparently public principles, which others can test and copy. In this way I proceed from the goal of rationality to morality as general solution and to Artificial Morality as a means to specify and implement this solution.

If I am correct, the class of entities that can be moral agents is determined by their functional abilities. This basic functionalist doctrine is widely accepted for other capacities. For example, there are functional prerequisites for calulating. The fossil-filled stone I use as a paperweight would make a poor computer. It contains lots of silicon but not in a form that can change and retain states easily. Similarly, we may ask: what sorts of things make good – that is rationally successful – agents?

Contractarians have always been somewhat friendlier to functionalism than other traditions in ethical theory. For example, Hobbes sees immediately that having created a new agent, the state or sovereign, his state of nature argument applies to these new agents (Hobbes 1968, Chap. XIII). Originally Rawls took a functional approach:

> The term 'person' is be construed variously depending on the circumstances. On some occasions it will mean human individuals, but in others it may refer to nations, provinces, business firms, churches, teams, and so on. The principles of justice apply in all these instances, although there is a certain logical priority to the case of human individuals. As I shall use the term 'person,' it will be ambiguous in the manner indicated.
>
> (Rawls 1958, p. 166)

Gauthier also has applied his argument for constrained maximization to states as well as human individuals (Gauthier 1984). None the less contractarians tend to half-hearted functionalism. The tradition barely tolerates non-human agents. Hobbes completes his second state of nature argument (applied to states) in a single sentence (instead of many pages) which is remarkable since it reaches the opposite conclusion from the first argument (international anarchy instead of a super-national sovereign). Rawls has dropped the application of his theory to non-human agents and recall that Gauthier grounds his rationality assumptions in appeals to rationality as essentially human (as I noted in Chapter 2). For the most part, contract theorists quantify over situations and principles, taking agents as fixed. They ask, in what situations do what principles best mediate co-operation for people? In contrast, Artificial Morality quantifies over types of agents as well as situations and principles, attempting to optimize over games, principles and agents.

I am a whole-hearted functionalist. I want to know what sorts of things are suited for moralized rational interaction. (What is required of agents and situations for moral agency to be a rational option? What moral principles suit these situations and capacities?) So far my functionalism has served to *simplify* my argument. I have been able to concentrate on the question of whether rational morality is possible quite apart from the further difficult question whether it was applicable to humans.[1] The time has come to pay the costs of this functionalist assumption. It cuts two ways, both adding to and deleting from the ontology of agents. I find that machines, states and firms are suitable rational moral agents but humans perhaps are not. Both conclusions are controversial; I shall take them up in turn.

11.2.1 Morality and formal organizations

I agree that would be objectionable if Artificial Morality applied to nothing at all. Is there any real thing that Artificial Morality *is* about? Yes; I think that it can be usefully applied to shed light on the controversial question of the moral standing of corporations. Artificial Morality may apply more readily to formal organizations because they have morally crucial capacities that individual people may lack. For example, firms and states may be constituted by public decision procedures, some of which commit them to various courses of action contrary to their interests, yet which are open to interest-based change.[2] On the other hand, the scale of organizations and the fact that we can stand outside them (as well as function in them as components) allows us to to see how something could make itself moral and more generally be moral using amoral parts. Since the idea of treating the state as a model of the individual is familiar from Plato's *Republic*, I should note a crucial difference. I will not claim that corporations are models of human individuals. I claim instead that they are models of adaptable rational agents, which, by satisfying my rational premise, are also capable of satisfying my moral conclusion. Whether humans can be so modelled remains on open question. I will argue that to the extent that formal organizations are like machines, Artificial Morality should apply to them.

Ladd's objection

The analogy between organizations and machines is not original. For example, Ladd (1970) invokes it to argue for a position quite contrary to mine:

> it will be evident from what I have said earlier that it is impossible to make compact with an organization. (Can we make a compact with a machine?) A compact is a bilateral promise and hence a compact can be made only between beings

that are capable of making promises. But a formal organization cannot make promises, for it cannot bind itself to a performance that might conflict with the pursuit of its goal. The principle of rationality, as applied to formal organizations, makes no provision for the principle that promises ought to be kept; indeed, if the keeping of promises, or of a particular promise, is inconsistent with the goals of the organization, that principle requires that they be broken.

In sum, we cannot make compacts with organizations because the standard of conduct which requires that promises be honored is that of individual conduct. It does not and cannot apply to a formal organization.

(Ladd 1970, pp. 504f.)

Ladd uses the analogy between machines and formal organizations to argue in the opposite direction from me. He assumes that it is obviously true that machines are incapable of moral constraint. Then he invokes the analogy between machines and formal organizations to conclude that organizations are incapable of entering moral relations. My argument critically addresses Ladd's assumption of machines' moral incapacity. Artificial Morality shows that when reduced to their functional minimum, moral relations are open to machines. The weakness in Ladd's argument is his failure to see that rationality is not limited to the direct connection between means and ends that I have characterized as straightforward maximization.[3] Notice that I *agree* with Ladd that straightforward maximizers are not moral. But I have argued that for machines which face unstable social co-operation (e.g. play the Prisoner's Dilemma), well-designed principles of moral constraint are rational. In particular it is rational for machines to be able to keep promises (e.g. to co-operate with promise-keepers). Now I can invoke the machine/organization analogy to refute Ladd's conclusion. It is similarly rational for organizations to restrain themselves, hence corporations may enter into moral compacts.

Furthermore, contrary to Ladd's claim, there are reasons to think that among formal organizations, business corporations *in particular* would become constrained instead of straightforward maximizers. Firms are subject to strong evolutionary pressures, the so-called 'discipline of the market'. If I am correct that responsively moral agents do substantively better, this should be reflected in the outcome of the market selection process, to the extent that it links survival and substantial success.[4] That is, market competition should select for moral (i.e. responsive co-operator) firms, not because their goals are moral (they need not be) but because some moral constraints are indirectly better means to market success. Ladd identifies his 'principle of rationality' with straightforward maximization on *a priori* grounds; I claim that this identification is refuted by this (conjectured) empirical market result.[5] Therefore we have more reason to expect to find artificially moral firms in the market environment than to find humans who are adapted in this way. Humans do not change (their basic constitutive principles) so fast nor are we subject to similar optimizing pressures; human suckers often survive. I conclude that corporations provide an example of the applicability of my abstract instrumentalist moral theory.

11.2.2 Can people be rational and moral?

I am now in a better position to answer the original objection that Artificial Morality does not apply to people or to anything that interests people. The previous section shows that my theory applies to firms and other formal organizations. Therefore even if artificial morality does not apply to people directly, it may apply to people indirectly, by showing how it is rational for the organizations that affect us so massively to become moral.

While it may be salutary to extend morality functionally to include non-human rational agents, it will no doubt seem objectionable to go further and *exclude* human agents. However, I must admit that there are some reasons why my principles may not be usable by human beings. First, we humans evidently are not cognitively transparent.[6] Second, we may lack the discriminating means of commitment that rational morality requires. Third, we humans cannot readily adapt our commitments, as our emotional mechanisms for fixing dispositions tend to have high inertia and momentum. Of course, much more needs to be said about the extent to which responsive moral principles can be beneficially used (directly) by people; I am simply sketching the worst case here.

However, even in the worst case where responsive principles cannot be used by humans, the objection to Artificial Morality is not fatal for two reasons. First, it is helpful to understand the 'logic' of co-operation and constraint in clear cases before wading into messier practical approximations. Second, as I noted in Chapter 3, in the case of AI and cognitive science there are good grounds for assuming that humans are the paradigm of intelligence. However, this paradigm case argument breaks down for rationality and morality. There is much evidence for failures of human practical rationality.[7] It should not be surprising if traditional human morality fares poorly in terms of rational performance. Hence there is less reason to take modelling human *moral* performance as the goal of Artificial Morality than there is to take modelling human cognitive performance as the goal of AI. Artificial Morality may lead us to discover techniques of communication and commitment that are morally effective but unavailable to unaided human beings.

11.3 TESTING ARTIFICIAL MORALITY

Having stressed how far we have come, it remains to be asked how close Artificial Morality approaches its goal. Are my theses true? Is it rational to be (artificially) moral? How could we find out more?

11.3.1 More games?

It seems obvious that adding more kinds of game to my tournament agenda would improve my rationality test. A rational player should be able to do well in all possible situations. In the 2×2 case, this amounts to some $(4!)^2 = 576$ ordinal game matrices (Rapoport *et al.* 1976, Chap. 2). Using all these games would also answer any suspicion of arbitrariness in the selection of games. However, there is a problem with adding more games to a tournament. Many of these matrices describe similar games and the repetition of similar games produces an iterated game, which, I have argued, is not a suitable test for moral constraint. Therefore I need to restrict the number of games to maintain the non-iterated character of my tournaments.[8]

Accordingly, I have limited the discussion to two games: Prisoner's Dilemma and Chicken, in order to maintain a sharp focus on the compliance problem. For example, other games might develop the important problem of distributive justice in bargaining, absent from the PD and barely represented in Chicken. In addition, I have not included straightforwardly constant-sum pure conflict games or pure co-ordination games.

There is a second reason that additional games should not be given too much weight. My argument has been *incremental*. I have proposed ways in which morally constrained players could do better than straightforward maximizers, but, following Gauthier, I have always kept the SM strategy available as the default. That is, if a reciprocal co-operator cannot apply its moral principles then it reverts to straightforward maximization. This general lexicographic strategy means that one could build a player who distinguishes the various games and uses my improved moral and indirect strategies precisely for those situations for which they are known to be better, and acts otherwise like a straightforward maximizer. Such a player should do no worse than the SM in new terrain, and better in the games that we have traversed so far. Therefore I do not want to give the impression that our argument is at risk of the discovery of some new game where moral players do disastrously worse than straightforward maximizers. Were there such a game, the indirect maximizer player should not adopt the moral strategy in that case; he should act like an amoral SM there. This incremental and conservative strategy suggests a high-level dominance argument: my moral players do better than SM in some situations and exactly the same everywhere else. This concludes the argument promised at the opening of the book. There are morally constrained players that sometimes do better and never do worse than the strategic players of the received theory.[9]

11.3.2 A Tournament Challenge

None the less I remain an empiricist. Having little faith in *a priori* arguments, I will not rely on this dominance argument in favour of moral engineering. Indeed, it would be self-defeating to do so. The whole point of Artificial Morality is the need to test the influence of an agent on the strategies it deploys. There may be costs to high-level adaptiveness, or to the pessimistic disposition to default to SM in unknown cases.

I prefer to put both my results and my framework to an empirical test by closing the main argument with a tournament challenge to my readers. This will test my results is an obvious way. If I am correct, my best player, an indirect maximizer who uses reciprocal co-operation in the Prisoner's Dilemma, and less broad co-operation in Chicken, will do well in a real tournament, so long as epistemic costs are low. Otherwise, I predict that less sophisticated moral strategies will do well. A tournament challenge also tests the framework proposed for Artificial Morality although more indirectly and at cross-purposes to the first test. A rich framework will allow and encourage surprising results, changing our conception both of players and the testing framework itself.

To find out more about participating in (the most recent version of) this tournament test, contact me, preferably by electronic mail message to this INTERNET address: artmoral@unixg.ubc.ca.

APPENDIX A:
A GLOSSARY OF ACRONYMS

The following acronyms are used several times. The parenthetical references point to introductory discussions of most items.

AM   Artificial Morality (§1.5)
ASM   *A priori* straightforward maximizer/maximization (§8.1.1)
BC   Broad co-operator/co-operation (§9.2.1)
CC   Conditional co-operator/co-operation (§4.2.1)
CM   Constrained maximizer/maximization (§4.2.1)
CUC   Co-operates with and only with unconditional co-operators (§5.2.5)
ESM   Empirical straightforward maximizer/maximization (§8.1.1)
IC   Indirect co-operator/co-operation (§7.3)
IM   Indirect maximizer/maximization (§7.2.5)
IPD   Iterated Prisoner's Dilemma (§3.2)
LBC   Less broad co-operator/co-operation (§9.3.2)
NCC   Narrow conditional co-operator/co-operation (§8.1.3)
NC   Narrow co-operator/co-operation (§9.2.1)
NRC   Narrower co-operator/co-operation (§9.3.2)
PD   Prisoner's Dilemma (§1.3.1)
RC   Reciprocal co-operator/co-operation (§5.1)
SM   Straightforward maximizer/maximization (§8.1)
TFT   Tit for Tat (§3.2)
UC   Unconditional co-operator/co-operation (§4.3)
UCP   Unconditional co-operator protector/protection (§6.3)
UD   Unconditional defector/defection (§4.3.2)
XPD   Extended Prisoner's Dilemma (§2.1.2)

The following alternatives and outcomes are defined by Figure 5.8.

C   Co-operative alternative
D   Defecting alternative

APPENDIX A

P	Punishment for mutual defection
R	Reward for mutual co-operation
S	Sucker's payoff for one-sided co-operation
T	Temptation to defect

APPENDIX B: PROLOG IMPLEMENTATIONS

This appendix provides more detail of several key features of my Prolog implementation of players and games.[1]

B.1 OPTIONAL TRANSPARENCY

In Chapter 4, I stressed that publicity was optional. I will now work out one way to implement this choice. It is easy to think of permissions as *filters* on the predicate subject to permission. To filter execution of the other player's **move2** predicate, I require players to invoke a new predicate, **pubmove2** that shadows the unfiltered predicate **move2**:

```
pubmove2(Player,Game,Other,Omove,Amove) :-
permit(Player,Game,Other,execute),
move2(Player,Game,Other,Omove,Amove).
```

The filtered predicate will fail unless it can pass the filter.[2] To see the difference that permission makes, consider UD1, who you will recall does not permit execution of his procedure.

```
?- pubmove2(ud1,pd,cc1,c,What).
⇒ No
?- move2(ud1,pd,cc1,c,What).
⇒ What = d
```

As a consequence of the failure of the **permit** query, CC1, which uses **pubmove2**, will choose *D* when paired with UD1, *not* because UD will choose *D*. Rather, CC1 can't find out what UD1 will do and defaults to *D*.

B.2 PREDICATES INTO FUNCTIONS

Players need not reveal their decision procedures but they may not lie about them. Let me show how veracity is enforced by our model. For example, here is part of a player, Tricky, that tries to trick CC1.

permit(tricky,Everyone,execute).
m2(tricky,Other,c,d).
m2(tricky,Other,c,c).

Tricky tries to exploit a source of indeterminacy in Prolog. Tricky's idea is to assure CC1 by satisfying her query about CC and still play D after CC1 plays C. Consider two queries:

  ?- m2(tricky,cc1,c,c).
⇒ **Yes**
  ?- m2(tricky,cc1,c,d).
⇒ **Yes**

It looks like Tricky will both co-operate and defect when playing with CC1. Isn't this contradictory? Not exactly. Both queries are true. Prolog has no way of knowing that C and D are contradictories.[3] Prolog implements logic generally. It knows nothing of truths specific to a particular domain until we add constraints in the form of additional premises to the Prolog database. We should not prohibit players from using more than one **m2** predicate. This would stop Tricky but it is too severe a restriction on programming in Prolog. Often the most intuitive way to write a procedure that must respond to many different players or patterns of response is to write many separate predicates, one for each context. Therefore I will try another tack.

Interpreting C and D as the alternative moves in a game demands that players have decision *functions*. Prolog predicates are not functions; as we have seen, Tricky's **m2** returns both C *and* D as results for the same arguments. Therefore I employ a filter that turns non-deterministic procedures into functions:

move2(Player,Other,Omove,Move) :-
  m2(Player,Other,Omove,X),!,X = Move.

This works by finding the first **m2** fact that matches the pattern of the first three arguments. (Notice that **X** is not the same variable as **Move**, which is returned as the value of **X**.) Should the **move** demanded not be what **X** points to, the so-called cut primitive, '!' blocks Prolog from going back and finding another instance of **m2** that satisfies the demand. In other words, asking **move2(tricky,cc1,c,c)** *doesn't* search for this complete pattern (which Tricky provides) but searches for the incomplete pattern **move2(tricky,cc1,c,X)** and then tests whether **X** = **c**. This is what stops Tricky from fooling CC1 with a procedure that Tricky will never get to use.

This filter bridges the gap between players who may have many **m2** procedures and a game that requires just one answer to the question: which of *D* exclusive-or *C* do you choose? Here is the difference it makes:

```
?- m2(tricky,cc1,c,d).
⇒ yes
?- move2(tricky,cc1,c,c).
⇒ no
```

Does this filter beg any important questions? It may seem to. One might think that players should be required to take on the job of discriminating the tricky players; I have the tournament block them. However, this criticism ignores the fact that in order to run a game we require players to have decision functions. The discipline exerted by my filter is required by the definition of a game and therefore seems unobjectionable. In any case, some tricky players are allowed; cf. Chapter 7.

Summarizing, my implementation of optional tranparency uses three predicates. Starting at the lowest level, players define **m1** and **m2** predicates. The tournament apparatus converts these into functions by constraining well-defined **move1** and **move2** predicates. Finally, if another player wishes to access a player's decision procedure, the first player must use the **pubmove1** and **pubmove2** predicates, which are filtered through the player's **permit** predicate. Note that a player may access its own decision procedure directly.

B.3 READING DECISION PROCEDURES

Players who use the device of reading quoted principles must also work around Prolog's backtracking to avoid being tricked by the order of a player's predicates. The **firstproc** is similiar to **move2** and **pubmove2**:

```
firstproc(Ego,Alter,Move,EgoProc):-
permit(Ego,Alter,read),   % permission filter
   clause(move(Ego,Alter,M1),EgoProc),% read first predicate
!,M1 = Move.              % don't backtrack
```

As defined in the text, **sc** uses **firstproc** to get the first principle only if it is co-operative, by this call:

firstproc(Ego,Alter,c,EgoProc)

B.4 HOW TO COPY A PRINCIPLE

Copying a principle with the appropriate substitutions is somewhat complicated but the underlying idea is particularly easy to represent in Prolog, because of its powerful variables and non-determinate execution. Intuitively, taking a copy of your principle seems related to the process of matching principles that I used in Chapter 4 to test principles for similarity. Prolog brings out this intuitive connection; the very same predicate can be used to match or to create a principle with substitutions. (The tester can be reversed to serve as a generator.)

```
%test cases
   m2(bret,X,c,c) :- m2(X,bret,d,d).
   m2(bart,X,c,c) :- m2(X,bart,d,d).
```

```
                                %examples of instantiated
                                   variables:
sameprinc(S,O,SP,OP):-          %S = bret, SP = m2(X,bret,d,d)
   SP = ..SPlist,               %SPlist = [m2,X,bret,d,d]
   sswap(S,O,SPlist,OPlist),    %OPlist = [m2,X,bart,d,d]
   OP = ..OPlist.               %SP = m2(X,bart,d,d)
```

```
?- clause(m2(bret,O1,A1,B1),C1,),   %query 1
   clause(m2(bart,O2,A2,B2),C2,),
   sameprinc(bret,bart,C1,C2).
```

```
?- clause(m2(bret,O1,A1,B1),C1,),   %query 2
   sameprinc(bret,bart,C1,C2).
```

Query 1 will return yes (actually by means of a lot of variable bindings) while query 2 will return:

$\Rightarrow$ O1 = X, A1 = c, B1 = c,C1 = m2(X,bret,d,d),C2 = m2(X,bart,d,d)

That is to say, **sameprinc** will create a principle that satisfies the condition that it match the given principle by means of swapping 'bret' and 'bart'.

The actual **copy** predicate used by Copycat is a bit more complicated:

```
copy(Self,Other1,Other2,Plan) :-
  examine(m2(Other2,Self,c,M),Tprinc),
  Tprinc = ..ListTp,
  swap(Self,Other2,ListTp,ListP1),
  subst(Other1,ListP1,Other2,ListP2),
  NewPrinc = ..ListP2,
  Plan = (m2(Self,Other1,c,M):-NewPrinc),!.
```

Two features make **copy** more complicated. Both allow it to deal with variables more flexibly. First, **copy** needs *three* names, while **sameprinc** worked with two. **Other2** selects who is copied from while **Other1** is the name put in the second slot of the copy. Why might they differ? One reason is that the copier may want to end up with a general principle. If he copies with **Other2** left in place, the principle will be *particular*, e.g:

m2(copycop1,rc1,c,c) :- m2(rc1,copycop1,d,d)

If one wants instead:

m2(copycop1,Other,c,c) :- m2(Other,copycop1,d,d)

one can get it by leaving **Other1** as a free variable. Second, the principle to be copied may contain a variable in the crucial last slot, which outputs the move selected. For example:

m2(rc,Other,c,M) :- (m2(Other,copycop1,d,d),M = c);M = d.

In order to link the **M** variable in the head of this rule to the variable in the body, it is necessary to *examine* the other's rule within **copy** and then build one's new rule (the value of the variable **Plan**) there as well.

NOTES

1 RATIONALITY AND MORALITY

1 I use 'world' to stress the need for a *rich* test – but 'ecosystem' is more appropriate for my simple robot agents.

2 Previously I called these things *agents* but this is confusing in two directions. Philosophers think of agents as richer things, the subjects of action theory. Computer scientists think of agents as more meagre things, the ingredients of which players might be built (cf. Minsky (1986)). My players fall between these two.

3 For other problems, other environments (that beg other questions) would be appropriate.

4 I could run it tomorrow if enough of you are interested. Indeed, I have used this test in several classes I teach, where grades are the prizes.

5 Compare Axelrod and Dion (1987), Kelly (1990) and Langton (1989).

6 I greatly oversimplify. See Danielson (1990c) for a less crude account.

7 A 'senior EC official' quoted in Leggett (1990, p. 9) expresses the latter perspective beautifully: 'If the IPCC scientists are right, then we are on the *Titanic*, and the only question that remains is whether we go first class or steerage. I prefer first class.'

8 These are conventionally labelled C (for co-operate) and D (for defect) respectively. The interaction of this pair of individual choices results in four possible social outcomes: both burn more, one burns less, etc. which each player ranks from best through good and bad to worst according to her own values. For example, we agree that both conserving is better than both continuing to burn much but we disagree about whether it is better that only I or only you shall continue burning cheap fuel.

9 The argument has the form of a constructive dilemma.

10 This fantasized classic technological challenge to morality is from Plato's *Republic*, 359c–360b. See the discussion in Gauthier (1986a, Chap. X) which links Plato's problem to the Prisoner's Dilemma.

11 Cf. Brand (1988).

12 The canonical story has two prisoners, separated by the prosecutor,

210

who face the alternatives of co-operating by keeping silent or defecting by confessing. The end of *The Postman Always Rings Twice* is an excellent fictional example. Luce and Raiffa (1957) is a good standard reference. Notice that co-operation for criminals is a *local* good; we, the larger population, hope to induce them to defect. Notice as well that the prisoners' situation is artificial in that it is structured by the action of a third party and supporting institutions. I will say little about the institutions that structure the situations studied in this book.

13 I am not claiming that all moral theories require unconditional co-operation. I will explore several that do not below. However some do; act utilitarianism is an example. If the scores in the PD represent utilities, than act utilitarians maximize the sum of scores; the strategy of unconditional co-operation does this. I return to this point below, in §2.1.4.

In earlier versions, I followed the convention of putting this contrast in terms of the moralist versus the egoist (cf. Watkins (1974) and Hardin (1988)). Some readers complained that egoism is a stronger motivational theory than my enterprise requires. They were right. Although 'egoism' is a good term for bringing in a wider audience, it carries too much philosophical baggage. At this stage, I should import as little motivational content as possible.

14 Cf. Nozick (1981, p. 543).

15 For reasons I take up in the next chapter, I will follow Gauthier's lead and focus on the possibility of a strictly speaking *moral* solution to the compliance problem.

16 This is slightly over-simplified; I will qualify it later, especially in Chapter 8.

17 The matrix simplifies matters in two ways. First, I assume that CM will always recognize SM because the situation is transparent. (Otherwise, the *CD* payoff would be lower than the *DD* payoff, yielding a payoff structure called the Assurance Game. This case is discussed in Gauthier (1975, p. 21).) I assume transparency in Part II and weaken the assumption in Part III. Second, I assume that CM and SM never co-operate together. Gauthier stresses the need for an additional disposition to refuse to co-operate with straightforward maximizers (Gauthier 1986a, p. 180). However, in sequential Prisoner's Dilemmas, SM would sometimes co-operate. I take this up in Chapter 8.

18 I have less confidence in other features of the theory as we move further from the core problem of compliance. For example, Gauthier's account of distributive justice which is based on bargaining theory is brilliant and his claim that rational agents must bargain from a basis induced by rights protecting persons and property is a striking innovation. Elsewhere I have registered doubts about this strategy (Danielson 1988); I shall not pursue them here. I focus quite narrowly on compliance in Part II by restricting myself to the Prisoner's Dilemma, where there is only one optimal outcome superior to joint defection, so no question of distribution arises.

Distributive questions enter in Part III when we consider the game of Chicken.

19 Contrast Rawls (1971, §2) which assumes 'strict compliance'.

20 The assumptions of strong game theory may be incoherent for more general reasons, that is, aside from the possibility of contracting into moral constraint. For example, common knowledge conflicts with the strategic problem of preference revelation in mixed-motive games; cf. Gibbard (1982).

21 I have developed this line of thinking further in Danielson (1991b).

22 Consider one example among many. Elster (1990), p. 875), writing on inducement via commitment in a sequential game (of Chicken): 'It would be a pointless play on words to say that [second], when behaving irrationally, is in fact being rational. Her irrationality is useful to her, but it is not the less irrational.' But compare the quote from Elster in §4.1, which indicates a wider usage of 'rational'.

23 It would perhaps be best to abjure use of the word 'rational' for a while, until things settle down, but I find this too difficult.

2 FUNDAMENTAL JUSTIFICATION AND GAMES

1 Gauthier (1986a, p. 5).

2 I owe the idea of fundamental justification to Nozick (1974, pp. 6–9).

3 That promising need not be strictly speaking moral is a theme in Hume that is developed by Hardin (1988).

4 Gibbard (1990, p. 795).

5 Cf. Gauthier (1986a, p. 169, n. 19); I return to the Iterated PD in the next chapter.

6 Gauthier (1987, p. 7); there is a similar story in Gauthier (1988a, §5).

7 The tree diagram is adapted from McClennen (1988, §5), who introduces an 'explicitly sequential' interaction problem. Note that McClennen's problem is not a full PD.

8 It greatly simplifies the comparison of the two theories that the basic version of utilitarianism, *act* utilitarianism, so closely parallels the received theory of rationality and shares an almost identical apparatus for describing situations. The main difference is the use, in classical utilitarianism, of values (utilities) that can be added together. Not all utilitarians always need such utilities; cf. Hardin (1988) for a helpful discussion which rejects counter-examples similar to the one I use in the text. Note that my use of interpersonally comparable scores favours utilitarianism; this strengthens my criticism.

9 That is what distinguishes sophisticated strategic thinking, appropriate to social interaction, from the simpler parametric situation of an agent against the natural world.

10 Deterrence (both nuclear and legal) are well documented problems for act utilitarians; Williams (1973, §6) presents the problem with characteristic insight.

11 This tradition lacks a self-acknowledged unity. Rawls reads Hobbes

out of the tradition and Hume reads himself out. But Hobbes is the founder of *rational* contractarianism and Gauthier (1979) argues for Hume's inclusion.

12   Cf. Sugden (1990, p. 769).

13   Cf. Gauthier (1986a, pp. 4f).

14   In this footnote I register some doubts about the political solution. It addresses one problem by giving us three more: (1) We must make a state (and trust some of us to run it). (2) We will likely need to supplement raw coercive power with authority relations that also call upon trust or something like it. (3) We must decide what the state will force (or order) us to do. Notice that each of these problems looks a lot like the original problem. The last is especially troubling. The state does not end the strategic jockeying for advantage; it moves it to a new arena. Is this more benign? A particularly deep and pessimistic model of the state has the players shifting to the game of petitioning the government, with the alternatives of *C* keeping its hands off and *D* taxing all to help me. The result is inevitable; the player-citizens are stuck with a state that grows like cancer, feeding off their strategic problem rather than solving it. (These arguments are based on Green (1988) and de Jasay (1989).) Political failure seems to parallel strategic and moral failure. However, this is a book on moral, not political, philosophy. I cannot explore the problems of the political alternative except to say briefly, as I have, why it is irrelevant to moral philosophy.

15   I use the term 'political', following the classification of solutions to the Prisoner's Dilemma in Parfit (1984), with hesitation because I am persuaded by Green (1988) that strictly political solutions depend on authority relations that share crucial internalist features with morality.

16   Yet contractarians are among the less humanistic of moral theorists. In the first version of his contract argument, Rawls (1958) allowed the account to range more widely and Gauthier (1984) applied morals by agreement to states.

17   This subsection may be skipped on a first reading.

18   I am indebted to Chris Morris for discussions that led me to and clarified the concept of fundamental justification. Cf. Morris (1988).

19   I can add, *ad hominem*, that many traditional moralists likely cannot imagine that morality could take the form proposed by Gauthier but this hardly counts as criticism.

20   Dennett (1978) defends the AI strategy that factors intelligence into generation and test using a similar argument.

21   See Rawls (1971, §22) for a perspicuous account of the 'circumstances of justice' that exclude pure conflict.

22   I address this problem in Part II; compare as well Morris (1990).

23   I have changed some names to suggest my preferred performance-enhancing drug.

24   McCullough's moral and virtuous machines may be treated together. Since neither can change the rules built into them, these rules may be considered part of their hardware; cf. Moor (1978).

3 NATURE AND ARTIFICE

1 Originally I was loath to admit this. Drexler (1986) and Brand (1988) have reassured me. Brand (p. 224) quotes Marvin Minsky: 'A couple of hundred years from now, maybe Isaac Asimov and Fred Pohl will be considered the important philosophers of the twentieth century, and the professional philosophers will almost all be forgotten, because they're just shallow and wrong, and their ideas aren't very powerful.'

2 'Did I tell you about the dream I had the other day? . . . '

3 It can liberate even further when we see how morality can reduce the role of 'struggle', a topic to which I shall return below, in §3.2.4.

4 I shall argue below that reciprocal altruism has little to do with genetics.

5 Cf. Dawkins (1976), who introduces the striking metaphor of organisms as robots programmed by their genes to play games like the Prisoner's Dilemma.

6 Hume (1960, p. 160).

7 Cf. Simon (1981, p. 27): 'Symbol systems are almost the quintessential artifacts, for adaptivity to an environment is their whole *raison d'être*.'

8 This, after all, is the methodological moral of Dawkin's metaphysical defence of egoism.

9 Mostly, they do *not*, a point to which I return below in §3.2.4.

10 The Extended game discussed in Chapter 2 was not iterated. Player II's move is terminal; she will not encounter player I again, as she likely would in an iterated game.

11 See Axelrod and Dion (1987) for the substantial literature that these results have generated and Carroll (1987) for a critique of the rationality of Tit for Tat.

12 Gauthier (1986a, pp. 169f. and n. 19). Compare Parfit (1984, §23), who denies that repeated cases should even be called 'Prisoner's Dilemmas'.

13 Thanks to Lew Lowther for raising this question.

14 This weakness of TFT was correctly predicted by Axelrod (1978).

15 See Campbell (1988b) p. 206 and note 12, respectively.

16 Trial-and-error learning is not directly penalized. It incurs these costs because it confuses some players, undermines the trust of others, or tries the patience of yet others.

17 The distinction between criterion and decision procedure is due to Bales (1971, p. 263), who applies it to utilitarianism. While TFT is a surpassingly simple rule of thumb, *how* an agent is to calculate the consequences of choice in an iterated situation is no simple matter. (See Axelrod (1978) for the details of several complex players.) Indeed, an agent learning in a field of other learning agents faces a complex problem of induction, involving the tracking of moving targets. However, this complexity is not a sign that the choice is other than straightforward. Similarly, how an agent is to arrive at the conclusion that a particular product or investment mix is best in a (competitive) market situation is also not simple. In both cases, the

complexity is a matter of discovering what is directly in the player's interest, not of indirectly constraining these interests with principles.

18 Thanks to my colleague Steve Savitt for pressing this question.

19 Gauthier (1986a, §IV.1); see Danielson (1988) for some doubts about this description.

20 The analogy is not perfect; the market is often structured by moral constraints while some of the IPDs Axelrod studied are natural situations. Of course we could alter this by using moral constraints – aiding identification, for example – to construct a situation allowing iteration through recognition, where there was none before. Then the analogy to the market would be stronger. Or, from the other side, we can note that the constraints against force and fraud that structure the market are often externally enforced and therefore not moral in the full sense.

21 Cf. Campbell (1988b, p. 206, n. 12) and Danielson (1988, p. 381, n. 13) for additional criticisms.

22 As Hardin (1985, p. 356) points out, Axelrod (1984, p. 216) is overly optimistic about directly applying his Tit for Tat solution to n-person games.

23 I owe this point to Miller and Drexler (1988).

24 Cf. Popper (1957) who stresses the technological form of predications with the concept of social engineering. This suggests another contrast: Artificial Morality is *individual* engineering.

25 An elementary but instructive example of this is Furguson (1981), which partially implements Asimov's Three Laws of Robotics in Prolog. Asimov's work shows how quickly one reaches deep problems with this small set of rules (Asimov 1950, p. 6):

1. A robot may not injure a human being, or, through inaction, allow a human being to come to harm.
2. A robot must obey the orders given to it by human beings except where such orders would conflict with the First Law.
3. A robot must protect its own existence as long as such protection does not conflict with the First or Second Law.

26 Do I – a partially retreaded philosopher – claim to understand Gauthier's theory so well? No. I probably distort morals by agreement, ignoring some of its humane content in my efforts to bend it towards Artificial Morality.

4 CONDITIONAL CO-OPERATION

1 I myself press other objections to CM later in Part II.

2 I stress this perspective to avoid misunderstanding. While I will defend Gauthier's broad theory, I do not follow his method, so my defence will not be internal to his theory, nor, perhaps, fully welcomed by Gauthier himself.

3 On formal vs substantive aims, cf. Parfit (1984, p. 9).

4 A particular utilitarian parallel is significant; I argue for rule

rationality in a way Harsanyi argues for rule utilitarianism:

> I will argue [that] act utilitarianism fails the basic utilitarian test: for a society governed by act utilitarian principles would reach a much lower level of social utility than a society governed by the rule utilitarian moral code would reach. (Harsanyi 1977, p. 44)

Like Harsanyi, I distinguish a neutral test, show the act and rule variants to be distinct, and conclude that a player following the rule variant does better by the test. (Note the change from society to player.) It is ironic to note that Harsanyi is a leading critic of the move from act to rule rationality.

5   The phrase is from Lyons (1965, p. 128).

6   Conditional co-operation comes from Michael Taylor's work; cf. Taylor (1987). The connection between constrained maximization and conditional co-operation is complicated by Gauthier's use of the phrases 'disposed' and 'like-disposed' (p. 169) which leave unclear the level of similarity intended. Is *any* disposition to co-operate sufficient or is a *conditional* disposition required? What I take to be the canonical specification of constrained maximization (on p. 167) indicates that the former suffices. Therefore constrained maximizers are conditional co-operators, as Gauthier (1988b, p. 399) agrees. But Gauthier also recommends sanctioning SM who co-operate; I take this complication up in Chapter 8. Cf. Danielson (1988, §III) for more detailed discussion; Sobel (1988) raises further difficulties.

7   My use of 'responsive' should not be taken to imply that these strategies are limited to iterated games. Narveson (1986b, p. 143) notes that 'the ordinary meaning of the term "response" . . . is a *reaction* to something perceived to *have happened* . . . it seems that the *only thing there is to respond to* here [in non-iterated situations] is the *disposition* of the other player.' I concur; later in this chapter we will see how this linkage is accomplished.

8   True, these are very crude *binary* signals but prices none the less. In Danielson and Roosen-Runge (1986) we consider how to give them more content.

9   Why 'demon'? Think of Maxwell's.

10 Notice that a variable is returned as part of the solution. Indeed, given the limited information in the query, Prolog has no way of determining that **ToWhom** may be bound to **uc1**.

11 See Figure 5.8.

12 I use unsubscripted integers appended to the principle name to distinguish possibly different implementations of a principle.

13 Appendix B, §B.2 explains the **m1** and **m2** predicates. The difference between **m1** and **move1** may be ignored for now.

14 The actual words used are, we should note, meaningless. Prolog types symbols as variables by their initial capital letter, so **Nothing** is true of just those things that **Everything** is.

15 See Haugeland (1987, Chap. 2) for a good account of this role.

16 There is an opportunity of extending our theory at this point. Some games only exist because they are managed or refereed; bookies broker bets, speculators span markets and courts need judges.

Therefore entrepreneurial opportunities arise for introducing new games, the profits flowing to which could be the payoffs of third parties to the new games. The games would become more complex and dynamic and less symmetrical. (Of course this is nothing new. What is Hobbes' sovereign but a third party that changes the game for the other players?) I consider this extension of the theory in Danielson (1990b).

17 Another exercise: I mentioned that CC1's **m2** is the same as Tit for Tat. How and why does CC1's **m1** differ from Tit for Tat?

18 For example, I would be pleased were you to quote this book in your own writing.

19 I could complete the standard set of permitted operations by allowing others to **write** to one's principles as well, but I shall not include this form of *effective teaching* in my models.

20 To be more precise, SM players need to know something about the other player, namely that she is rational and what her preferences over the outcomes are. Therefore the received theory should not object to my providing players with pointers to their co-players in my implementations of **move1** and **move2**.

21 Note also that some of the reasons to deny publicity may be weaker than they first appear. Some existing players can publicize their minds (for example, formal organizations consisting of public operating procedures). Also some opposition to access to other minds comes from unfounded scepticism; since others surely have minds, why is reading them impossible? Similarly, behaviourism still exerts a powerful methodological pull. But we have been engaged in engineering on the *cognitive* level for this entire chapter.

22 This is a clear illustration of Prolog's backtracking mechanism. The first time, **P2** is bound to the first player fact, **uc1**. When I reject this choice (by pressing ';'), I force Prolog to try to satisfy the query in an alternative way. Since **move1** and **move2** are functions, they can only be satisfied in one way. Therefore we end up with the next way to satisfy **player(P2)**, namely with **ud1**.

23 Campbell (1988a, pp. 350f.); Campbell suggests a solution to the coherence problem, to which I will return in §4.4.3. Also, Campbell is well aware that his criticism is limited to the non-sequential PD; cf. p. 351, quoted below.

24 Smith (1991, p. 240); I have simplified the argument by substituting 'co-operate' for Smith's more complex 'form the intention to build and then carry out this intention'.

25 Paradoxically this means that CC players implemented in this way will *only* succeed in co-operating when interacting with unconditional co-operators. Since this is precisely the case that I will criticize in §5.1, CC's procedural success is coincident with its substantive failure.

26 Campbell (1988a, p. 351) makes the same point in regard to Gauthier's account of the CM disposition:

> Notice that it won't do to construe Gauthier's second clause ["she does cooperate should she expect an actual practice or activity to

be beneficial" (Gauthier 1986a, p. 167)] as implying that a CM does cooperate should she expect mutual cooperation to be beneficial *if it were to occur*. For then a CM would cooperate with and be exploited by a known SM. A CM must expect the cooperation to be *actual* before her readiness to cooperate issues in her cooperation.

27 I return to this difference in Chapter 8.

28 A substantively rational player must be able to co-operate with some dissimilar players as well as with players similar to herself. This discrimination task calls on procedures more complex than matching. To simplify the task of constructing a coherent symmetrical strategy, I temporarily drop concern with substantive rationality and focus on procedural matters in this subsection.

29 Symmetrical metastrategies are introduced in Howard (1974). Cf. Danielson (1991a) and Smith (1991, p. 242, n. 18) for criticism of my earlier appeal to metastrategies. Notice that the definition of selfsame co-operation guarantees that both will co-operate in case of a match (in contrast to Smith's account of CM, according to which CM allows joint defection).

30 She may be overly cautious in doing this since her procedure should break any fatal loops.

31 However, it will not co-operate with SC1. This creates a co-ordination problem to which I shall return in Chapter 7.

32 A risk remains; quoting players can be thrown into a loop because transparency *is* voluntary. For example, a cautious player may make the other player's co-operation a condition even on granting permission to read her procedure. I return to risks like this in Chapter 8.

33 Campbell may agree that this is one way to secure a non-circular R as he writes, 'Perhaps Gauthier would prefer to specify R as the property of being ready to cooperate in achieving a fair optimal outcome' (Campbell 1988a, p. 351). However this does not spell out the solution; does readiness refer to a disposition? How are dispositions related to actions?

5 RECIPROCAL CO-OPERATION

1 While CC makes the most of the bad situation where SM is present it does not make the best of a generally good situation where predatory benefits are freely available. In Lyons' terms (discussed in §4.2), CC meets minimizing conditions but it does not meet maximizing conditions.

2 This assumption is problematic because it is analogous to Campbell's assumption to which I objected in §4.4.3. It is possible that a player is more responsive as player II than as player I. Possible, but unlikely, since the strategic distance between the two roles in the XPD is smaller than between the XPD and the PD (which was objectionable in Campbell). But there are epistemic and motivational differences, so players could differ in these roles, as the strategy ESM, to be introduced in Chapter 8, demonstrates.

3 Another implementation of RC, RC2, defines herself negatively by defecting if the other player would return a C for a D. You might take designing this variant as an exercise. It has some advantages which I take up in Chapter 8.

4 Peter Roosen-Runge made me take notice of this problem.

5 Gauthier (1988b, pp. 400–1); I discuss the continuation of this passage in Chapter 6. Dawkins (1976, p. 201) also notes the dangers unconditional co-operators pose for responsive players.

6 Dawkins (1976, p. 80); I have adapted these results by adding my own strategy labels. Since Maynard Smith and Price used a game of Chicken instead of Prisoner's Dilemma, some differences should be noted. In the game of Chicken (which I take up in Part III), hawk, who always defects, is distinct from bully who is an SM; prober-retaliator is only 'almost an ESS' because in the iterated sequential game in Maynard Smith and Price (1973), where knowledge is acquired by probing (defecting), prober-retaliator pays epistemic costs which RC does not pay in our transparent model. I introduce these costs in Chapter 8.

7 Once players react to player's principles (as Smith's king-breaker does), complexity explodes and there are infinitely many agents to consider. A diagonal argument establishes this result. Begin with the two simple strategies, UC and UD. There are four ways to react to this pair: C with both, which is UC again, C with UC and D with UD, D with UC and C with UD and D with both, which is UD again. Now we have four strategies, two of which are new. Each of these four strategies needs to be specified further according to the two possible answers to the question whether it co-operates with each of the two new strategies. This is the diagonal generator which yields sixteen strategies; starting with CCCC and CCCD and ending with DDDC and DDDD. Then the process continues, since there are now twelve new strategies, responses to which need to be specified. The diagonal thickens. The source of this complexity cannot be avoided, as the instrumentally attractive RC is similar to Smith's king-breaker in the crucial complicating respect. Both are metastrategies: strategies responsive to the other's choice of strategy.

8 Granted, this is a bit circular, since we are deciding on the standard to be used *within* this filter, but not, I think, viciously so.

9 Of course we do not exclude the possibility that an agent should try to anticipate these further population additions but it is not irrational to choose S now and find that S is overtaken by events later. It would be irrational to choose S at the later point.

10 Axelrod (1984) uses a variation on evolutionary stability that differs from my test in (among other ways) counting the results of self-play. I argued in Danielson (1986) that this assumption is inappropriate for moral theory. I add that it becomes less appropriate as we consider small numbers, as I do here. Allowing self-play simplifies the test but it introduces a systematic error related to *population* size: it inflates the influence of the diagonal outcomes by $(pop - 1)^2/pop^2$. This error is

negligible in large populations but significant in very small populations. In particular, it is crucial to the question of how moral constraint could rationally ever get started.

11 The ESS test requires newcomers to do better, so CC and RC can invade SM only if newcomers arrive in clusters; cf. Axelrod (1984, Chap. 3). Allowing drift means I soften the effect of banning self-play. I defend the use of drift in §5.2.4.

12 But notice that I do not assume that an entrant is the best possible agent for a slot; evolution does not optimize.

13 Axelrod (1984)'s ecological test assumes that players can clone themselves. I argued in Danielson (1986) that this assumption is inappropriate for moral theory. I provide some simple models of players that learn in Chapter 7.

14 Gauthier makes stronger assumptions tying preferences to survival: 'Now suckers are unlikely to do well in the struggle for survival, so that our maximizer may not expect to find many around' (Gauthier 1985, p. 85). This assumption tends to support Gauthier's derivation of CC by depriving RC of UC fodder.

15 For the idea of 'moral hysteresis', cf. Elster (1984, p. 147).

16 Cf. Narveson (1988b) on SM as a disposition.

17 See Chapter 8.

18 CUC takes symbiotic co-operation to the extreme of self-sacrifice.

19 The received theory appeals to a prior non-strategic preference-measuring session at this point. But wouldn't the upcoming strategic interaction corrupt the pre-interaction, given the forward-looking cleverness of strategic agents? (Strategy corrupts and pure strategic thinking corrupts absolutely.) Compare my criticism of Gauthier's proviso on appropriation in Danielson (1988) in this respect.

20 See Sen (1986).

21 I oversimplify to make a point. RC's behaviour is *too complex* to capture at the level of behaviour with the concept of a preference over actions. RC is a complex metastrategy: it reveals well-defined preferences (if we persist with this term at all) only over options that include other's strategies as well.

6 A MORAL MONSTER

1 The received theory of rationality commits this methodological offence when it defends DD as the 'solution' to the Prisoner's Dilemma.

2 I called reciprocal co-operation a 'schmoral' principle to mark its morally dubious status.

3 Cf. §5.3.

4 See, for example, Sayre-McCord (1991).

5 Gauthier (1986a, Chap. VI); Gauthier does distinguish two strategies *within* constrained maximization, broad and narrow compliance, which I take up in Part III.

6 What makes it *retributive* (instead of deterrent) is the inability to alter

the other player's behaviour. See Regan (1980, p. 73) for an argument against punishment where expectations cannot be altered.

7   I shall return to this suggestion in Chapter 8.

8   This makes RC out to be slightly more discriminating than it is. When I introduce subspecies of SM in Chapter 8, RC will co-operate with some morally sensitive but unconstrained players.

9   Contrast this more consistently punitive principle: 'I will cooperate; I will join in punishing any defection; I will treat any member who does not join in punishing as a defector' (Maynard Smith 1984, pp. 68f.).

10 Looking ahead, the results of Chapter 8 ensure that populations will be mixed, so toleration is an endemic problem.

11 I do not claim that this particular test is unique; thanks to Calvin Normore for raising this point. The test discussed in this section adds to the argument in Danielson (1991a).

12 I stress again that I choose this moral test because it is appropriate to Gauthier's own standard of impartiality. I do not claim that it is the best moral measure. For example, I introduce a more general consequentialistic measure in Danielson (1986) which can be applied here. Take our tournament result matrix with empty self-play diagonals. Add the columns to get the score for others, then add in the row sums to get the score to the player itself. Sum these figures to get a moral measure that gives equal weight to self and others. (Self figures in so heavily because each player is one-half of its inter-actions.) In our running example of a small tournament, UC and CC each score 14 and RC and UD each score 11 by this measure. CC does surprisingly well by this measure, since it scores as high as UC on a measure that should favour UC.

13 Gauthier (1988b, p. 401); see the longer quotation in §5.2.2. I originally made these points in Danielson (1988).

14 While Gauthier defends RC as protecting itself indirectly from SM, he sees that this rationale does not hold under the conditions of full transparency that I have assumed so far, where SM can never exploit RC; cf. Gauthier (1988b, p. 401) quoted above in §5.2.2.

15 A more deontological principle that focuses against acts of exploit-ation (rather than my principle that aims at protecting innocents) will be less critical of CC because of CC's indirect relation to the exploitation of UC. CC encourages UC and fails to sanction RC but in so doing leaves these two agents to create the criticizable relation.

16 Indeed, UCP makes a *double* point of this. The first condition would assure co-operation with her twin but I add the second condition to foil tricky predators who co-operate *only* with unconditional co-operators.

17 As we have already seen, in the presence of unconditional co-operators, CC is not morally impressive, since it fails to defend UC. But this is not a failure of impartiality and it is not captured by my discrimination test.

18 UCP embodies what Axelrod (1986) calls a *metanorm* supporting co-operation.

19 Note that CC and RC do not *sanction* UD, since this is their best

option; §9.1.1 discusses this further.

20 This conclusion is stronger than that of the earlier version of the argument in Danielson (1991a), where I underplay UCP's problem of limiting the entry of UC into the protected population. It will likely be weakened again when we turn to less transparent situations in Chapter 8.

21 One subtlety: what if there is no UC to protect? There are two ways UCP could go in this case. *Easy-going* UCP drops the issue and becomes a CC. *Hard-nosed* UCP is concerned to protect any UC that might arise, so he switches to a counter-factual test, which I will not explore. UCP1 is easy-going.

22 Only 'may' because this depends on where a UC player is located in the roster of players. If the UC player comes up before any looping player, **ucp1**'s test will not cause any loopers to meet.

7 FLEXIBLE PLAYERS

1 I discuss this latter possibility in Danielson (1990b).

2 Thanks to Lew Lowther for forcing this problem to my attention.

3 I ignore for now the strategic advantage, in more complex situations, that players may derive by remaining fixed (on a principle that serves their interests differentially) while allowing others to adapt to them. This is a topic in Chapters 9 and 10.

4 I have used the built-in predicates for simplicity here but they are not suitable for a real tournament, as they allow a player to alter another's mind without permission. I will correct this later in the chapter.

Readers familiar with procedural programming languages will have noticed that Prolog makes it awkward to do one of procedural computing's fundamental operations, namely changing the contents of memory. This is appropriate when you recall that the ideal of Prolog is descriptive (not changing things) and logical (mustn't change the premises). By introducing **retract** and **asserta** I leave both ideals behind.

5 It turns out to be more difficult to decide what Flipflop1 should do with her own kind.

6 In nature this has had some fabulous effects, such as bamboo and locusts timed to flower and fly at long intervals with lengths which are *prime* numbers of years all presumably aimed at throwing off predators who would otherwise be able to figure out when to be waiting (Gould 1977, Chap. 11).

7 The test needs to be more complex. Players can consist of layers of predicates; this hierarchy needs to be searched all the way down to primitive operations.

8 The premise is only *weakened*, not discharged. While I allow players to change their principles, I still require that procedures be effective so long as they are in place. Therefore deception that involves saying that one will co-operate and actually defecting still is impossible. I bar this deeper deception by blocking any information that would allow

players to differentiate a **move** query coming from another player from a similar query coming from the tournament apparatus.

9   One can imagine other models that would admit of more primitive kinds of transmission; it is not clear that the following count as *learning*. Parents can clone themselves or they can directly program their offspring. (These are different as the latter but not the former permits parents to program children with principles *different* from their own and so opens up the possibility of additional variation and also exploitation.) Cf. Trivers (1978b).

10   See Haugeland (1987, p. 11) for a good short account of the priority of structured knowledge representation to learning.

11   For example, see Winston (1984, Chap. 11).

12   Cf. Denning (1986) and, more speculatively, Henson (1987).

13   An exercise: construct an improved Serveme. Hint: consider Flip-flop1's state as a copy-resistant context.

14   $>$ = means greater than or equal to. The simpler **S1** $>$ = **S2, O1** $>$ = **O2** is too weak a test; it will pass principles which are not better. Finally note that Gauthier requires **S1** $>$ **S2**.

15   I will not speculate how to implement a standard that will allow a player to learn UCP.

16   Parfit's own discussion (Parfit 1984, pp. 19–23) deserves more attention.

8 INFORMATION AND ITS COSTS

1   Cf. Gauthier (1991).

2   RC1 will only co-operate with ESM1 if the latter is transparent; I return to this point below.

3   There is no need for a *commitment* to defect in the Prisoner's Dilemma. This is not the case in the game of Chicken, taken up in Chapter 9.

4   Gauthier (1986a, p. 180) gives this impression but sequential interactions are not discussed in *Morals by Agreement*. The discussion of sequential interaction in Gauthier (1987, §10) introduces an agent like ASM 'so committed to the orthodox view of feasibility that the no promise–no aid plan is best' but suggests that with ESM partial co-operation is appropriate. Gauthier (1991) stresses the primacy of constraint disengaged from mutuality.

5   Refusing to co-operate with an ESM who would co-operate is a form of sanction. As we saw in Chapter 6 and will see again in Chapter 10, sanctioning raises both substantive and moral issues. For example, NCC can only hurt ESM by hurting itself as well. Here I am concerned only with the procedural aspect.

6   There is a risk of the use of the term 'risk' here; we tend to ignore the risk of not making a prediction and settling, as ASM does, for a pessimistic maximizing strategy.

7   RC2 has another interesting feature: it may trick simple learners, who only learn one principle at a time, into learning something else. This opens up possibilities in indirect exploitation through learning,

in the case where RC teaches others to CC, which leaves RC some UC to exploit.

8 In Chapter 5, §5.2 I defended the presence of UC by appeal to population *drift*. Scrutiny costs allow me to make their presence less arbitrary. Am I making my present argument too easy by ignoring the fact that UC pays exposure costs? I think not; what more could be done to UC than SM already does? CC risks an SM cracking CC's conditional test after exposure; UC has already paid these costs by allowing exploitation.

9 For example, might not a procedurally defective CC sometimes mistakenly exploit UC, so the 'costs' of scrutiny should be *added* to the CC/UC cell?

10 Thanks to Alex Kean for the program that produced these results.

11 I am heavily indebted to Frank (1988, Chap. 3) for this discussion of differential costs of scrutiny. His model is more general than mine and differs in other ways as well. For example, he deals with voluntary interactions. He does not stress the polymorphic split between UC and CC, perhaps because he is concerned to establish that not all agents will be SM.

9 CHICKEN

1 Recall the plan to sketch several parallel developments of Artificial Morality in Part III. This chapter does not fully incorporate the results of the previous two. In particular it does not incorporate the costs of information into the new game it introduces. I return to questions of learning at the end of the discussion of Chicken.

2 But not *overturn* them, as we shall see in the final chapter.

3 Taylor and Ward (1983, p. 350); see also de Jasay (1989) and Hampton (1987). My friend, Allan Cobb, who deserves my thanks for supporting this project in many ways, first directed me to the game of Chicken as a corrective for overemphasis on the Prisoner's Dilemma.

4 The aggression of RC to UC is an exception that needs a special explanation, namely that UC are encouraged by CC or CUP.

5 However, as we saw in Chapter 6, sanctions are needed for stronger moralities such as CUP.

6 This section is based on Danielson (1989).

7 Cf. Narveson (1988c) for a related objection.

8 It is usual to generate Chicken by reversing the Sucker and Punishment payoffs from the PD. But, my standard payoff set, $\{T=3, R=2, P=1, S=0\}$, leaves the sums of the payoff in three of the quadrants equal and violates the constraint that joint co-operation should be better than alternating exploitation and acquiescence. Since, as we shall see momentarily in the text, the equilibrium strategy in the extended game is alternate CD and DC, the standard payoffs would leave the 'co-operative' CC outcome no better than the 'non-co-operative' equilibrium. Therefore I boost the two highest payoffs, so that $R > (T+S)/2$; $3 > (4+1)/2$, giving the payoff

set of {4,3,1,0} for the Chicken matrix. The cost of this change is that some of what I will say will not be true in virtue of the ordinal structure of the game alone. Since this is just to say that purely ordinal Chicken may be more tractable than my version, there should be no methodological objection to my change since it makes it more difficult to show that morality is rational and, by making CD relatively worse than CC, favours Gauthier's moral solution over mine.

9   I am indebted here to Gauthier (1987).

10 I return to the moral evaluation of outcomes in Chicken in the next chapter.

11   Roughly, the principle of risk dominance says that Row, by insisting on [the D alternative] (where he gets more), faces a larger risk than Column, should agreement be impossible. Similarly, Column faces a larger risk than Row if he insists on [the D alternative]. There is, however, another equilibrium pair in this game, namely the mixed strategy pair $(0.5,0.5),(0.5,0.5)$, which gives each player [2.0]. Here the risk is equalized. This strategy pair constitutes Harsanyi's solution of this game.

(Rapoport *et al.* 1976, p. 47)

Note however that the argument for risk dominance assumes a contest between symmetrical straightforward maximizers and relies heavily on the need to preserve consistent expectations as Harsanyi (1986) makes clear. Brams (1976, §5.3) provides an account of the controversy between Harsanyi and Howard over Harsanyi's proposed solution. Gauthier (1986a, pp. 73f.) defends the use of maximin strategies (in an asymmetrical game of Chicken) which stresses the importance in the received theory of 'generating the [consistent] expectations [the agents] seek.'

12 The idea of equal rationality is not unproblematic. We encountered it in §8.3 and I will return to it below in §9.3.1.

13 These labels are intended to parallel Gauthier's categories of broad and narrow compliance which are introduced in §9.3.

14 The tables report average results of roles I and II.

15 Narrow co-operators face a problem similar to that which led the unconditional co-operator protector of Chapter 6 to contemplate controlling the population of UC agents. We shall explore below a more drastic solution to the problem.

16 These exactly equal scores are an artefact of my payoff matrix; equality here has no significance.

17 Leaving aside UCP, to whom I shall return below.

18 I should qualify this criticism, given the close relation between morality and rationality in Gauthier's theory and his particular sensitivity to one form of this criticism: 'were I to become convinced that an appeal to equal rationality was either a concealed moral appeal, or inadmissible on some other ground, then I should have to abandon much of the core argument of *Morals by Agreement*' (Gauthier 1988a, p.186). I am not claiming that Gauthier rejects unequal bargains as irrational when the real basis for his claim is that

they are immoral. I am claiming that equal bargaining is a moral principle which it may be rational to hold.

19 Elster (1984, §1.4) makes a similar argument against the possibility of a rationally mixed population following strategies like BC and UD.

20 Kitcher (1985, p. 89) calls this strategy 'Clever UD, the strategy of attacking exactly those animals that can be defeated without injury to the attacker'.

21 Kraus and Coleman (1987, p. 734) quoting Gauthier (1986b, p. 13).

10 DISCRIMINATION, FAIRNESS AND SANCTIONS

1 I have constructed players for such fully generalized games but their programs are very difficult for humans to understand. I do not remark on this to deprecate human cognitive capacities. (If god had intended us to read computer programs he wouldn't have given us computers to run them.) On the contrary, I am making an arcane methodological point. The complications introduced by general game descriptions do not prove much more difficult for other players to understand. (Unlike us, they don't mind if c is replaced by [[3,3][1,4]].) If the general form *were* more difficult for artificial players, my simplifications would beg an important question by assuming away some complexity. (Artificial players would need us humans to describe situations for them in morally – or at least strategically – relevant terms.)

2 Again I assume, as in §5.1, that I's **move2** is available and relevant to II's decision. This linkage assumption breaks down in the case of ASM, who is less responsive when playing role I than role II.

3 If the code is the same, why do I differentiate two players with different principles and names? Because the contextual change from the PD to Chicken makes these strategies different. (Two differences: in the PD, RC does not aim at fair outcomes but exploits UC; NRC but not RC is willing to take a loss for the sake of making the world safe for morality.) As I mentioned earlier, I have been assuming that players will have the means to identify the game they are playing; I have left this discrimination task aside so as not to burden the coding. Therefore it is quite possible, as Gauthier would seem to recommend, to play NRC in Chicken and not play RC, but instead CC, in the PD.

4 Why is co-operation ambiguous in Chicken? The number of co-operative outcomes depends on the height of the non-co-operative baseline. Is DD the appropriate baseline for comparison? Not obviously; the baseline should be the non-co-operative expectation, and arguably that is 2.5, not 1, which excludes all but CC as co-operative outcomes. However there are two reasons to admit DC and CD as co-operative outcomes. First, we have been using Chicken as a simplified model of more complicated cases where there are a range of co-operative outcomes in dispute. Second, the higher SM/SM baseline of 2.5 is hardly secure enough to form a basis for excluding CD as co-operative. Recall that only straightforward maximizers

achieve it with each other and, therefore, it ignores that others will (find it rational to) threaten straightforward maximizers. In particular, against a UD, the expectation of non-co-operation is 0. (For example, in the environment of the sample of players in Figure 10.1, the averages are ASM1 = 0.9 and ESM1 = 1.5.) Therefore I conclude that the emphasis on multiple Pareto-superior outcomes in Chicken is appropriate.

5   I could implement Gauthier's maximin relative concession standard in Prolog, but it would be complicated because the **result** predicate doesn't return enough of the outcome matrix and would need to be extensively modified to get the extra parameters that Gauthier's ratios require.

11 CONCLUSION

1   As I noted in Chapter 3, the cognitive engineering branch of artificial intelligence has a parallel research strategy. For example some mechanized chess strategies, depending on enormous tables or high-speed tree searches, although unusable by humans, are none the less quite intelligent. Similarly, the resolution technique used by Prolog to prove theorems produces results some identify as the crowning achievement of intelligence by a brute force method quite repellent to most logicians.

2   I hasten to add the obvious qualifiers that not all firms and states are rational, open or adaptable. Cf. Doyle (1983). Also, there are well-known problems in attempting to ground collective preferences to individual preferences, which I will not go into here. Another foundational regress threatens; I take preferences as given at whatever level the theory of rationality addresses.

3   In fairness to Ladd, I add that this assumption is widely shared by defenders of the received theory of rational choice.

4   The whole discussion of corporate responsibility presupposes that market behaviour is not completely constrained by moral and legal rules, else it would be impossible for irresponsible firms to gain from force and fraud.

5   I note several limits on this rough argument. Firms that are too small may not be able to adopt responsive moral methods. For example, my local Mom and Pop candy store is too closely identified with Mom and Pop to change its structure. At the other extreme, very large firms can influence their environment and they might be selected for the ability to corrupt political institutions rather than for market success. To develop this point as a matter of empirical economics is beyond my ability.

6   There are ready evolutionary explanations of why we are not; cf. Trivers (1978a).

7   Cf. Tversky and Kahneman (1986) and the large literature this research has incited.

8   Iteration effects can be achieved even between dissimilar games. I

noted in Chapter 5 Smith's criticism of R. Campbell's attempt to link the PD with the strategically more tractable IPD. Similarly one might also be able to link PD and Chicken. Although PD and Chicken are different, they can yield strategic information relevant to each other. A related point is that similarity of games is relative to the cognitive capacities of the players. For example, a player incapable of interpersonal comparison of utilities will identify as similar games that an interpersonally comparing agent will see as distinct. In general, agents with simpler minds will identify games that more complex agents will distinguish.

9　Those who find the conclusions of Part III disturbing now have a way out. A player could follow my recommendations for the Prisoner's Dilemma and do something else (more or less moral) in Chicken.

APPENDIX B: PROLOG IMPLEMENTATIONS

1　Neither the text nor this appendix attempts to teach the language Prolog. For this you should consult a text on Prolog, for example: Bratko (1986), Clocksin and Mellish (1984), Rowe (1988) or Sterling and Shapiro (1986).

2　I have added an argument slot for the game further to specify permission. For example, a player may allow execution in the XPD but not in a game of pure conflict of interests.

3　The property represented by **m2** could be: the last argument comes earlier in the alphabet than the first letter of the first argument.

BIBLIOGRAPHY

Asimov, Isaac (1950) *I, Robot*. Fawcett, New York.
Axelrod, Robert (1978) 'Artificial intelligence and the iterated prisoner's dilemma'. Discussion Paper 120, Institute of Public Policy Studies, University of Michigan, Ann Arbor, Mich.
—— (1984) *The Evolution of Cooperation*. Basic Books, New York.
—— (1986) 'An evolutionary approach to norms'. *American Political Science Review*, 80:1095–1111.
—— and Dion, D. (1987) 'Bibliography of the evolution of cooperation'. Institute of Public Policy Studies, University of Michigan, Ann Arbor, Mich.
Bales, R.E. (1971) 'Act utilitarianism: account of right-making characteristics or decision-making procedure'. *American Philosophical Quarterly*, 8:257–65.
Binmore, Ken (1987) 'Modeling rational agents'. *Economics and Philosophy*, 3:179–214.
Brams, Steven J. (1976) *Paradoxes in Politics*. Macmillan, New York.
Brand, Stewart (1988) *The Media Lab: Inventing the Future at M.I.T.* Penguin, New York.
Bratko, I. (1986) *Prolog Programming for Artificial Intelligence*. Addison-Wesley, Reading, Mass.
Buchanan, James (1975) *The Limits of Liberty: Between Anarchy and Leviathan*. University of Chicago Press, Chicago.
Campbell, Donald T. (1975) 'On the conflicts between biological and social evolution and between psychology and moral tradition'. *American Psychologist*, 30:1103–26.
—— (1986) 'Rationality and utility from the standpoint of evolutionary biology'. *Journal of Business*, 59(4):S355–S365.
Campbell, Richmond (1985a) 'Introduction'. In R. Campbell and L. Sowden (eds), *Paradoxes of Rationality and Co-operation*. University of British Columbia Press, Vancouver, B.C.
—— (1985b) 'Sociobiology and the possibility of ethical naturalism'. In David Copp and David Zimmerman (eds), *Morality, Reason and Truth*. Rowman & Allanheld, Totowa, N.J.
—— (1988a) 'Gauthier's theory of morals by agreement'. *The Philosophical Quarterly*, 38(152):342–64.

—— (1988b) 'Moral justification and freedom'. *The Journal of Philosophy*, 85(4):192–213.

Carroll, John W. (1987) 'Indefinite terminating points and the iterated prisoner's dilemma'. *Theory and Decision*, 22:247–56.

Clocksin, W.F. and Mellish, C.S. (1984) *Programming in Prolog*. Springer-Verlag, Berlin, 2nd edn.

Danielson, Peter (1986) 'The moral and ethical significance of tit for tat'. *Dialogue*, 25.

—— (1988) 'The visible hand of morality'. *Canadian Journal of Philosophy*, 18:357–84.

—— (1989) 'The rights of chickens: a rational foundation for libertarianism?' Presented at the American Association for the Philosophic Study of Society meeting with the APA Eastern Division.

—— (1990a) 'Morality, rationality and politics: Solving the Greenhouse Dilemma'. Presented at the conference on Moral Philosophy in the Public Domain, University of British Columbia, Vancouver, B.C..

—— (1990b) 'Artificial morality: Prolog and the prisoner's dilemma'. Presented at the Fourth Annual Conference on Computers and Philosophy, Stanford University, August 1990.

—— (1991a) 'Closing the compliance dilemma'. In Peter Vallentyne (ed.), *Contractarianism and Rational Choice: Essays on Gauthier*. Cambridge University Press, Cambridge.

—— (1991b) 'Is game theory good for ethics: artificial high fidelity'. Presented at the American Philosophical Association, Pacific Division Meeting, San Francisco, March.

—— and Roosen-Runge, Peter (1986) 'Conditional commitment: How to strengthen one's moral principles by weakening them'. Discussion Paper, York University.

Davis, Lawrence H. (1985) 'Prisoners, paradox, and rationality'. In R. Campbell and L. Sowden (eds), *Paradoxes of Rationality and Co-operation*. University of British Columbia Press, Vancouver, B.C.

Dawkins, Richard (1976) *The Selfish Gene*. Oxford University Press, New York.

—— (1986) *The Blind Watchmaker*. Basic Books, New York.

de Jasay, Anthony (1989) *Social Contract, Free Ride*. Clarendon Press, Oxford.

Dennett, Daniel (1978) 'Why the law of effect won't go away'. In *Brainstorms*, Bradford Books, MIT Press, Cambridge, Mass., pp. 71–89.

—— (1981) 'Intentional systems'. In John Haugeland (ed.), *Mind Design*, MIT Press, Cambridge, Mass., pp. 220–42.

—— (1984) *Elbow Room: The Varieties of Free Will Worth Wanting*. Bradford Books, MIT Press, Cambridge, Mass.

—— (1988) 'When philosophers encounter artificial intelligence'. *Daedalus*, 117:283–95.

Denning, Peter J. (1986) 'Computer viruses'. In Charles Dunlop and Bob Kling (eds), *Computerization and Controversy*. Academic Press, San Diego.

Doyle, Michael W. (1983) 'Kant, liberal legacies, and foreign affairs, part I'. *Philosophy and Public Affairs*, 12:205–35.

Drexler, K. Eric (1986) *Engines of Creation*. Anchor Press, New York.

Dworkin, R.M. (1977) 'Is law a system of rules?' In R. M. Dworkin (ed.), *Philosophy of Law*. Oxford University Press, New York.

Elster, Jon (1984) *Ulysses and the Sirens: Studies in Rationality and Irrationality*. Cambridge University Press, Cambridge, 2nd edn.

—— (1985) 'Rationality, morality, and collective action'. *Ethics*, 96:136–55.

—— (1986a) 'Introduction'. In Jon Elster (ed.), *Rational Choice*. New York University Press, New York.

—— (1986b) 'The market and the forum'. In Jon Elster and Aanund Hylland (eds), *Foundations of Social Choice Theory*. Cambridge University Press, Cambridge.

—— (1990) 'Norms of revenge'. *Ethics*, 100:862–85.

Frank, R. (1988) *Passions within Reason*. W. H. Norton & Co., New York.

Frayn, Michael (1965) *The Tin Men*. Ace, New York.

Furguson, Ron (1981) 'Prolog: A step towards the ultimate computer language'. *Byte*, 6:384–99.

Gauthier, David P. (1975) 'Reason and maximization'. *Canadian Journal of Philosophy*, 4:411–33.

—— (1979) 'David Hume, contractarian'. *The Philosophical Review*, 88(1):3–38.

—— (1984) 'Deterrence, maximization, and rationality'. In D. MacLean (ed.), *The Security Gamble: Deterrence Dilemmas in the Nuclear Age*, Rowman & Allanheld, Totowa, N.J., pp. 101–22.

—— (1985) 'The unity of reason'. *Ethics*, 96:74–88.

—— (1986a) *Morals by Agreement*. Oxford University Press, Oxford.

—— (1986b) 'Reply to Kraus/Coleman'. Paper read at American Philosophical Association.

—— (1987) 'Economic man and the rational reasoner'. Paper given at York University.

—— (1988a) 'Morality, rational choice and semantic representation'. *Social Philosophy and Policy*, 5:173–221.

—— (1988b) 'Moral artifice'. *Canadian Journal of Philosophy*, 18:385–418.

—— (1991) 'Rational constraint: some last words'. In Peter Vallentyne (ed.), *Contractarianism and Rational Choice: Essays on Gauthier*. Cambridge University Press, Cambridge.

Gibbard, Allan (1982) 'Manipulation of voting schemes: a general result'. In Brian Barry and Russell Hardin (eds), *Rational Man and Irrational Society?* Sage Publications, Beverly Hills, Calif.

—— (1990) 'Norms, discussion, and ritual: evolutionary puzzles'. *Ethics*, 100:787–802.

Gould, Stephen J. (1977) *Ever Since Darwin:Reflections in Natural History*. W. W. Norton & Co., New York.

—— (1980) *The Panda's Thumb: More Reflections in Natural History*. W. W. Norton & Co., New York.

Green, Leslie (1988) *The Authority of the State*. Oxford University Press, Oxford.

Hampton, Jean (1987) 'Free rider problems in the production of collective goods'. *Economics and Philosophy*, 3:245–73.

Hardin, Russell (1985) 'Individual sanctions, collective benefits'. In R. Campbell and L. Sowden (eds), *Paradoxes of Rationality and Co-operation*. University of British Columbia Press, Vancouver, B.C.

—— (1988) *Morality within the Limits of Reason*. University of Chicago Press, Chicago.

Harsanyi, John C. (1977) 'Rule utilitarianism and decision theory'. *Erkenntnis*, 11:25–53.

—— (1986) 'Advances in understanding rational behavior'. In Jon Elster (ed.), *Rational Choice*. New York University Press, New York.

Haugeland, John (1987) *Artificial Intelligence: The Very Idea*. MIT Press, Cambridge, Mass.

Hayek, F.A. (1988) *The Fatal Conceit: The Errors of Socialism*. University of Chicago Press, Chicago.

Henson, Keith (1987) 'Memetics: the science of information viruses'. *Whole Earth Review*, Dec. 1987, 57:50–5.

Hillis, W. Daniel (1988) 'Intelligence as an emergent behavior'. *Daedalus*, 117:175–89.

Hirshleifer, Jack (1987) 'The emotions as guarantors of threats and promises'. In John Dupré (ed.), *The Latest on the Best*. Bradford Books, MIT Press, Cambridge, Mass.

Hobbes, Thomas (1968) *Leviathan*. Penguin Books, Harmondsworth, Middx.

Hofstadter, Douglas R. (1985) *Metamagical Themas*. Basic Books, New York.

Howard. Nigel (1971) *Paradoxes of Rationality: Theory of Metagames and Political Behavior*. MIT Press, Cambridge, Mass.

—— (1974) ' "General" metagames: an extension of the metagame concept'. In Anatol Rapoport (ed.), *Game Theory as a Theory of Conflict Resolution*, D. Reidel, Dordrecht-Holland, pp. 261–83.

Hume, David (1960) 'Of the original contract'. In Ernest Barker (ed.), *Social Contract*, Oxford University Press, New York.

Kavka, Gregory (1986) *Hobbesian Moral and Political Theory*. Princeton University Press, Princeton, N.J.

Kelly, Kevin (1990) 'Perpetual novelty: selected notes from the second artificial life conference'. *Whole Earth Review*, 67:20–9.

Kitcher, Philip (1985) *Vaulting Ambition*. MIT Press, Cambridge, Mass.

Kraus, Jody S. and Coleman, Jules L. (1987) 'Morality and the theory of rational choice'. *Ethics*, 97:715–49.

Ladd, John (1970) 'Morality and the ideal of rationality in formal organizations'. *Monist*, 54:488–516.

Langton, Christopher G. (ed.) (1989) *Artificial Life: The Proceedings of an Interdisciplinary Workshop on the Synthesis and Simulation of Living Systems*, held September, 1987 in Los Alamos, New Mexico. Addison-Wesley, Redwood City, Calif.

Leggett, Jeremy (1990) 'Introduction'. In Jeremy Leggett (ed.), *Global Warming: The Greenpeace Report*. Oxford University Press, New York.

BIBLIOGRAPHY

Leiber, Justin (1985) *Can Animals and Machines be Persons?*. Hackett Publishing Company, Indianapolis.

Lewis, David (1979) 'Newcomb's problem is a prisoner's dilemma'. *Philosophy and Public Affairs*, 8:235–40. Reprinted in R. Campbell and L. Sowden (eds), *Paradoxes of Rationality and Co-operation*. University of British Columbia Press, Vancouver, B.C.

Luce, R. Duncan and Raiffa, Howard (1957) *Games and Decisions*. John Wiley & Sons, New York.

Lyons, David (1965) *The Forms and Limits of Utilitarianism*. Clarendon Press, Oxford.

McCarthy, John (1988) 'Mathematical logic in artificial intelligence'. *Daedalus*, 117:297–311.

McClennen, Ned (1988) 'Constrained maximization and resolute choice'. *Social Philosophy and Policy*, 5:95–118.

McCullough, Warren G. (1965) 'Toward some circuitry of ethical robots or an observational science of the genesis of social evaluation in the mind-like behavior of artifacts'. In *Embodiments of Mind*. MIT Press, Cambridge, Mass.

Maynard Smith, John (1984) 'The evolution of animal intelligence'. In Christopher Hookway (ed.), *Minds, Machines and Evolution*. Cambridge University Press, Cambridge.

—— and Price, G. R. (1973) 'The logic of animal conflict'. *Nature*, 246:15–18.

Miller, Mark S. and Drexler, K. Eric (1988a) 'Comparative ecology: a computational perspective'. In B. A. Huberman (ed.), *The Ecology of Computation*, Elsevier Science Publishers, B.V., Amsterdam, pp. 51–76.

Minsky, Marvin (1986) *The Society of Mind*. Simon & Schuster, New York.

Moor, J. (1978) 'Three myths of computer science'. *British Journal for Philosophy of Science*, 29:213–22.

Morris, Christopher (1988) 'The relation between self-interest and justice in contractarian ethics'. *Social Philosophy and Policy*, 5:119–53, 1988.

—— (1991) 'The scope of rational choice, contractarian morality'. In Peter Vallentyne (ed.), *Contractarianism and Rational Choice: Essays on Gauthier*. Cambridge University Press, Cambridge.

Narveson, Jan (1988a) 'Justifying a morality'. In Douglas Odegard (ed.), *Ethics and Justification*, Academic Printing & Publishing, Edmonton, Alberta, pp. 257–76.

—— (1988b) *The Libertarian Idea*. Temple University Press, Philadelphia.

—— (1988c) 'McDonald and McDougall, pride and gain, and justice'. *Dialogue*, 27:503–6.

Nozick, Robert (1969) 'Newcomb's problem and two principles of choice'. In N. Rescher (ed.), *Essays in Honor of Carl Hempel*. D. Reidel Publishing Co., Dordrecht.

—— (1974) *Anarchy, State, and Utopia*. Basic Books, New York.

—— (1981) *Philosophical Explanations*. Harvard University Press, Cambridge, Mass.

Oldenquist, Andrew (1980) 'The possibility of selfishness'. *American Philosophical Quarterly*, 17:25–33.

BIBLIOGRAPHY

Parfit, Derek (1984) *Reasons and Persons*. Oxford University Press, Oxford.

Pettit, Philip (1986) 'Free riding and foul dealing'. *Journal of Philosophy*, 83(7):361–79.

Popper, Karl L. (1957) *The Poverty of Historicism*. Routledge & Kegan Paul, London.

Rapoport, Anatol, Guyer, Melvin J. and Gordan, David G. (1976) *The 2 × 2 Game*. University of Michigan Press, Ann Arbor, Mich.

Rawls, John (1958) 'Justice as fairness'. *The Philosophical Review*, LXVII(2):164–94.

—— (1971) *A Theory of Justice*. Harvard University Press, Cambridge, Mass.

Regan, Donald H. (1980) *Utilitarianism and Co-operation*. Oxford University Press, Oxford.

Resnik, Michael D. (1987) *Choices: An Introduction to Decision Theory*. University of Minnesota Press, Minneapolis, Minn.

Ripstein, Arthur (1987) 'Foundationalism in political theory'. *Philosophy and Public Affairs*, 16:115–37.

Robbinett, Jane (1991) 'Ethics in invisible communities: Looking at network security in our changing society'. *Computer Research News*, Jan. 1991.

Rowe, Neil C. (1988) *Artificial Intelligence Through Prolog*. Prentice Hall, Englewood Cliffs, N.J.

Sayre-McCord, Geoffrey (1991) 'Deception and reasons to be moral'. In Peter Vallentyne (ed.), *Contractarianism and Rational Choice: Essays on Gauthier*. Cambridge University Press, Cambridge.

Schmidtz, David (1991) *The Limits of Government: An Essay on the Public Goods Argument*. Westview Press, Boulder.

Searle, John (1981) 'Minds, brains, and programs'. In John Haugeland (ed.), *Mind Design*. MIT Press, Cambridge, Mass.

Sen, Amartya (1986) 'Behaviour and the concept of preference'. In Jon Elster (ed.), *Rational Choice*. New York University Press, New York.

Simon, Herbert A. (1981) *The Sciences of the Artificial*. MIT Press, Cambridge, Mass., 2nd edn.

Smith, Holly (1991) 'Deriving morality from rationality'. In Peter Vallentyne (ed.), *Contractarianism and Rational Choice: Essays on Gauthier*. Cambridge University Press, Cambridge.

Sobel, Jordan Howard (1985a) 'Not every prisoner's dilemma is a Newcomb problem'. In R. Campbell and L. Sowden (eds), *Paradoxes of Rationality and Co-operation*. University of British Columbia Press, Vancouver, B.C.

—— (1985b) 'Utility maximizers in iterated prisoner's dilemma'. In R. Campbell and L. Sowden (eds), *Paradoxes of Rationality and Co-operation*. University of British Columbia Press, Vancouver, B.C.

—— (1988) 'Maximizing, optimizing, and prospering'. *Dialogue*, 27:233–62.

Sterling, L. and Shapiro, E. (1986) *The Art of Prolog*. MIT Press, Cambridge, Mass.

Sugden, Robert (1990) 'Contractarianism and norms'. *Ethics*, 100:768–86.

Taylor, Michael (1987) *The Possibility of Cooperation*. Cambridge University Press, Cambridge.

—— and Ward, Hugh (1983) 'Chickens, whales, and lumpy goods: alternative models of public goods provision'. *Political Studies*, 30:350–70.

Trivers, R. L. (1978a) 'The evolution of reciprocal altruism'. In T. H. Clutton-Brock and Paul Harvey (eds), *Readings in Sociobiology*. W. H. Freeman, San Francisco.

—— (1978b) 'Parent-offspring conflict'. In T. H. Clutton-Brock and Paul Harvey (eds), *Readings in Sociobiology*. W. H. Freeman, San Francisco.

Turing, Alan (1937) 'On computable numbers, with an application to the entscheidungsproblem'. *Proceedings of the London Mathematical Society*, 42. Translated in *The Undecidable*, ed. Martin Davis, Raven Press, New York, 1965.

—— (1953) 'Computing machinery and intelligence'. *Mind*, LIX(236).

Tversky, Amos and Kahneman, Daniel (1986) 'The framing of decisions and the psychology of choice'. In Jon Elster (ed.), *Rational Choice*. New York University Press, New York.

Vallentyne, Peter (ed.) (1991) *Contractarianism and Rational Choice: Essays on Gauthier*. Cambridge University Press, Cambridge.

Watkins, J. (1974) 'Comment: self-interest and morality'. In S. Körner (ed.), *Practical Reason*. Oxford University Press, Oxford.

Williams, Bernard (1973) 'A critique of utilitarianism'. In J. C. C. Smart and B. Williams, *Utilitarianism: For and Against*. Cambridge University Press, Cambridge.

Winston, Patrick Henry (1984) *Artificial Intelligence*. Addison-Wesley, Reading, Mass., 2nd edn.

INDEX

Printed in the United States
by Baker & Taylor Publisher Services